CASEBOOK SERIES

JANE AUSTEN: *Emma* (Revised) David Lodge
JANE AUSTEN: *'Northanger Abbey' & 'Persuasion'* B. C. Southam
JANE AUSTEN: *'Sense and Sensibility', 'Pride and Prejudice' & 'Mansfield Park'*
B. C. Southam
BECKETT: *Waiting for Godot* Ruby Cohn
WILLIAM BLAKE: *Songs of Innocence and Experience* Margaret Bottrall
CHARLOTTE BRONTE: *'Jane Eyre' & 'Villette'* Miriam Allott
EMILY BRONTE: *Wuthering Heights* (Revised) Miriam Allott
BROWNING: *'Men and Women' & Other Poems* J. R. Watson
CHAUCER: *The Canterbury Tales* J. J. Anderson
COLERIDGE: *'The Ancient Mariner' & Other Poems* Alun R. Jones & W. Tydeman
CONRAD: *'Heart of Darkness', 'Nostromo' & 'Under Western Eyes'* C. B. Cox
CONRAD: *The Secret Agent* Ian Watt
DICKENS: *Bleak House* A. E. Dyson
DICKENS: *'Hard Times', 'Great Expectations' & 'Our Mutual Friend'* Norman Page
DICKENS: *'Dombey and Son' & 'Little Dorrit'* Alan Shelston
DONNE: *Songs and Sonets* Julian Lovelock
GEORGE ELIOT: *Middlemarch* Patrick Swinden
GEORGE ELIOT: *'The Mill on the Floss' & 'Silas Marner'* R. P. Draper
T. S. ELIOT: *'Prufrock', 'Gerontion' & 'Ash Wednesday'* B. C. Southam
T. S. ELIOT: *The Waste Land* C. B. Cox & Arnold P. Hinchliffe
T. S. ELIOT: *Plays* Arnold P. Hinchliffe
HENRY FIELDING: *Tom Jones* Neil Compton
E.M. FORSTER: *A Passage to India* Malcolm Bradbury
WILLIAM GOLDING: *Novels 1954–64* Norman Page
HARDY: *The Tragic Novels* (Revised) R. P. Draper
HARDY: *Poems* James Gibson & Trevor Johnson
HARDY: *Three Pastoral Novels* R. P. Draper
GERARD MANLEY HOPKINS: *Poems* Margaret Bottrall
HENRY JAMES: *'Washington Square' & 'The Portrait of a Lady'* Alan Shelton
JONSON: *Volpone* Jonas A. Barish
JONSON: *'Every Man in his Humour' & 'The Alchemist'* R. V. Holdsworth
JAMES JOYCE: *'Dubliners' & 'A Portrait of the Artist as a Young Man'* Morris Beja
KEATS: *Odes* G.S. Fraser
KEATS: *Narrative Poems* John Spencer Hill
D.H. LAWRENCE: *Sons and Lovers* Gamini Salgado
D.H. LAWRENCE: *'The Rainbow' & 'Women in Love'* Colin Clarke
LOWRY: *Under the Volcano* Gordon Bowker
MARLOWE: *Doctor Faustus* John Jump
MARLOWE: *'Tamburlaine the Great', 'Edward II' & 'The Jew of Malta'* J. R. Brown
MARLOWE: *Poems* Arthur Pollard
MAUPASSANT: *In the Hall of Mirrors* T. Harris
MILTON: *Paradise Lost* A. E. Dyson & Julian Lovelock
O'CASEY: *'Juno and the Paycock', 'The Plough and the Stars' & 'The Shadow of a
Gunman'* Ronald Ayling
EUGENE O'NEILL: *Three Plays* Normand Berlin
JOHN OSBORNE: *Look Back in Anger* John Russell Taylor
PINTER: *'The Birthday Party' & Other Plays* Michael Scott
POPE: *The Rape of the Lock* John Dixon Hunt
SHAKESPEARE: *A Midsummer Night's Dream* Antony Price
SHAKESPEARE: *Antony and Cleopatra* (Revised) John Russell Brown
SHAKESPEARE: *Coriolanus* B. A. Brockman

Thomas Hardy

Poems

A CASEBOOK

EDITED BY

JAMES GIBSON

and

TREVOR JOHNSON

MACMILLAN

First published 1979 by
THE MACMILLAN PRESS LTD
Houndmills, Basingstoke, Hampshire RG21 2XS
and London
Companies and representatives
throughout the world

ISBN 0–333–23107–4

A catalogue record for this book is available
from the British Library.

Printed in Hong Kong

12 11 10 9 8 7
01 00 99 98 97

CONTENTS

ACKNOWLEDGEMENTS

The editor and publishers wish to thank the following, who have kindly given permission for the use of copyright material: Howard Baker, extract from 'Hardy's Certitude' from *The Southern Review* (1940), by permission of the author. Jean Brooks, extracts from 'The Homeliest of Heart-Stirrings: Shorter Lyrics' from *Thomas Hardy: The Poetic Structure* (1971), by permission of Paul Elek Limited. Douglas Brown, extract from 'Thomas Hardy' 1954, by permission of Longman Group Limited. Lord David Cecil, extracts from 'The Hardy Mood' from *Thomas Hardy and the Modern World 1974*, (ed.) F. Pinion, by permission of the author. E. K. Chambers, review of Thomas Hardy's Poetry from *The Athenaeum* (14 January 1899), by permission of the University of Oxford. C. B. Cox and A. E. Dyson, extract from *Modern Poetry* (1963), by permission of Edward Arnold (Publishers) Limited. Walter de la Mare, extract from *Private View* (1953), by permission of The Literary Trustees of Walter de la Mare and The Society of Authors. Professor Frank Giordano, extracts from 'Hardy's Farewell to Fiction: The Structure of "Wessex Heights"' from *The Thomas Hardy Year Book*, No. 5 (1975), by permission of the author. Samuel Hynes, extract 'The Hardy Style' from *The Pattern of Hardy's Poetry*, by permission of the author. Philip Larkin, article from *The Listener* (25 July 1968), by permission of the author. C. Day Lewis, extract from 'The Lyrical Poetry of Thomas Hardy' (The Warton Lecture, 6 June 1951, 'Proceedings of the British Academy') by permission of A. D. Peters & Company Limited. F. L. Lucas, extract from *Ten Victorian Poets*, by permission of Cambridge University Press. Kenneth Marsden, extracts from *The Poems of Thomas Hardy* (1969), by permission of The Athlone Press of the University of London. John Middleton Murry, extract from *Aspects of Literature*, by permission of The Society of Authors as the literary representatives of the Estate of John Middleton Murry. William W. Morgan, extract from an article 'The Partial Vision: Hardy's Idea of Dramatic Poetry' from *Tennessee Studies in Literature*, Volume XX, (Nineteenth-Century British Issue) edited by Richard M. Kelly and Allison R. Ensor, by permission of University of Tennessee Press, Copyright © 1975, by the University of Tennessee Press. Dr. I. A. Richards, extract from *Science and Poetry* (1926), by permission of the author. L. E. W. Smith, extract from Thomas Hardy's 'The Impercipient' from *Critical Survey* (1964), by permission of the author. Lytton Strachey, review of Thomas Hardy's poetry from *The New Statesman* (19 December 1914), by permission of

The New Statesman & Nation Publishing Company Limited.

Every effort has been made to trace all the copyright holders, but in some cases this has been unsuccessful. The publishers apologise for any unintentional discourtesy.

GENERAL EDITOR'S PREFACE

The Casebook series, launched in 1968, has become a well-regarded library of critical studies. The central concern of the series remains the 'single-author' volume, but suggestions from the academic community have led to an extension of the original plan, to include occasional volumes on such general themes as literary 'schools' and genres.

Each volume in the central category deals either with one well-known and influential work by an individual author, or with closely related works by one writer. The main section consists of critical readings, mostly modern, collected from books and journals. A selection of reviews and comments by the author's contemporaries is also included, and sometimes comment from the author himself. The Editor's Introduction charts the reputation of the work or works from the first appearance to the present time.

Volumes in the 'general theme' category are variable in structure but follow the basic purpose of the series in presenting an integrated selection of readings, with an Introduction which explores the theme and discusses the literary and critical issues involved.

A single volume can represent no more than a small selection of critical opinions. Some critics are excluded for reasons of space, and it is hoped that readers will pursue the suggestions for further reading in the Select Bibliography. Other contributions are severed from their original context, to which many readers will wish to turn. Indeed, if they take a hint from the critics represented here, they certainly will.

A. E. DYSON

But criticism is so easy, and art so hard
THOMAS HARDY

PUBLISHER'S NOTE

In the Introduction and the ensuing selection, the numbers in square brackets inserted after poem-titles and verse-quotations relate to the numbering of poems in *The Complete Poems*, edited by James Gibson (1976): e.g., 'A Meeting with Despair' [34].

Where a poem also appears in *Poems of Thomas Hardy: A New Selection*, edited by T. R. M. Creighton (1974; revised edition 1977), this is indicated by the addition of an asterisk: e.g., 'Hap' [4*].

EDITORS' NOTE

Occasionally, in early reviews reproduced here, the attentive reader will discern discrepancies between early and later forms of certain poems. Hardy was an assiduous reviser, and it has been thought advisable to retain the poem-texts as they were originally quoted in criticism contemporary with their first publication. Those wishing to explore such variations are recommended to consult the *Variorum Edition* (see Select Bibliography).

INTRODUCTION

When *Wessex Poems* first appeared in 1898, some critics, as Hardy drily observed, took umbrage at his 'having taken the liberty to adopt another vehicle of expression than prose-fiction without consulting them'.[1] However, even if we agree with Hazlitt that 'The business of reviewers is to watch poets; not of poets to watch reviewers', it may be conceded that there was some excuse for the tentative and confused response apparent even in the more favourable early estimates of Hardy's poetry. Not that there was any dearth of comment: his fame as a novelist ensured widespread reviews. But, aside from its marked idiosyncrasies of style and vocabulary – more marked here indeed than in any subsequent volume – and the addition of his own curiously emblematic illustrations, *Wessex Poems* certainly presented a good many pieces which were strongly reminiscent, in terms of theme and plot, of his novels and short stories. Moreover, since the apparently despairing estimate of human destiny which had been so marked and so execrated a feature of *Jude the Obscure* in 1895 was readily discernible again in such poems as 'Hap' [4*], 'Her Dilemma' [12*] and 'A Meeting with Despair' [34], those critics for whom any stigma will serve to beat a dogma did not have to look far for a target.

Hardy was to pursue a running skirmish for over twenty years with those who persisted in using his poetry as a stalking horse for attacks on his supposed theological or philosophical positions, echoes of which can be heard in the extracts from his observations on poetry, including his own poetry, which form Part One of this Casebook, and which are often of an epigrammatic sharpness and concision to make one feel that T. S. Eliot had some justification for saying that only poets should criticise poetry.

Not many critics were as crudely offensive as the anonymous *Saturday Review* writer of 1899† who said: 'It is impossible to understand why the bulk of this volume was published at all – why [Hardy] did not himself burn the verse'; and, in case that was insufficiently damnatory, proceeded to categories some of the ballads as 'the most astounding balderdash that ever found its way into a book of verse'. All

---

A dagger (†) indicates critical material discussed in the Introduction which is included in this selection.

the same, it is difficult to find a note of unalloyed enthusiasm among any of the other reviewers of *Wessex Poems*. Even the usually perceptive and scholarly Edmund Chambers† – later to become one of the most distinguished Shakespearean scholars – though he was receptive to Hardy's innovations in language and not averse from his 'sombre irony and mournful music', finds it necessary to rebuke him for his 'woodenness of rhythm and a needlessly inflated diction'. Others were less charitable. Though most found something to commend, all found more to condemn. But a genuine perplexity was widespread, perhaps the commonest reaction being the one Hardy sardonically noted in our opening quotation.

However, when *Poems of the Past and the Present* appeared in 1901, it was no longer possible to dismiss Hardy's verse as an aberration typical of an era when 'housemaids turn lady-novelists and lady-journalists turn amateur housemaids', as one reviewer of *Wessex Poems* had sourly put it.[2] Nevertheless, serious and detailed discussion was still far to seek, and Hardy was entitled to grumble, as he did, not that his poetry was disliked, but that Edwardian reviewing lacked a professional discipline and was often, even at a simple factual level, inaccurate. Thus Herbert Warren, later well-known as a vice-chancellor of Oxford University, summed up *Poems of the Past and the Present* as being 'of much the same size and character' as *Wessex Poems*.[3] As it not only contains twice as many poems, but many of them break entirely new ground ('Poems of Pilgrimage' and the Boer War poems, for example), one must question Warren's thoroughness; and when he says of 'At a Lunar Eclipse' [79*] that, though a fine thought, 'forcibly expressed', it is 'barely poetry', one is driven to reject his judgement, since this is a particularly good example of Hardy's impeccable handling of a traditional and strict form, the sonnet, and a worse instance could hardly have been cited as evidence of his unorthodoxy.

For virtually the whole of his poetic career, Hardy had to put up with the kind of comment exemplified in the anonymous *Athenaeum* piece of January 1902.† Its glib generalisation (mostly unsubstantiated by appropriate quotation), its casual, patronising tone – Hardy is 'wholly devoid of the faculty of self-criticism' (in fact, he was one of the most assiduous of revisers) – are not at all untypical of much that passed for criticism at the time. In 1904, to complicate matters, he disturbed the placid waters of Edwardian literature by launching upon them that vast and singular enterprise, *The Dynasts*. Its publication in three parts (Part II in 1906, Part III in 1908) exacerbated the controversy about his philosophy; and if, on the whole, it tended to establish his reputation as a poet, it also created a hiatus in the publication, if not the composition, of his lyrical poetry.

Even so, one would have expected the arrival of *Time's Laughingstocks* in 1909 to have attracted a good deal more attention than it did, for the last poems of Meredith (who died in that year) and an unremarkable collection by Laurence Binyon made up virtually the whole of the competition at the time of publication. The quality of the response, however, is distinctly higher than before. Far more searching and perceptive than anything that had appeared earlier are the *Athenaeum* piece of 1910† – which makes very high claims for Hardy's dour honesty and exceptional sensitivity to beauty, that together produce 'the ultimate dignity of artistic faithfulness' – and a review by Edward Thomas in the *Daily Chronicle* in December 1909.[4] Thomas here speaks of Hardy's 'austere, condensed and fateful manner', observes his fascination with verse form and his pervading sense of the 'misery and fraudulence of life', but concludes that, though 'the book contains ninety-nine reasons for not living . . . it is not a book of despair'. It is a pity that these two appraisals did not, in the event, set the tone for subsequent criticism.

That was left for Lytton Strachey, then the *enfant terrible* of the *New Statesman*'s review pages, to do, upon the appearance in November 1914 of *Satires of Circumstance*: a literary event not unnaturally somewhat overshadowed by the outbreak of the First World War four months before. In his *New Statesman* review† Strachey is, as ever, shrewd, witty and eminently readable, and he does not allow any niggling concern for accuracy to inhibit his talent for the telling phrase. The crux of his contention is that Hardy writes a kind of unpoetic verse, a 'flat and undistinguished' and 'clumsy collection of vocables' in which 'cacophony is incarnate': a kind of verse which, against the grain of all previous assumptions about poetry, is nevertheless incongruously effective in solving the 'secret of touching our marrow-bones'. This interesting but, to say the least, highly debatable paradox offered so easy an escape-route from the painful chore of actually thinking about Hardy's poetry *ab initio* that it became something of a critical commonplace in later years, substantially hampering the emergence of a more balanced and probing approach. It would have been a great deal better for a deeper understanding of Hardy's poetry if Edward Thomas's far more modest, as it was also far more profound, voice had been listened to more widely. It is at least possible that the revised and expanded version (1915)† of his *Poetry and Drama* piece of 1913 was partly intended as a riposte to Strachey. Brief as it is, Thomas's appraisal is remarkable not only for its accurate comparison of Hardy with Donne, and its directing our attention to Hardy's ability to 'mingle elements unexpectedly' (Samuel Johnson's *discordia concors*), but also for the poems Thomas chooses to exemplify his comments: poems like 'Julie-Jane' [205*], for instance, that have only recently begun to be seen as characteristic of Hardy at his best. As far as we know, Hardy never saw this essay, though he did read its writer's poetry, published after Thomas's death in action in 1917, and admired it.

It is noticeable that neither Thomas nor Strachey, nor any one else for that matter, gave much attention at the time of publication to that section of *Satires of Circumstance*, the 'Poems of 1912–13', which even those who care little for Hardy's verse would concede contains some of the greatest love-poetry in the language. These poems in the collection receive only a bare mention in the *Times Literary Supplement* article of mid-January 1915,† and many years were to elapse before they were granted anything like their critical due. The 'Poems of 1912–13', in fact, exemplify that unobtrusiveness, that unwillingness to adopt an opulent or, in his own phrase, 'jewelled', manner which was, we suspect, a powerful factor in the slowness of Hardy's climb to general public acceptance as a poet. The immediate, though diverse, appeal of the early works of Yeats, of Kipling, of Masefield and of Rupert Brooke was lacking – and designedly so. The popularity of 'Weathers' [512*] – 'This is the weather the cuckoo likes' – as an anthology piece is the exception that neatly proves the rule.

By this time books on Hardy were beginning to appear. Of those that devoted some space to the poetry we think that Harold Child's (1916)† – though brief and unambitious – is the best, not least because of his unhesitating identification of the 'Poems of 1912–13' as 'the most musically and suggestively beautiful poems Hardy ever wrote'. Though Child praises Hardy for his simplicity and intensity, and, perceptively, dwells on the poetry's 'fidelity to the author's precise meaning', he is uneasy about the diction; he fails, as many did, to see that for Hardy *what* he had to say was always the pre-eminent consideration, to which style and language must take a subservient place. Lascelles Abercrombie, in an uncharacteristically loose and perfunctory chapter of his book on Hardy (1912),[5] complains about the poet's failure in the management of 'the nameless excitations' of words – a comment that must stem, one feels, from a view of poetry as pure sound or 'music'. And the same complaint is heard in an otherwise generous assessment by Sir Arthur Quiller-Couch, who by this time was lecturing on Hardy at Cambridge. However, in two or three pages 'Q' gives perhaps the best account of Hardy as a countryman, 'most autochthonous of living writers'.[6] And indeed there begins to be apparent, from the end of the Great War and the publication of the first version of *Collected Poems* in 1919, a move away from the piecemeal reviewing of each successive volume towards a more ambitious and conspectual view of Hardy's poetical *oeuvre* – though we have still thought it sensible to include a contemporary review (1918) † of *Moments of Vision* (published in 1917), and would cite that on *Winter Words* (1928) in the *Times Literary Supplement*[7] as an interesting assessment of Hardy's last individual book of poems.

Some of the best criticism of the poetry is, in fact, clustered in the years 1918–20. The only reason for our not including the essay of 1918 by Edmund Gosse,[8] who had been a friend of Hardy's for some forty years, is that it is readily available in R. G. Cox's *Thomas Hardy: The Critical Heritage*. (See Select Bibliography.) Gosse's attempts to trace a chronological development in Hardy are not very productive perhaps, but he conducts an admirable defence of the 'metrical peculiarities', and discriminates nicely between Hardy's 'profoundly tragic' observation and the 'romantic peevishness' of, say, Shelley – interestingly citing Crabbe's poetry as an illuminating point of comparison.

To Middleton Murry (1919) † belongs much of the credit for the more perceptive appraisal of Hardy. He unhesitatingly asserts that Hardy is 'a great poet', uttering 'the cry of the universe'. From the first, says Murry, Hardy 'held aloof from the general conspiracy to forget . . . denying no element of his profound experience'. Post-war critics were naturally less eager than their predecessors to label Hardy a cynic or pessimist. Murry was also the first to insist on the magnificence of the love-poetry, singling out 'After a Journey' [289*] as an example of 'the quality of life that is vocal, gathered into a moment of time with a vista of years'. I. A. Richards (1926),† usually an adversary of Murry's, generously acknowledged the quality of his judgement of Hardy; and perhaps Murry's aphorism – 'The great poet remembers both rose and thorn; and it is beyond his power to remember them otherwise than together' – is, of all comments on Hardy, the one we can least afford to forget.

Walter de la Mare – whose own poetry Hardy admired and whose genius for the macabre was so like Hardy's, though generally they are far removed from each other in technique and language – contributed, in the *Times Literary Supplement* (late November 1919),† another original and profound survey. Though far from adulatory ('Never was the tinder of the mind more hospitable to the feeblest of actuality's sparks' is a sample of his sub-acid manner), he warmly praises Hardy's 'scope, his multifarious range of theme'; and, of the style, he memorably observes that 'Difficulty, seeming impossibility, is the breath of Mr Hardy's nostrils as a craftsman'. That is praise from one well qualified to give it. For all that critical opinion was still far from uniformly persuaded of Hardy's claim to immortality as a poet, the tide was certainly on the turn.

It is a significant, as well as a touching, sidelight on his character that so many of the young writers who had survived the holocaust – T. E. Lawrence, Siegfried Sassoon, Edmund Blunden and Robert Graves, with others less famous—should have sought out Hardy in the post-war years and been befriended by him. Profoundly disillusioned by the experience of the trenches, their ears were sharp to catch the faintest note of patriotic humbug or romantic claptrap. They found in his poems and in the old man himself an austere yet far from humourless integrity, an entire absence of chauvinism and vindictiveness, a comprehensive pity, together with a whole-hearted admiration for those virtues which the war, however terrible, had disclosed. It was as if he had already divined what they had discovered empirically; and, although his influence is only rarely discernible overtly in their work, he became a kind of spiritual grandfather to them. His refusal to edit experience was perhaps his most abiding and valuable legacy to his successors.

But there had also been a change of poetic climate. Hardy was no longer an innovator. His last three volumes display no signs of the times; if what was wanted in poetry was something *pour épater les bourgeois*, or an involved obscurity of manner, it was not to be found in the collections Hardy compiled in the last six years of his life: *Late Lyrics and Earlier* (1922: the year of T. S. Eliot's *The Waste Land*); *Human Shows, Far Phantasies* (1925: the year of Ezra Pound's *A Draft of XVI Cantos*; and *Winter Words* (1928: posthumously published in the Macmillan list that included Yeats's *The Tower*). Indeed, in a poem in *Late Lyrics and Earlier* – 'An Ancient to Ancients' [660*] – he issued a gentle rebuke to contemporary young men in a hurry. He was now the *doyen* of English letters – recipient of the Order of Merit and of an Honorary Fellowship at a Cambridge College—but he would rather have had his poetry read than respected, and he had moreover a wholesome respect for tradition, continuing to admire Tennyson for all that he had never attempted to emulate him.

The *London Mercury*, a new and very influential literary magazine, paid Hardy the compliment (as he, always modest, saw it) of printing one of his poems in its first issue (January 1920); and in 1922, among several other pieces about Hardy, a fine tribute to him, 'Mr Hardy's Old Age', was written by the magazine's editor, Sir John Squire.[9] His remark, 'Everything is behind him and nothing is before him', is perhaps obvious enough, though not always remembered; but when Squire added that 'the contemplation of transience and the regret of things gone is the mainspring of half our deepest emotion, and the source of half our poetry', he reminds us succinctly of one of the most distinctive qualities of Hardy's verse, which is far more significantly retrospective in mood than any *oeuvre* of similar size. No criticism that ignores Hardy's engagement with Time can hope to be adequate. The *London Mercury* also printed R. W. King's essay of 1925 † which is really the first substantial attempt to tackle the whole of Hardy's work in verse up to *Human Shows* . . . , and deserves credit for its methodical and sensible approach.

Hardy's death in January 1928, followed in November by the posthumous publication of *Winter Words in Various Moods and Metres*, inevitably brought a spate of obituary tributes. Of these, where the poetry is concerned, much the best is the leading article (unsigned, but now identified as being by Arthur S. MacDowall) in the *Times Literary Supplement* of 26 January 1928.† Thoughtful and finely expressed, its sensitive generalisations nevertheless mark the end of a phase in the criticism of Hardy's poetry which had lasted for nearly thirty years, and had been typified by the prevalance of hit-or-miss reviewing, often both perfunctory and patronising, content to repeat the shibboleths of earlier commentators. Really sustained and probing comment was rare indeed, and, until quite recently, recovery from this bad start was anything but swift. The monumental secondary bibliography by Gerber and Davis[10] includes some 3,150 items dealing with Hardy's work up to 1968. Of these, less than 300 have to do with the poetry (apart from *The Dynasts*), and more than half of these entries relate to contemporary reviews and are commonly very brief notices. In addition to those included in this Casebook there was a handful of pioneering articles which attempted something more ambitious, some of which we mention later; and, certainly, in the last years of his life and thereafter, it was felt by writers of books on Hardy that some comment on his poetry was expedient, if only for completeness's sake. Samuel Chew, for example, devoted part of his book (1921)[11] to the poems. He was rewarded by his subject by some vigorous, if irritable, annotations; Hardy was far from indifferent to what was written about his work. To be fair, Chew's book is much better than most of its predecessors.

After Hardy's death his prose did not fall into the trough of disregard which often awaits long-lived writers, but for the poetry the bibliography tells a tale of neglect. Probably the lack of a really representative and substantial selection from the poems contributed to this. Hardy's own *Chosen Poems* (compiled 1927, published 1929) is perhaps over-idiosyncratic and certainly over-modest; nor did G. M. Young's *Selected Poems* (1940) adequately fill the gap.

In 1932, however, a judgement on Hardy's poetry which was to prove exceedingly influential appeared in F. R. Leavis's first book, *New Bearings in English Poetry*.[12] There are, in fact, only six pages on Hardy in the chapter surveying the situation at the end of the First World War; and the tone of Leavis's remarks is far from uniformly commendatory. Hardy is 'truly a Victorian . . . with the earth firm under his feet . . . a naive poet of simple attitudes and outlook. . . . His originality . . . went, indeed, with a naive conservatism'; he displays a 'precritical innocence', and his 'rank as a major poet rests upon a dozen poems'. Here is what we may call the Inspired Rustic theory of Hardy's achievement; like a literary Douanier Rousseau, he hardly knew what he was doing when he created a masterpiece. A careful study of Hardy's own remarks in Part One of this Casebook will go far to suggest that much of Leavis's argument is tendentious. But Leavis did 'value some poems very highly indeed; the six he lists out of his dozen include at least four that everyone would agree on, and his brief analysis of 'The Voice' [285*] – like his later superb critique (1952)[13] of 'After a Journey' [289*] – evinces a fine capacity to define one aspect of Hardy's genius: what he calls the 'poignancy of love and its hopelessness, and the cruelty of time'. All the same, the overall effect of Leavis's comments was, we feel, mischievous in that it made it possible for readers to suppose that a very brief encounter indeed was all that was needed to experience Hardy as a poet. Moreover, Leavis was to become a routine starting point for many later critics, some of whom do no more than briskly cite as received and incontrovertible wisdom the passage we have instanced. We regret that we have been denied permission to include anything of the late Dr Leavis's in this selection.

Two books on Hardy published between the wars deserve special notice. That by Dr E. C. Hickson (1931)[14] is a scholarly and exhaustive analysis of the versification, in which she draws attention to the exceptionally wide range of metrical device and stanzaic forms employed by Hardy. The other, Arthur S. MacDowall's *Thomas Hardy: A Critical Study* (1931), † which has been unaccountably neglected, is the first to devote a proportionate share of its contents to the poetry, of which it treats both thoroughly and sensitively. MacDowall may seem to us now to labour his points a little, but he deserves credit for breaking so much new ground, so painstakingly. Apart from these two studies, there is very little in book-form during the interwar period. H. C. Duffin (1921)[15] and W. R. Rutland (1938)[16] have valuable contributions to make on the novels but are plainly not in sympathy with the poems. We include F. L. Lucas's lively essay (1940) † more because of its insistence on Hardy's truthfulness, his 'hatred of cant', than because of any particularly profound analysis.

With a mordant irony he would have been the first to notice, the centenary of Hardy's birth (2 June 1840) coincided with the beginning of the Battle of Britain. It is a token of his enduring power that even events as cataclysmic as any in *The Dynasts* did not preclude a throng of tributes. But, so far as the poetry is concerned, it was from across the Atlantic that the most significant contribution came.

It is not too much to say that the Hardy issue (Summer 1940) of the *Southern Review*[17] is the great watershed in the study of Hardy's poetry. Certainly, in terms both of direction and emphasis, nothing was to be the same again. The authority of the contributors was indisputable; the sheer weight of comment (eight of the fourteen substantial essays deal with Hardy's verse) and the diversity of opinion are at once stimulating and, taken as a whole, an impressive testimony to his range. The essay by W. H. Auden is one of the two or three best tributes ever paid by one great poet to another; it is readily available in the volume on Hardy edited by A. J. Guerard. (See Select Bibliography.) That by Howard Baker † identifies very precisely what its writer terms Hardy's 'fundamental quality': a 'simple humanity'. Jacques Barzun and Delmore Schwartz each treat persuasively more ideological aspects of the verse. John Crowe Ransom has a rather diffuse piece; F. R. Leavis reiterates with additions his earlier contentions; and R. P. Blackmur writes on the 'Shorter Poems'; each qualifies his praise pretty sharply, however. Blackmur's essay has become something of a *locus classicus* for subsequent accounts of Hardy's briefer lyrics – Douglas Brown (1954) using as a springboard, so to speak, its telling exegesis of 'Last Words to a Dumb Friend' [619*]; J. I. M. Stewart (1971)[18] citing it with warm approval. But these few pages, which include an all too brief commendation of the 'Poems of 1912–13', are preceded by many which can only be labelled depreciating. It is what he sees as Hardy's wilful break with tradition in favour of a stubborn 'adherence to his personal and crotchety obsessions' that excites Blackmur's opposition, and he virtually denies success to Hardy except when his 'personal rhythm' finds a 'liberating subject', almost always when 'responding directly and personally to death or the dead'. It is hardly the whole truth, but it is one of the judgements that demand attention. Even so, and however subtly, Blackmur's position represents a reworking of the Strachey–Leavis theme: that of a prolific, unselective minor talent blundering into an uncovenanted magnificence now and then, when theme and eccentric manner chance to harmonise. This is a view shared, rather surprisingly, by Edmund Blunden, whose otherwise excellent book appeared in 1941.[19]

The war years tended to throw critical emphasis back on Hardy's prose, perhaps because that very 'parochialism' which he said was vital to a great novelist now appealed more than ever to an islanded and embattled people – though his treatment of war in poetry was curiously prophetic of the tone adopted by many of the poets of the Second World War. It was not until 1947, almost fifty years àfter the publication of *Winter Words*, that there appeared the first critical book to concern itself wholly with the evaluation of Hardy's verse: J. G. Southworth's *The Poetry of Hardy*.[20] His earlier sections, on ideas, influences and technique, are satisfactory, but Part III, 'The Achievement', is confusing and lukewarm at best,.offers no sustained attempt to examine meaningfully earlier strictures, and cannot be said to have done much to increase understanding or enthusiasm. Quiller-Couch once said: 'Tendencies didn't write the "Ode to Autumn"; Keats wrote it!' – a minatory remark which several of Hardy's critics might have profitably heeded.

   Much more of lasting value can be found, we suggest, in the small but elegant compass of Cecil Day Lewis's Warton Lecture (1951). † By no means indulgent (he speaks of Hardy's 'potted melodramas' and accepts that he wrote 'many bad poems'), he brings to bear the insight of a poet, at his best a very good poet indeed, and conducts a telling defence of Hardy's 'great technical skill', his 'critical judgement', his 'balance and congruence', while insisting, above all, on his 'tenderness'. It is no coincidence that Day Lewis wrote two of the best poems about Hardy, one in a loving pastiche of his style, and he is undoubtedly the best corrective to the more Apollonian critics like Blackmur and Leavis. Those new to Hardy would do well to begin with Day Lewis and Auden.

   From about 1950 the trickle of books and articles on Hardy has grown steadily into a river, of which a very sizeable tributary is now devoted to the poetry, while general books on his work increasingly assign a fair share of their attention to his verse. An increasing and, on the whole, welcome trend towards specialisation is also noticeable, and a good deal of useful background material has been published. For example, Emma Hardy's *Some Recollections*, edited by Evelyn Hardy and Robert Gittings (1961),[21] illuminates several of the 'Poems of 1912–13' most effectively. The writers of articles now tend to concern themselves with manageable themes instead of trying to draw out Leviathan with a hook; the actual achievement of individual poems or groups of poems is scrutinised, the text receives its proper due, and there is much less fishing in the Tom Tiddler's Pool of Hardy's Ideas and Philosophy. All this is admirable. Yet it presents us here with a dilemma, since to mention everything would strengthen the resemblance of this Introduction to an annotated bibliography! We therefore propose to treat first of books, all of which are fairly accessible, of course; and then, more selectively, to deal with articles. Our policy for inclusion now becomes subject to criteria of general usefulness balanced against varying critical approaches. For earlier work we felt it was worth the attempt to be broadly representative.

   The books mentioned above, together with those listed in the Select Bibliography and the Notes to this Introduction, all have much to offer. The chapter from Jean Brooks's study (1971),† however, with its combination of close textual analysis and scholarly breadth of reference, together with Samuel Hynes's pointed analysis (1956)† of Hardy's style and Kenneth Marsden's careful probing of his vocabulary (1969),† are, we think, particularly good examples of the recent upsurge of sound critical comment on the poetry. Paul Zietlow's book *Moments of Vision* (1974)[22] also merits close reading, especially for its stressing a too-often

undervalued aspect of Hardy's achievement. Tom Paulin's study of
'perception' in the poetry (1975)[23] may also be commended. Hardy's
classical status is accepted by all these critics, who gain a good deal by
not having first to cut away the brushwood round the temple. Perhaps
they were assisted in this by a somewhat earlier generation of general
books on Hardy, of which the best was that by the late Douglas Brown
(1954)† – already mentioned – which contains brilliant and seminally
detailed treatment of several key poems. The section on the 'Poems of
1912–13' in Irving Howe's study (1967)[24] is hard to better as a general
statement of their quality; and Trevor Johnson's book (1968)[25] surveys
the field methodically and concisely.

As for the articles: these tend mostly to fall into three categories. First
is the explanatory or elucidatory, like those by Evelyn Hardy[26] and
James O. Bailey,[27] sometimes reporting discoveries relevant to the text.
We have not included anything of this kind because Bailey and Pinion
have, between them, subsumed practically all of this material into their
handbooks. (See Select Bibliography.) Most of the articles published up
to around 1950 were of this kind, but the results of this necessary
pioneering are now readily available.

Secondly, there is a fairly small group of articles concerned with close
textual analysis, focussing on one or two poems only. Of these we would
single out the illuminating treatment by C. B. Cox and A. E. Dyson
(1963)† of one of Hardy's greatest poems, 'After a Journey' [289*],
which Douglas Brown, in the book already mentioned, and David
Holbrook (1977)[28] also treat with skill and perception; while it is on this
poem too that F. R. Leavis, as already mentioned, writes what we think
is his best criticism of Hardy. The piece by L. E. W. Smith (1964)†
shows, succinctly, how a less familiar lyric – 'The Impercipient' [44*]—
may be brought to life by a tactful employment of exegesis. Hardy is
generally lacking in the kind of complexity or 'ambiguity' that,
sometimes more than any intrinsic force in a poem, attracts the
analytically disposed. But there is plenty of scope here for good work to
be done.

Thirdly come the exploratory or inductive articles, which attempt to
break new ground, to effect a synthesis or advance an hypothesis; and
the vast preponderance of these are, of course, recent. In our selection
we have quite deliberately attempted to indicate some of the
approaches, now very diverse, that critics have taken, feeling that, even
if in our opinion some of them have allowed their reach to exceed their
grasp, those who wish to study Hardy's poetry other than superficially
will gain from grappling with theories that necessitate constant returns
to the text. It seems best to let such articles speak for themselves; there is
little purpose in attempting to summarise such pieces as that by Thom
Gunn (1972).† At the risk of being invidious, it may be better to

instance some of those we do not have room for, along with other writers who are represented in this Casebook.

Early articles, or chapters, were published by Joseph Beach (1936),[29] Mark Van Doren (1930),[30] George Elliott (1928),[31] John Livingston Lowes (1926)[32] and Lionel Stevenson (1932)[33] – all from America, where appreciation of Hardy's poetry and readiness to study it in detail were of earlier growth than in Britain. David Daiches (1936)[34] – who was working in America at the time – Ifor Evans (1933)[35] and Charles Williams (1936)[36] are perhaps the best of the British pioneers, together with Vivian de Sola Pinto, whose admirable and original comparison of Hardy with Housman (1939) was later incorporated into his book *Crisis in English Poetry* (1951).[37] For manna in the critical wilderness of 1940–50 (aside from the *Southern Review* issue of 1940) we must look to Vere Collins (1942),[38] Marion Roberts (1944)[39] and, especially, Sir Maurice Bowra whose sparkling and acute Byron Lecture of 1947[40] gave a much-needed lift to Hardy's poetical reputation at a time when it was in the doldrums.

Finally, amid a much greater profusion of possibilities since the 1950s, we may cite as deserving attention the work of John Bayley (1976),[41] Jonathan Dollimore (1975),[42] Hillis Miller (1968; 1970),[43] Roy Morrell (1965),[44] Harold Orel (1971; 1974; and especially his book of 1976),[45] David Perkins (1959)[46] and Yvor Winters (1967),[47] together with other pieces by contributors to this selection.

In so far as all the more recent critics share (with the exception of Yvor Winters, perhaps) certain assumptions about Hardy's poetry – a conviction that he knew what he was about, a close regard to words on the page, a disinclination to equate idiosyncrasy with eccentricity, and a steady awareness of the essential humanity which is, paradoxically, the true root of the sardonic and satirical strain in him – they may be said to have given, collectively, the kind of firm direction to the study of Hardy's poems which was lacking for so long. It is easier now, of course, to avoid pitfalls; there are good anthologies, and the publication of the *Complete Poems* has helped here. Among critical appraisals of this, now the standard edition, we would mention the review article by Robert Gittings (1976)[48] because what Gittings (who is Hardy's best biographer so far) has to say is especially significant in regard to the use of the main events in Hardy's life as the poet's own mythological system.

The Variorum Edition of the Complete Poems has now been published, and it increases the opportunities for students of Hardy to examine his many emendations: which are such as to deal the death-blow to the contention that he brought off his successes by happy accident. James O. Bailey and Frank B. Pinion between them have exhaustively annotated every poem; Lennart Björk's edition of the *Notebooks* (1974)[49] is of great value; and we now have the first volume of the *Collected Letters*, edited by R. L. Purdy and Michael Millgate.[50]

All this is evidence of the recognition of Hardy as one of the major English poets. But, for all the lively and illuminating discussion of the last decade, we do not think that Philip Larkin's magisterial complaint of 1966, 'Wanted: Good Hardy Critic',[51] has yet been answered. The fact remains that there is still a streak of diffidence, a smack of apology, in the manner in which even his most fervent admirers assume to advance his claims. The itch to classify, the urge to delimit, are perhaps symptoms of a quite proper deference before so large, so Protean, a body of work as Hardy's. But, for the critic's baptism, '*manet oceanus*', as George Saintsbury once remarked; and some one, some day, will have to take the plunge and try to tell us just where and how Hardy triumphs, and why – without paying too much attention to taking out insurance policies on what his predecessors have said.

NOTES

Hardy('s) and Thomas Hardy('s) are here abbreviated throughout to H('s) and TH ('s).

1. Florence Hardy, *Life of TH* (London: 1962), p. 299.
2. Unsigned review in *The Academy* (14 Jan. 1899).
3. T. H. Warren, *Spectator* (5 April 1902).
4. Edward Thomas, *Daily Chronicle* (7 Dec. 1909).
5. Lascelles Abercrombie, *TH* (London: 1912), ch. VII.
6. Sir Arthur Quiller-Couch, *Studies in Literature*, 1st series (Cambridge: 1919), p. 201.
7. Unsigned review in *TLS* (4 Oct. 1928).
8. Edmund Gosse, 'Mr H's Lyrical Poems', *Edinburgh Review*, CCVII (April 1918); see also his 'Mr H's Last Poem', *The Times* (13 Sept. 1928).
9. Sir John Squire, 'Mr H's Old Age', *London Mercury* (July 1922); reprinted in his *Essays on Poetry* (London: 1924).
10. Helmut E. Gerber and W. Eugene Davis, *TH: An Annotated Bibliography of Writings about Him* (Urbana, Ill: 1973).
11. Samuel Chew, *TH, Poet and Novelist* (New York: 1921).
12. F. R. Leavis, *New Bearings in English Poetry* (London: 1932), pp. 56–62.
13. Idem, 'Reality and Sincerity', *Scrutiny*, XIX, 2 (1952); reprinted in his *The Living Principle: 'English' as a Discipline of Thought* (London: 1975), pp. 127–54.
14. E. C. Hickson, *The Versification of TH* (Philadelphia: 1931).
15. H. C. Duffin, *TH: A Study* (London: 1921); material on poems added in later edition.
16. W. R. Rutland, *TH: A Study of His Writings and Their Background* (Oxford: 1938).
17. Special centenary issue on H, *Southern Review*, VI (Summer 1940).
18. J. I. M. Stewart, *TH: A Critical Biography* (London: 1971).

19. Edmund Blunden, *TH* (London: 1941).

20. J. G. Southworth, *The Poetry of H* (New York: 1947).

21. Emma Hardy, *Some Recollections*, edited by Evelyn Hardy and Robert Gittings (Oxford: 1961).

22. Paul Zietlow, *Moments of Vision: The Poetry of H* (Cambridge, Mass: 1974). See also his 'The Tentative Mode in H's Poetry', *Victorian Poetry* (Summer 1967).

23. T. Paulin, *TH: The Poetry of Perception* (London: 1975).

24. Irving Howe, *TH* (New York: 1967). See also his 'The Short Poems of TH', *Southern Review* (October 1960).

25. H. A. T. Johnson, *TH* (London: 1968). See also his 'TH and the Respectable Muse', *Thomas Hardy Year Book*, I (1970); and 'Despite Time's Derision: TH, Donne and the 1912–13 Poems', *THYB*, VI (1978).

26. Evelyn Hardy, 'H: Some Unpublished Poems', *London Magazine*, III (1956); and 'H: An Unpublished Poem', *TLS* (2 June 1966).

27. James O. Bailey, 'Evolutionary Meliorism in the Poetry of H', *Studies in Philology* (July 1963); 'Autobiography in H's Poems', and 'H's "Poems of Pilgrimage"', both in *English Literature in Transition*, IX, 4 (1966); 'Fact and Fiction in H's Poetry', *CEA Critic* (March 1968); 'H in the Modern World', in F. B. Pinion (ed.), *TH and the Modern World* (Thomas Hardy Society, Dorchester: 1974).

28. David Holbrook, 'Despite Time's Derision: A Reading of "After a Journey"', in his *Lost Bearings in English Poetry* (London: 1977). Versions of this appreciation of the poem were previously published, in a symposium on existentialism, in *Tract*, 16 and 17, and in *New Universities Quarterly*, 29, No. 4 (Autumn 1975).

29. Joseph W. Beach, *The Concept of Nature in Nineteenth-Century Poetry* (New York: 1936).

30. Mark Van Doren, many reviews and articles, especially his *Modern Writers at Work* (New York: 1930), and *The Happy Critic* (Edinburgh and London: 1961).

31. George R. Elliott, 'H's Poetry and the Ghostly Moving Picture', *South Atlantic Quarterly* (July 1928); and 'Spectral Etchings in H's Poetry', *PMLA* (Dec. 1928).

32. John Livingston Lowes, 'Two Readings of Earth (H and Meredith)', *Yale Review* (April 1926).

33. Lionel Stevenson, *Darwin Among the Poets* (Chicago: 1936).

34. David Daiches, *Poetry in the Modern World* (Chicago: 1936).

35. Ifor Evans, *English Poetry in the Later Nineteenth Century* (London: 1933).

36. Charles Williams, *Poetry at Present* (Oxford: 1936).

37. Vivian de Sola Pinto, *Realism in English Poetry* (London: 1939); and *Crisis in English Poetry* (London: 1951).

38. Vere H. Collins, 'The Love Poetry of TH', *Essays and Studies* (1942).

39. Marion Roberts, 'The Dramatic Element in H's Poetry', *Queen's Quarterly* (Winter 1944); see also her article of the same title in *Kenyon Review*, XXII (Spring 1960).

40. Sir Maurice Bowra, *The Lyrical Poetry of H* (The Byron Lecture, University of Nottingham: 1947).

41. John Bayley, 'Separation and Non-Communication as Features of H's Poetry', *Agenda*, No. 14 (1976).

42. Jonathan Dollimore, 'The Poetry of TH and Edward Thomas', *Critical Quarterly* (Autumn 1975).

43. J. Hillis Miller, ' "Wessex Heights": The Persistence of the Past in H's Poetry', *Critical Quarterly* (Winter 1968); and *TH: Distance and Desire* (Cambridge, Mass: 1970).

44. Roy Morrell, *The Will and the Way* (Singapore: 1965).

45. Harold Orel, 'Trends in Critical Views Towards H's Poetry', *English Literature in Transition*, xiv, 5 (1971); 'H, War and the Years of Pax Britannica', in *TH and the Modern World* (1974: see note 27 above); 'After *The Dynasts*: H's Relationship to Christianity', in *Budmouth Essays* (Thomas Hardy Society, Dorchester: 1976); and *The Final Years of TH 1912–1928* (London: 1976). See also his *H's Personal Writings* (London: 1967).

46. David Perkins, 'H and the Poetry of Isolation', *J. of English Literary History* (June 1959).

47. Yvor Winters, *Forms of Discovery* (Chicago: 1967).

48. Robert Gittings, 'The Complete Poems of TH', *Encounter* (July 1976). An edited version of this review is included in L. St John Butler (ed.), *TH After Fifty Years* (London: 1977). Gittings's two biographies are *Young TH* (London: 1975) and *The Older H* (London: 1978).

49. Lennart A. Björk (ed.), *The Literary Notes of TH* (Göteborg: 1974).

50. R. L. Purdy and Michael Millgate (eds), *Collected Letters of TH*, vol. 1 (Oxford: 1978).

51. Philip Larkin, 'Wanted: Good Hardy Critic', *Critical Quarterly* (Summer 1966).

PART ONE

Hardy on Poetry

EXTRACTS FROM *NOTEBOOKS*, *THE LIFE*, CORRESPONDENCE AND PREFACES TO COLLECTIONS OF VERSE

THE most prosaic man becomes a poem when you stand by his grave at his funeral and think of him.

> *The First Notebook*, 29 May 1871: R. H. Taylor (ed.), *The Personal Notebooks of TH* (London: 1979), p. 10.

☆

READ again Addison, Macaulay, Newman, Sterne, Defoe, Lamb, Gibbon, Burke, *Times* leaders, etc., in a study of style. Am more and more confirmed in an idea I have long held, as a matter of common sense, long before I thought of any old aphorism bearing on the subject: 'Ars est celare artem'. The whole secret of a living style and the difference between it and a dead style, lies in not having too much style – being, in fact, a little careless, or rather seeming to be, here and there. It brings wonderful life into the writing:

> A sweet disorder in the dress . . .
> A careless shoe-string, in whose tie
> I see a wild civility,
> Do more bewitch me than when art
> Is too precise in every part.

Otherwise your style is like worn half-pence – all the fresh images rounded off by rubbing, and no crispness or movement at all.

It is, of course, simply a carrying into prose the knowledge I have acquired in poetry – that inexact rhymes and rhythms now and then are far more pleasing than correct ones.

> F. E. Hardy, *The Life of TH* (London: 2 vols, 1928 and 1930; new edition, 1 vol., 1962, p. 105): comment of 1875.

☆

THERE is enough poetry in what is left [in life], after all the false romance has been abstracted, to make a sweet pattern: *e.g.* the poem by H. Coleridge:

> She is not fair to outward view.

So, then, if Nature's defects must be looked in the face and transcribed, whence arises the *art* in poetry and novel-writing? which must certainly show art, or it becomes merely mechanical reporting. I think the art lies in making these defects the basis of a hitherto unperceived beauty, by irradiating them with 'the light that never was' on their surface, but is seen to be latent in them by the spiritual eye.

Life, p. 114 (1877).

☆

SINCE coming into contact with Leslie Stephen about 1873, as has been shown, Hardy had been much influenced by his philosophy, and also by his criticism. He quotes the following sentence from Stephen in his note-book under the date of 1 July 1879:

'The ultimate aim of the poet should be to touch our hearts by showing his own, and not to exhibit his learning, or his fine taste, or his skill in mimicking the notes of his predecessors.' That Hardy adhered pretty closely to this principle when he resumed the writing of poetry can hardly be denied.

Life, p. 128 (1879).

☆

THE business of the poet and novelist is to show the sorriness underlying the grandest things, and the grandeur underlying the sorriest things.

Life, p. 171 (1885).

☆

To find beauty in ugliness is the province of the poet.

Life, p. 213 (1888).

☆

POETRY. Perhaps I can express more fully in verse ideas and emotions which run counter to the inert crystallized opinion – hard as a rock – which the vast body of men have vested interests in supporting. To cry out in a passionate poem that (for instance) the Supreme Mover or Movers, the Prime Force or Forces, must be either limited in power, unknowing, or cruel – which is obvious enough, and has been for centuries – will cause them merely a shake of the head; but to put it in argumentative prose will make them sneer, or foam, and set all the literary contortionists jumping upon me, a harmless agnostic, as if I were a clamorous atheist, which in their crass illiteracy they seem to think is the same thing . . . . If Galileo had said in verse that the world moved, the Inquisition might have let him alone.

Life, pp. 284–5 (1896).

☆

[The reception of *Wessex Poems*]

IN short, this was a particular instance of the general and rather appalling conclusion to which he came – had indeed known before – that a volume of poetry, by clever manipulation, can be made to support any *a priori* theory about its quality. Presuppose its outstanding feature to be the defects aforesaid; instances can be found. Presuppose, as here was done, that it is overloaded with derivations from the Latin or Greek when really below the average in such words; they can be found. Presuppose that Wordsworth is unorthodox; instances can be found; that Byron is devout; instances can also be found. (The foregoing paragraphs are abridged from memoranda which Hardy set down, apparently for publication; though he never published them.)

He wrote somewhere: 'There is no new poetry; but the new poet – if he carry the flame on further (and if not he is no new poet) – comes with a new note. And that new note it is that troubles the critical waters.

'Poetry is emotion put into measure. The emotion must come by nature, but the measure can be acquired by art.'

In the reception of this and later volumes of Hardy's poems there was, he said, as regards form, the inevitable ascription to ignorance of what was really choice after full knowledge. That the author loved the art of concealing art was undiscerned. For instance, as to rhythm. Years earlier he had decided that too regular a beat was bad art. He had fortified himself in his opinion by thinking of the analogy of architecture, between which art and that of poetry he had discovered, to use his own words, that there existed a close and curious parallel, both arts, unlike some others, having to carry a rational content inside their artistic form. He knew that in architecture cunning irregularity is of enormous worth, and it is obvious that he carried on into his verse, perhaps in part unconsciously, the Gothic art-principle in which he had been trained – the principle of spontaneity found in mouldings, tracery, and such like – resulting in the 'unforeseen' (as it has been called) character of his metres and stanzas, that of stress rather than of syllable, poetic texture rather than poetic veneer; the latter kind of thing, under the name of 'constructed ornament', being what he, in common with every Gothic student, had been taught to avoid as the plague. He shaped his poetry accordingly, introducing metrical pauses, and reversed beats; and found for his trouble that some particular line of a poem exemplifying this principle was greeted with a would-be jocular remark that such a line 'did not make for immortality'. The same critic might have gone to one of our cathedrals (to follow up the analogy of architecture), and on discovering that the carved leafage of some capital or spandrel in the best period of Gothic art strayed freakishly out of its bounds over the moulding, where by rule it had no business to be, or that the enrichments of a string-course were not accurately spaced; or that there was a sudden blank in a wall where a window was to be expected from formal measurement, have declared with equally merry conviction, 'This does not make for immortality'.

One case of the kind, in which the poem 'On Sturminster Foot-Bridge' [426] was quoted with the remark that one could make as good music as that out of a milk-cart, betrayed the reviewer's ignorance of any perception that the metre was intended to be onomatopoeic, plainly as it was shown; and another in the same tone disclosed that the reviewer had tried to scan the author's sapphics as heroics.

If any proof were wanted that Hardy was not at this time and later the apprentice at verse that he was supposed to be, it could be found in an examination of his studies over many years. Among his papers were quantities of notes on rhythm and metre: with outlines and experiments in innumerable original measures, some of which he adopted from time to time. These verse skeletons were mostly blank, and only designated by the usual marks for long and short syllables, accentuations, etc., but they were occasionally made up of 'nonsense verses' – such as, he said, were written when he was a boy by students of Latin prosody with the aid of a 'Gradus'.

Lastly, Hardy had a born sense of humour, even a too keen sense occasionally: but his poetry was sometimes placed by editors in the hands of reviewers deficient in that quality. Even if they were acustomed to Dickensian humour they were not to Swiftian. Hence it unfortunately happened that verses of a satirical, dry, caustic, or farcical cast were regarded by them with the deepest seriousness. In one case the tragic nature of his verse was instanced by the ballad called 'The Bride-Night Fire' or 'The Fire at Tranter Sweatley's' [48*]; the criticism being by an accomplished old friend of his own, Frederic Harrison, who deplored the painful nature of the bridegroom's end in leaving only a bone behind him. This piece of work Hardy had written and published when quite a young man, and had hesitated to reprint because of its too pronounced obviousness as a jest.

But he had looked the before-mentioned obstacles in the face, and their consideration did not move him much. He had written his poems entirely because he liked doing them, without any ulterior thought; because he wanted to say the things they contained and would contain.

He offered his publishers to take on his own shoulders the risk of producing the volume, so that if nobody bought it they should not be out of pocket. They were kind enough to refuse this offer, and took the risk on themselves; and fortunately they did not suffer.

A more serious meditation of Hardy's at this time than that on critics was the following:

'*January* (1899). No man's poetry can be truly judged till its last line is written. What is the last line? The death of the poet. And hence there is this quaint consolation to any writer of verse – that it may be imperishable for all that anybody can tell him to the contrary; and that if worthless he can never know it, unless he be a greater adept at self-criticism than poets usually are.'

Life, pp. 300–2 (1899).

☆

IN a pocket-book of this date [1900] appears a diagram illustrating 'the language of verse':

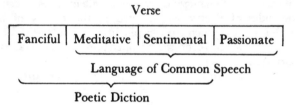

and the following note thereon:

The confusion of thought to be observed in Wordsworth's teaching in his essay in the Appendix to *Lyrical Ballads* seems to arise chiefly out of his use of the word "imagination". He should have put the matter somewhat like this: In works of *passion and sentiment* (not "imagination and sentiment") the language of verse is the language of prose. In works of *fancy* (or *imagination*), "poetic diction" (of the real kind) is proper, and even necessary. The diagram illustrates my meaning.

Life, p. 306 (1900).

☆

PICTURES. My weakness has always been to prefer the large intention of an unskilful artist to the trivial intention of an accomplished one: in other words, I am more interested in the high ideas of a feeble executant than in the high execution of a feeble thinker.

Life, p. 310 (1901).

☆

POETRY. There is a latent music in the sincere utterance of deep emotion, however expressed, which fills the place of the actual word-music in rhythmic phraseology on thinner emotive subjects, or on subjects with next to none at all. And supposing a total poetic effect to be represented by a unit, its component fractions may be either, say:

> Emotion three-quarters, plus Expression one quarter, or
> Emotion one quarter, plus Expression three-quarters.

This suggested conception seems to me to be the only one which explains all cases, including those instances of verse that apparently infringe all rules, and yet bring unreasoned convictions that they are poetry.

Life, p. 311 (1901).

☆

WHAT a pity there is no school or science of criticism, – especially in respect of verse . . . You might deliver an excellent series of lectures on the Vicissitudes of Poetry as exhibited in the history of English Literature – instancing such a queer phenomenon as that of Vaughan for example, who for two centuries dropped into oblivion, and was then only resurrected.

Letter to Quiller Couch (22 December 1916)

☆

FOR as long as I can remember my instinctive feeling has been to avoid the jewelled line in poetry as being effeminate.

Letter to Edmund Gosse (4 February 1919)

☆

. . . THE characteristic of all great poetry – the general perfectly reduced to the particular.

Hardy talking to Elliott Felkin about Robert Browning's 'The Statue and the Bust' (21 July 1919)

☆

IT was my hope to add to these volumes of verse as many more as would make a fairly comprehensive cycle of the whole. I had wished that those in dramatic, ballad, and narrative form should include most of the cardinal situations which occur in social and public life, and those in lyric form a round of emotional experiences of some completeness. But

The petty done, the undone vast!

The more written the more seems to remain to be written; and the night cometh. I realize that these hopes and plans, except possibly to the extent of a volume or two, must remain unfulfilled.

> from the General Preface to the 'Wessex Edition of Thomas Hardy's Works in Prose and Verse' (London, 1912).

☆

HERE is a sentence from the *Edinburgh Review* of a short time back which I might have written myself: 'The division [of poems] into separate groups [ballad, lyrical, narrative, &c.] is frequently a question of the preponderance, not of the exclusive possession, of certain aesthetic elements.'

> *Life*, p. 359 (1912).

☆

IN these days when the literature of narrative and verse seems to be losing its qualities as an art, and to be assuming a structureless and conglomerate character, it is a privilege that we should have come into our midst a writer [Anatole France] who is faithful to the principles that make for permanence, who never forgets the value of organic form and symmetry, the force of reserve, and the emphasis of understatement, even in his lighter works.

> *Life*, p. 363 (1913).

☆

—TURNING now to my verse – to myself the more individual part of my literary fruitage – I would say that, unlike some of the fiction, nothing interfered with the writer's freedom in respect of its form or content. Several of the poems – indeed many – were produced before novel-writing had been thought of as a pursuit; but few saw the light till all the novels had been published. . . .

The few volumes filled by the verse cover a producing period of some eighteen years first and last, while the seventeen or more volumes of novels represent correspondingly about four-and-twenty years. One is reminded by this disproportion in time and result how much more concise and quintessential expression becomes when given in rhythmic form than when shaped in the language of prose. . . .

> from the Introduction to the Mellstock Edition of *The Collected Poems* (London, 1919).

☆

HAVING at last, I think, finished with the personal points that I was recommended to notice, I will forsake the immediate object of this

Preface; and, leaving *Late Lyrics* to whatever fate it deserves, digress for a few moments to more general considerations. The thoughts of any man of letters concerned to keep poetry alive cannot but run uncomfortably on the precarious prospects of English verse at the present day. Verily the hazards and casualties surrounding the birth and setting forth of almost every modern creation in numbers are ominously like those of one of Shelley's paper-boats on a windy lake. And a forward conjecture scarcely permits the hope of a better time, unless men's tendencies should change. So indeed of all art, literature, and 'high thinking' nowadays. Whether owing to the barbarizing of taste in the younger minds by the dark madness of the late war, the unabashed cultivation of selfishness in all classes, the plethoric growth of knowledge simultaneously with the stunting of wisdom, 'a degrading thirst after outrageous stimulation' (to quote Wordsworth again), or from any other cause, we seem threatened with a new Dark Age.

I formerly thought, like other much exercised writers, that so far as literature was concerned a partial cause might be impotent or mischievous criticism; the satirizing of individuality, the lack of whole-seeing in contemporary estimates of poetry and kindred work, the knowingness affected by junior reviewers, the overgrowth of meticulousness in their peerings for an opinion, as if it were a cultivated habit in them to scrutinize the tool-marks and be blind to the building, to hearken for the key-creaks and be deaf to the diapason, to judge the landscape by a nocturnal exploration with a flash-lantern. In other words, to carry on the old game of sampling the poem or drama by quoting the worst line or worst passage only, in ignorance or not of Coleridge's proof that a versification of any length neither can be nor ought to be all poetry; of reading meanings into a book that its author never dreamt of writing there. I might go on interminably.

But I do not now think any such temporary obstructions to be the cause of the hazard, for these negligences and ignorances, though they may have stifled a few true poets in the run of generations, disperse like stricken leaves before the wind of next week, and are no more heard of again in the region of letters than their writers themselves. No: we may be convinced that something of the deeper sort mentioned must be the cause.

In any event poetry, pure literature in general, religion – I include religion, in its essential and undogmatic sense, because poetry and religion touch each other, or rather modulate into each other; are, indeed, often but different names for the same thing – these, I say, the visible signs of mental and emotional life, must like all other things keep moving, becoming; even though at present, when belief in witches of Endor is displacing the Darwinian theory and 'the truth that shall make you free', men's minds appear, as above noted, to be moving backwards rather than on. I speak somewhat sweepingly, and should except many thoughtful writers in verse and prose; also men in certain worthy but small bodies of various denominations, and perhaps in the homely quarter where advance might have been the very least expected a few years back – the English Church – if one reads it rightly as showing evidence of 'removing those things that are shaken', in accordance with the wise Epistolary recommendation to the Hebrews. For since the historic and once august hierarchy of Rome some generation ago lost its chance of being the religion of the future by doing otherwise, and throwing over the little band of New Catholics who were making a struggle for continuity by applying the principle of evolution to their own faith, joining hands with modern science, and outflanking the hesitating English instinct towards liturgical restatement (a flank march which I at the time quite expected to witness, with the gathering of many millions of waiting agnostics into its fold); since then, one may ask, what other purely English establishment than the Church, of sufficient dignity and footing, with such strength of old association, such scope for transmutability, such architectural spell, is left in this country to keep the shreds of morality together?*

It may indeed be a forlorn hope, a mere dream, that of an alliance between religion, which must be retained unless the world is to perish, and complete rationality, which must come, unless also the world is to perish, by means of the interfusing effect of poetry – 'the breath and finer spirit of all knowledge; the impassioned expression of science', as it was defined by an English poet who was quite orthodox in his ideas. But if it be true, as Comte argued, that advance is never in a straight line, but in a looped orbit, we may, in the aforesaid ominous moving backward, be doing it *pour mieux sauter*, drawing back for a spring. I repeat that I forlornly hope so, notwithstanding the supercilious regard of hope by Schopenhauer, von Hartmann, and other philosophers down to Einstein who have my respect. But one dares not prophesy. Physical, chronological, and other contingencies keep me in these days from critical studies and literary circles

> Where once we held debate, a band
> Of youthful friends, on mind and art

(if one may quote Tennyson in this century). Hence I cannot know how

---

* However, one must not be too sanguine in reading signs, and since the above was written evidence that the Church will go far in the removal of 'things that are shaken' has not been encouraging.

things are going so well as I used to know them, and the aforesaid limitations must quite prevent my knowing henceforward.

from the Apology to *Late Lyrics and Earlier* (London: 1922)

☆

[From Mrs Hardy's last chapter of the *Life*.]

SPEAKING about ambition T. said to-day that he had done all that he meant to do, but he did not know whether it had been worth doing.

His only ambition, so far as he could remember, was to have some poem or poems in a good anthology like the Golden Treasury.

The model he had set before him was 'Drink to me only', by Ben Jonson.

Life, p. 444 (1927).

PART TWO

Critical Comment up to 1928

The Saturday Review (1899) on Wessex Poems

Mr Hardy enjoys a great reputation for his very clear, and sometimes powerful, presentation of the limited life of the country folk who live in a backwater out of the main stream of the world. Even more, his work has for some years been one of the important influences determining the estimate of life of many thoughtful, if imperfectly educated, people. We come, therefore, to anything he chooses to publish predisposed to respect. But as we read this curious and wearisome volume, these many slovenly, slipshod, uncouth verses, stilted in sentiment, poorly conceived and worse wrought, our respect lessens to vanishing-point, and we lay it down with the feeling strong upon us that Mr Hardy has, by his own deliberate act, discredited that judgement and presentation of life on which his reputation rested. It is impossible to understand why the bulk of this volume was published at all – why he did not himself burn the verse, lest it should fall into the hands of the indiscreet literary executor, and mar his fame when he was dead.

The pieces of verse at the beginning of the volume are expressions of the feelings natural to every thoughtful young man coming to his first grips with life, and finding that his imaginings surpass its possibilities. There are the lines to the lady-love who has changed to grosser clay; there is the thought that suffering is more bitter because it falls from blind chance, and not from the flattering, if painful, action of some malignant deity; there is the lament that Nature is indifferent; that the children of a lady who has married another will not be so 'high-purposed' as they would have been had she married Mr Hardy; and there is the revulsion from love. The feelings do not ring quite sincere; they are not strongly felt; they are, in truth, the outpourings in verse common to all the weak, undeveloped natures of intelligent young men, and it is the custom to lock them away, or burn them. Only two of them, 'The Heiress and the Architect' [49], and 'Neutral Tones' [9*], show any forecast of Mr Hardy's mature strength.

Then comes a very pleasant ballad 'Valenciennes', with two really good stanzas in it:

> I never hear the zummer hums
> O'bees; and don' know when the cuckoo comes;
> But night and day I hear the bombs
> We threw at Valencieën.

and

> O' wild wet nights, when all seems sad,
> My wownds come back, as though new wownds I'd had;
> But yet – at times I'm sort o' glad
> I fout at Valencieën.　　　　　　　　[20*]

There is in it a genuine realisation of the pathos of the old, shell-deafened pensioner's plight, the true insight into his feelings, and naturally the right form comes.

Of four of the other ballads it can only be said that they are some of the most amazing balderdash that ever found its way into a book of verse. In 'San Sebastian' [21*] a sergeant, harrowed by remorse, tells the story of the siege of that city, and how Heaven has punished him for ravishing a young girl during the sack of it, by giving his daughter her eyes. In 'Leipzig' a Casterbridge workman tells the story of Napoleon's defeat, as it was told him by his German mother,

> When she used to sing and pirouette,
> And touse the tambourine
>
> To the march that yon street-fiddler plies.　　　　[24*]

In 'The Peasant's Confession' an improbable peasant tells how he led astray and killed an officer, who told him the gist of the orders he was carrying from Napoleon to Grouchy. The stories of the siege and of the battles are alike bald, mechanical and lacking in spirit; while that essential quality of the ballad, a lilting easy flow, is entirely wanting. Consider such a verse as:

> With Gordon, Canning, Blackman, Ompteda,
> L'Estrange, Delancey, Packe,
> Grose, D'Oyly, Stables, Morice, Howard, Hay,
> Von Schwerin, Watzdorf, Boek.　　　　　　[25*]

Even worse than these three is 'The Alarm' [26]. 'The Dance at the Phoenix', save for the idiotic lines

> But each with charger, sword, and gun,
> Had bluffed the Biscay wave,　　　　　　[28]

is far better. It is better in story, and has the real ballad ring. While 'My Cicely' [31*] is exceedingly interesting; for it is instinct with the feeling

of Poe, and there sounds through it a far-away, faint echo of his peculiar
music.

Mr Hardy is hardly more fortunate with the poems which purport to
be dramatic, than with his ballads of the wars of Napoleon. The
situations in 'The Burghers' [23 *], when the husband surprises the flying
lovers, and when he gives them gold and jewels for their livelihood,
afford admirable opportunities for the display of dramatic power; but
such is the poorness, the clumsiness rather, of the treatment that they
lose all their inherent dramatic force, and are entirely unreal, lifeless
and flat. The scene too in 'Her Death and After', where the lover, for the
sake of the dead wife's neglected child, blackens her name, and declares
falsely to her husband that he is the child's father, is even more unreal.
Consider the bald infelicity of this ending of their dialogue:

> '– Sir, I've nothing more to say,'

> 'Save that, if you'll hand me my little maid,
> I'll take her, and rear her, and spare you toil.
> Think it more than a friendly act none can;
> > I'm a lonely man,
> > While you've a large pot to boil.

> 'If not, and you'll put it to ball or blade –
> To-night, to-morrow night, anywhere –
> I'll meet you here . . . But think of it,
> > And in season fit
> > Let me hear from you again.'   [27]

Mr Hardy reaches a higher level in the verse which he calls
'personative' in conception. Such verses as 'Friends Beyond' [36*],
'Thoughts of Ph-a' [38*], 'In a Eweleaze near Weatherbury' [47], are
instinct with the intimate, penetrating charm of real feeling, completely, strongly felt; they have the value of originality of sentiment and
idea; and were the form equal to the matter, they would be poetry. Last
of all comes a veritable poem, 'I Look Into My Glass' [52*]. It is an
original thought realised and felt completely; and the expression is so
clear and simple, that it will surely live when the rest of the book has
been forgotten. . . .

SOURCE: unsigned review in *The Saturday Review* (7 January
1899), LXXXVII, 19.

E. K. Chambers (1899) on *Wessex Poems*

It is not often that a writer at an advanced, if not quite the eleventh, hour essays two new arts at a blow. Nevertheless, this is the case with Mr Hardy, who has not only published a volume of poetry, but has also adorned it with thirty drawings and designs from his own pencil. These illustrations, which recall the fact that Mr Hardy was originally apprenticed in an architect's office, are thoroughly in keeping with some of the most marked characteristics of the book itself. Primitive in execution, and frequently inspired by a somewhat grim mortuary imagination, they are still full of poetry, and show a real sense of the decorative values of architectural outline and nocturnal landscape. Even without the verses, they are a new light on Wessex.

As for the verses themselves, many of which date back to the sixties, while some are of yesterday, it is difficult to say the proper word. Much that Mr Hardy has amused himself by collecting is quite trifling, conceived in the crude ferments of youth, and expressed with woodenness of rhythm and a needlessly inflated diction. On the other hand, there are certain things which stand out unmistakably, not from their fellows merely, but from the ruck of modern verse as a whole. Two or three of these, which take more or less of a ballad form, are vigorous studies of types of Wessex character, and are marked by the observation and saturnine humour which one would naturally expect from the writer of Mr Hardy's novels. Such are 'The Fire at Tranter Sweatley's' [i.e., 'The Bride-Night Fire', 48* – Eds], one of the few pieces in the volume which have been printed before, and 'Valenciennes' [20*], in which 'Corp'l Tullidge' recalls the great fight and its disastrous results to his own hearing [quotes last six stanzas].

The majority, however, of Mr Hardy's small cluster of really remarkable poems, even though they may be dramatic in their setting, are not so in their intention. They are personal utterances, voicing a matured and deliberate judgement on life, which has, indeed, found expression more than once in his novels. More than anything it was this that gave offence to the narrower minds in *Tess of the D'Urbervilles*. 'The President of the Immortals had finished his sport with Tess': this is the note upon which the tragedy ends. And this is the note, too, more or less, of all the poems in which Mr Hardy really speaks, is really convincing. The tragedy of life as the outcome of the sport of freakish destinies: this is briefly the conception which dominates his inmost thought. And the mood of melancholy, or perhaps rather melancholic irritation, to which such a conception gives rise, is the one from which his verse must well, if it is to attain anything beyond a mediocre inspiration. From this spring the sombre irony and mournful music of what is perhaps his finest single effort, 'My Cicely'. A Londoner, hearing of the death of his Wessex love, sets out to visit her grave. The description of the journey is magnificent. . . . On arriving, he learns that the dead lady is but a namesake. His has married beneath her, and keeps a hostel on the very road by which he had come. He had seen her, unrecognising, as with liquor-fired face and thick accents she had jested with the tapsters:

> I backed on the Highway: but passed not
>   The hostel. Within there
> Too mocking to Love's re-expression
>   Was Time's repartee!

He deludes himself with the fond belief that the dead one, 'she of the garth', was his real love, 'the true one':

> So, lest I disturb my choice vision,
>   I shun the West Highway,
> Even now, when the knaps ring with rhythms
>   From blackbird and bee;

> And feel that with slumber half-conscious
>   She rests in the church-hay,
> Her spirit unsoiled as in youth-time
>   When lovers were we.   [31*]

Equally uncompromising in its pessimism is 'Friends Beyond' [36*], with its dream – as all these things are but dreams – of the cessation of life, the deadening of desire, in the grave. Here, again, the touch of Wessex makes the treatment singularly effective. . . .

We do not conceal our opinion that Mr Hardy's success in poetry is of a very narrow range. He is entirely dependent for his inspiration upon this curiously intense and somewhat dismal vision of life, which is upon him almost as an obsession. Where he is not carried along by this, his movement is faltering, and his touch prosaic. But within such close limits his achievement seems to us to be considerable, and to be of a kind with which modern poetry can ill afford to dispense. There is no finish or artifice about it: the note struck is strenuous, austere, forcible; it is writing that should help to give backbone to a literature which certainly errs on the side of flabbiness. And this applies to diction as well as sentiment. Very little of this volume is actually in dialect, but, on the other hand, Mr Hardy is liberal in the introduction of vigorous and unworn provincialisms. Such forms, for instance, as 'lynchet', 'church-hay' and 'knaps', to cull only from the poems quoted in this article, should do something to renew and refresh a somewhat wilted vocabulary.

SOURCE: review in *The Athenaeum* (14 January 1899).

The Academy (1901) on *Poems of the Past and the Present*

In Mr Hardy's new volume of poetry, even more than in his *Wessex Poems*, we are in the company of a profoundly serious sympathiser with human nature, a disillusioned observer of life, a frustrated searcher after divine purposes; while the curious mastery of sombre measures and grave and intricate rhyming schemes is even more noticeable – so much so that Mr Hardy (like his friend and fellow-countryman, William Barnes, before him) seems often to have set himself difficulties for the mere pleasure of overcoming them, without in any way injuring the argument of the poem. But in no other way, save in an occasional mention of the same localities, is Barnes suggested. Between the lyrical cheerfulness and simple piety of the singer of Blackmoor Vale and Mr Hardy's gloomy recognition of chaos and wrong the widest gulf is fixed. Barnes was, after Burns, perhaps as good an example of the natural poet as could be found. Mr Hardy is too selfconscious, too deliberately rhetorical, too monotonously disenchanted, for the word poet to spring naturally to our lips at all in connection with this book. There is more of sheer poetry in his novels. Mr Hardy has his lyrical moments, as we shall show later, although we feel that he has had difficulty in urging his vocabulary to keep pace with them; and we know perfectly well that, under happier conditions, he could sing with the best. But the time is not now. To-day it seems as if his world-weariness, his sense of the transitoriness, the illusion, of all happiness, so preoccupy him that for poetry pure and simple he has no time. He feels too strongly. His melancholia is so absorbing that anything extraneous, anything that might divert his mind towards something frankly beautiful or joyous, must be eschewed.

We are not complaining – we are merely stating the case. For this is a very remarkable book, which, personally, we would not have altered. Mr Hardy's hopelessness is no pose; it is the genuine condition of mind reached, probably very unwillingly, by a sincere student of life, and expressed with great power and lucidity. No other living writer could have written this book.

Let us give, without further remarks, some idea of the character of the work. On page 111 is a poem 'To an Unborn Pauper Child' suggested by the sentence of a magistrate: 'She must go to the Union House to have her baby.' We quote three stanzas:

> Had I the circuit of all souls
> Ere their terrestrial chart unrolls,
>   And thou wert free
>   To cease, or be,
> Then would I tell thee all I know,
> And put it to thee: Wilt thou take Life so?
>
> Fain would I, dear, find some shut plot
> Of earth's wide world for thee, where not
>   One tear, one qualm,
>   Should break the calm.
> But I am weak as thou and bare;
> No man can move the stony gods to spare!
>
> Vain vow! No hint of mine may hence
> To theeward fly: to thy locked sense
>   Explain none can
>   Life's dismal plan:
> Thou wilt thy ignorant entry make
> Though skies spout fire and blood and nations quake.   [91*]

The prominent notes of Mr Hardy's thought are struck there: the helplessness of man, the unavoidability of destiny, the carelessness of the gods. It is wrong to say that he sees no good in life; on the contrary, he sees much. The very fact that men and women, the sport of Fate, can be friendly to each other – that they are subject, in a word, to such an impulse as that which has prompted Mr Hardy himself to address the unborn pauper child in these kindly verses – would probably be to him sufficient reason for continuing the present scheme of things, however awry. Hence the effect of the book, though sad, is also sweet, for we remember no work that, between the lines, so urges kindness and tolerance between man and man. When Heaven is blind and hard let us be doubly watchful and considerate – that is Mr Hardy's implicit moral.

Take these stanzas from another poem, 'The Bedridden Peasant to an Unknowing God':

> That some disaster cleft Thy scheme
> And tore us wide apart,

So that no cry can cross, I deem;
   For Thou art broad of heart,

And would'st not shape and shut us in
   Where voice can not be heard:
'Tis plain Thou meant'st that we should win
   Thy succour by a word.

Might but Thy sense flash down the skies
   Like man's from clime to clime,
Thou would'st not let me agonize
   Through my remaining time;

But, seeing how much Thy creatures bear –
   Lame, starved or maimed, or blind –
Thou'dst heal the ills with quickest care
   Of me and all my kind.

Then, since Thou mak'st not these things be,
   But these things dost not know,
I'll praise Thee as were shown to me
   The mercies Thou would'st show!   [88*]

It is a very beautiful, a very Christian, type of Agnosticism that can prompt such a poem as that. Indeed, it has been left to Mr Hardy, among non-believers, to construct a new gospel of kindliness, a spiritualised 'service of man.' The ordinary agnostic who has serious thought for his fellows offers a hard materialism in the place of the religion in which he finds no solace. Mr Hardy, who is not ordinary, might be called an unbelieving mystic. This little poem, 'The Subalterns,' illustrates what we mean:

'Poor wanderer,' said the leaden sky,
   'I fain would lighten thee,
But there be laws in force on high
   Which say it must not be.'

'I would not freeze thee, shorn one,' cried
   The North, 'knew I but how
To warm my breath, to slack my stride;
   But I am ruled as thou.'

'To-morrow I attack thee, wight,'
   Said Sickness. 'Yet I swear

> I bear thy little ark no spite,
>> But am bid enter there.'

> 'Come hither, Son,' I heard Death say;
>> 'I did not will a grave
> Should end thy pilgrimage to-day,
>> But I, too, am a slave.'

> We smiled upon each other then,
>> And life to me wore less
> That fell contour it wore ere when
>> They owned their passiveness. [84*]

Two other poems might be mentioned in this connection, wherein Mr Hardy, for whom, the readers of *Wessex Poems* will remember, the dead have always a romantic fascination, sets up what is to us a new theory of life in the grave. This poem, dated 1899, first states the theory:

HIS IMMORTALITY

> I saw a dead man's finer part
> Shining within each faithful heart
> Of those bereft. Then said I: 'This must be
>> His immortality.'

> I looked there on a later day,
> And still his soul outshaped, as when in clay,
> Its life in theirs. But less its shine excelled
>> Than when I first beheld.

> His fellow-yearsman passed, and then
> In later hearts I looked for him again;
> And found him – shrunk, alas! into a thin
>> And spectral mannikin.

> Lastly I ask – now aged and chill –
> If aught of him remain unperished still;
> And find, in me alone, a feeble spark,
>> Dying amid the dark. [109*]

In the poem that follows it, 'The To-Be-Forgotten' [110*], the idea is carried further, the dead in the churchyard being overheard to complain, not of their first death, which is bearable, but of that second

and final and dreaded death, when the last friend in whom their
memory is being kept sweet on earth dies also.

We cannot think Mr Hardy always successful. The poem describing
the dream in which he visits Heaven to wrest from God some answer to
the cry of the sons of earth is not what it should be. So tremendous an
idea should be expressed finally the first time. Mr Hardy has not given it
the best form nor the dignity we expect from his verse. Again, 'The
Ruined Maid' is a mistake. The poem has six stanzas, but the first says
all. Thus:

> 'O 'Melia, my dear, this does everything crown! –
> Who could have supposed I should meet you in Town?
> And whence such fair garments, such prosperi-ty?'
> 'O didn't you know I'd been ruined?' said she.   [128*]

The rest is anti-climax.

We have left ourselves no space wherein to remark upon Mr Hardy's
war poems, which bear, as might be expected, rather upon those left
behind than those at the front: the grief of the wives and widows, with a
reminder, hardly to be avoided by one of Mr Hardy's temperament, of
the circumstance that the struggle is raging in the year of our Lord 1901.
Nor have we left ourselves room to say anything of Mr Hardy's poems of
frustrated love, that persistent subject of his thoughts. There are several
remarkable ironical lyrics on this theme (one sweetly tender lament,
entitled 'To Lizbie Browne' [94]), and a curiously chilling ballad, 'The
Return to Athelhall' [124][1]; but the *Wessex Poems* had perhaps finer
work in the same manner. Neither have we noticed Mr Hardy's
exercises in translation, or the dainty French forms which were popular
some twenty years ago, and which he handles with much skill but rather
too much gravity.

We prefer to end our remarks by quoting two other short poems
complete. This sonnet, a kind of verse for which Mr Hardy's deliberate
movement and heavily Latinised vocabulary especially suit him, seems
to us worthy to stand in any collection devoted to that measure:

IN THE OLD THEATRE, FIESOLE
(*April*, 1887)

I traced the Circus whose gray stones incline
Where Rome and dim Etruria interjoin,
Till came a child who showed an ancient coin
That bore the image of a Constantine.

She lightly passed; nor did she once opine
How, better than all books, she had raised for me

In swift perspective Europe's history
Through the vast years of Cæsar's sceptred line.

For in my distant plot of English loam
'Twas but to delve, and straightway there to find
Coins of like impress. As with one half blind
Whom common simples cure, her act flashed home
In that mute moment to my opened mind
The power, the pride, the reach of perished Rome.   [67*]

We quote now one of Mr Hardy's reflective lyrics, a very memorable little poem:

MUTE OPINION

I traversed a dominion
Whose spokesmen spoke out strong
Their purpose and opinion
Through pulpit, press, and song.
I scarce had means to note there
A large-eyed few, and dumb,
Who thought not as those thought there
That stirred the heat and hum.

When, grown a Shade, beholding
That land in lifetime trode,
To learn if its unfolding
Fulfilled its clamoured code,
I saw, in web unbroken,
Its history outwrought
Not as the loud has spoken
But as the dumb had thought.   [90*]

In these poems, as in his last volume, Mr Hardy seeks to give poetic form to the poetry of the last majestic sentence of *Tess*.

SOURCE: unsigned review in *The Academy* (23 November 1901)

NOTE

1. The poem-title was later revised to 'The Dame of Athelhall' [Eds].

The Athenaeum (1902) on *Poems of the Past and the Present*

Mr Hardy's *Wessex Poems* were perplexing in the unevenness of their literary quality. They contained much that was inconsiderable and that failed to distinguish itself from the most commonplace productions of early Victorian art. On the other hand, there were a few things that stood out on a far higher level, had caught the local colouring of the large pastoral life familiar in the same writer's tales, and gave characteristic expression to his austere and melancholy philosophy. So far as these went, they were true poetry – individual, dignified, direct. They suggested a temperament which had never learnt, as professed poets to some extent learn, to evoke the rhythmic mood at will, but which was stirred from time to time, perhaps at rare intervals, by some inner fluctuation of its own to this kind of utterance. It must be owned with regret that but few such moments seem to have gone to the making of *Poems of the Past and the Present*. Mr Hardy is a great master of English. That he should have considered that the large majority of the verses in this volume give worthy form to his thoughts and feelings can only show that he is almost wholly devoid of the faculty of self-criticism. The diction is persistently clumsy, full of ugly neologisms, with neither the simplicity of untutored song nor that of consummate art. The matter is colourless and abstract, although Mr Hardy's strength lies essentially in the actual and the concrete. Wessex is barred out, save for a stanza here and there which only awakes expectation in vain. Of course, there is a strong personality energising. To say that this never asserts itself and masters the refractory medium would be to go too far. But such occasions now come more seldom, and are more brief than a reader of *Wessex Poems* would look for. Those who formed the highest hopes from the earlier book will close the present one with a sense of disappointment, and with a conviction that if Mr Hardy is deserting novel – writing for poetry, he is wholly mistaking his vocation.

The preface affords an amusing instance of just that failure to comprehend the enigma of himself which we notice in Mr Hardy. He says of the personal element in his poems:

It will probably be found, therefore, to possess little cohesion of thought or harmony of colouring. I do not greatly regret this. Unadjusted impressions have their value, and the road to a true philosophy of life seems to lie in humbly recording diverse readings of its phenomena as they are forced upon us by chance and change.

This is arguable enough as an æsthetic or even a philosophic point of view; but as a criticism of Mr Hardy's verse it is surely inapplicable. So far as he claims hearing at all, he presents not diverse readings of the phenomena of life, but a single reading repeated in various accents almost to monotony. It is a vision of the irony of life that alone inspires him, an irony which he almost always feels tragically, the expression of which is by turns grim, cynical, melancholy, resigned, and which more than once rises, in intention at least, to the sublimity of an indictment. It takes a lower form in an amused sense of the limitations of human sympathies or judgement:

I

There is a house with ivied walls,
And mullioned windows worn and old,
And the long dwellers in those halls
Have souls that know but sordid calls,
    And daily dream of gold.

II

In blazing brick and plated show
Not far away a 'villa' gleams,
And here a family few may know,
With book and pencil, viol and bow,
    Lead inner lives of dreams.

III

The philosophic passers say,
'See that old mansion mossed and fair,
Poetic souls therein are they:
And O that gaudy box! Away,
    You vulgar people there.'   [130]

The same spirit of irony, more sombre and more passionate, informs what is probably the most successful poem in the book, and, at the same time, one of the few fine poems suggested by the present war. It is called 'The Souls of the Slain' [62*] . . . [and the] whole of [it] is so singularly, both in dignity of image and harmony of rhythm, above the standard of most of its companions as strongly to confirm the theory expressed above concerning the spontaneous and incalculable character of Mr Hardy's rare inspirations. There is only one other poem in the volume which we are willing to quote after it:

THE COMET AT YALBURY OR YELL'HAM

I

It bends far over Yell'ham Plain,
    And we, from Yell'ham Height,
Stand and regard its fiery train,
    So soon to swim from sight.

II

It will return long years hence, when
    As now its strange swift shine
Will fall on Yell'ham; but not then
    On that sweet form of thine.   [120]

Surely this is very charming – an epithet, it must be confessed, not often applicable to Mr Hardy's verse, even at its best. The workmanship is more finished, the sentiment more genial, than is his wont. The sadness is that of melancholy, not of disillusion.

SOURCE: unsigned review in *The Athenaeum* (4 January 1902), No. 3871.

The Athenaeum (1910) on *Time's Laughingstocks and Other Verses*

The main impression left upon the mind after perusal of Mr Hardy's new volume is admiration, mingled with some perplexity, at his mastery of technique. It is surprising that gifts so high should be contentedly devoted to subjects on the whole so narrow; and as we consider the manner in which these subjects are handled, we are confronted by a further problem; for how is it possible for a writer to be at the same time so poetic and so casual?

A poem, to be a poem, must be couched in language which, without error either of defect or excess, fulfils the artistic possibilities of its theme; and three parts of the theme must be looked for in the mental and emotional attitude of the producer. Poetry aims on the whole at expressing the idea of an ordered and lasting beauty and turns to human life and human ideals as the material in which the principles it seeks are manifested. Undying beauty and persistent aspiration, both established in fulfilment or recognition of unalterable law, inspire poetry, and dictate the measured cadence, the grave contour, eloquence, and impassioned diction which one associates with all that is loftiest and most splendid in poetic achievement. But if the poet, looking upon human life, decides that an abiding beauty is not what is mainly to be found there, and that ideals are so seldom realised that it is hypocrisy to be serious about them, he has still to make the artistic expression of his thought appropriate to its content; and although measure on the one hand, and passion on the other, cannot be dispensed with, both must submit to a disguise. The position is indeed strange; for unless beauty be both worshipped and claimed, the impulse to poetic expression is unintelligible. A perplexing task awaits the craftsman whose duty it is to decry in the course of his work the very instincts that brought it into being, and to build a permanent edifice out of materials which he will not himself allow to be good for anything but a house of cards. The truth seems to be that this attitude – which closely resembles Mr Hardy's – is the outcome of a sensitiveness or idealism pushed to excess. Beauty and perfection are so passionately worshipped, so imperatively demanded, that the poet is conscious only of the imperfection of things as they are, and his own unreasonableness in expecting them to be anything but imperfect.

Mr Hardy pursues his course with excellent skill, avoiding every pitfall. His poetic tact is unsurpassable. The temper he writes in is exactly that which could alone give credibility, artistic justice, and a natural appeal to the point of view he is expressing. That point of view is, in one word, disillusionment, and centres upon the disillusionment of love. For love, as Mr Hardy throughout implies, is founded upon constancy, and his pictures of inconstancy, of animality even, derive their meaning and value from their background, from the quality which they exalt by presupposing.

That which makes man's love the lighter and the woman's burn no
    brighter
Came to pass with us inevitably while slipped the shortening year . . . .
And there stands your father's dwelling with its blank bleak windows
    telling
That the vows of man and maid are flimsy, frail, and insincere.
                                                            [182*]

What is the force of such a passage as this, if not the easy nonchalance, the unconscious, conversational tone given to a statement against which every fibre of poetry in us stiffens and rebels? If it were less casual, might it not be almost offensive? As it is, we can only admire; while the magic of language conquers the sceptical sing-song.

If we were asked to name the man whose work Mr Hardy's most resembles on its technical side, we should without hesitation name

Browning. It would be easy to quote a score of passages out of this volume which might have been written by either of them:

> We kissed at the barrier, and passing through
> She left me, and moment by moment got
> Smaller and smaller . . .   [170*]

or,

> Yet I wonder,
> Will it sunder
>   Her from me?
> Will she guess that
> I said 'Yes,' – that
>   His I'd be,
> Ere I thought she might not see him as I see?   [206]

and, with the exception of a word or two here and there, several entire poems. The difference between them is that Mr Hardy, in using these queer conversational forms, almost always manages to convey, not only a sense of propriety in them, which is frequent in Browning also, but a pleasing illusion that the language has adapted itself by magic to his merely momentary needs. How often in completing his more eccentric patterns Browning jumps and struggles, like an unruly child, against the stern restraint of his mother-tongue! Mr Hardy, whether the line is long or short and the rhyme in one or two or three syllables, is always at his ease:

> We Christmas-carolled down the Vale, and up the Vale, and round the
>   Vale,
> We played and sang that night as we were yearly wont to do –
> A carol in the minor key, a carol in the major D,
> Then at each house: 'Good wishes: many Christmas joys to you!'
>   [212]

When he roughens the metre, it is because he wishes, not because he is forced, to do so; and now and then he draws an overwhelming effect from deliberate violation of his scheme:

> O vision appalling
> When the one believed-in thing
>   Is seen falling, falling,
> With all to which hope can cling.   [174*]

Mr Hardy is, in fact, casual or conversational in tone, but not in workmanship.

The quality we have pointed to – power under the mask of nonchalance – performs a still more important service in Mr Hardy's verse than any we have yet mentioned. There is an obvious poetic appeal, a sentiment of easy pathos, attached to unrealisable desire. Effort, consistency, and other forces that tend to bring desires to realisation or to correct their bearings, operate in a humdrum manner. The poet cannot be bothered with them. If, for example, lovers insist on marrying and 'settling down,' the lyric poet wishes them good-day, and if he has a touch of petulance in him, as on this topic Mr Hardy has undeniably, he will have nothing to do with their children either.

However, our point is that, if the poetry of the unrealisable is taken as a mainspring of inspiration, the danger besetting the poet will be that of overtaxing its resources, and revealing, to those who come to him for refreshment, how shallow they are. Mr Hardy is not beyond reproach on this point, so far as the matter of his volume is concerned; but the faultlessness of his manner redeems the mistake. The sensitiveness to beauty which his writing reveals, and the contained idealism which unsuccessfully hides itself under the cloak of the religious or social revolutionary, never tempt him into a fatal extravagance, never draw him over the line that separates the poet from the cynic and the sentimentalist. Maintaining thus a perfect equilibrium, bringing to his themes the utmost illumination of which they are susceptible, avoiding at once the snares of false enchantment and facile indignation, he achieves the poetry of irony:

> I saw him steal the light away
>   That haunted in her eye:
> It went so gently none could say
> More than that it was there one day
>   And missing by-and-by.
>
> I watched her longer, and he stole
>   Her lily tincts and rose;
> All her young sprightliness of soul
> Next fell beneath his cold control,
>   And disappeared like those.
>
> I asked: 'Why do you serve her so,
>   Do you, for some glad day,
> Hoard these her sweets –?' He said, 'O no,
> They charm not me; I bid Time throw
>   Each promptly to decay.'

Said I: 'We call that cruelty –
   We, your poor human kind.'
He mused. 'The thought is new to me.
Forsooth, though I men's master be,
   Theirs is the teaching mind!'   [232*]

A noble poem inscribed 'G. M. (1828–1909)' stimulates what must in
any case have been a natural impulse – the impulse to compare Mr
Hardy's poetry with that of another great writer of our time who, like
Mr Hardy, was less known as a poet than as a novelist:

   He was of those whose wit can shake
   And riddle to the very core
   The counterfeits that Time will break.   [243*]

It is interesting that, in his tribute to Meredith, Mr Hardy should have
singled out for remark, among many qualities that distinguished the
master's work, the great and salient quality which he shares with him.
Like Meredith, Mr Hardy, whatever else he disbelieves in, believes in
the strength and permanence of truth. Like Meredith, he aims at
adhering in his poetry with scrupulous care to the facts which he
believes to be before him. His conception of what the facts are is as
different from Meredith's as it could be, and perhaps it is a conception
which provides poetic material more readily. But Mr Hardy will not,
any more than would Meredith, have poetry at the expense of truth;
and thus the same influence which curbed Meredith's optimism, curbs
Mr Hardy's pessimism, and where Meredith denied wings to Aspiration, Mr Hardy offers no laurel to Despair.

   O sweet sincerity! –
   Where modern methods be
   What scope for thine and thee?

   Life may be sad past saying,
   Its greens for ever graying,
   Its faiths to dust decaying;

   And youth may have foreknown it,
   And riper seasons shown it,
   But custom cries: 'Disown it:

   Say ye rejoice, though grieving,
   Believe, while unbelieving,
   Behold, without perceiving!'

> – Yet, would men look at true things,
> And unilluded view things,
> And count to bear undue things,
>
> The real might mend the seeming,
> Facts better their foredeeming,
> And Life its disesteeming. [233]

Mr Hardy's picture, therefore, however dark, has the ultimate dignity of artistic faithfulness, and this noble quality governs both his attitude to his conceptions and his treatment of details. His execution has everywhere a vibrating precision, even when the mood is languorous; everywhere we have the pleasure as we read of feeling that a definite effect was intended, and has been produced with exquisite delicacy. Thus it comes about that the same faculty which has made Mr Hardy a master of rustic tragedy, and which has placed the great drama of history within his grasp, enables him also to handle the subtlest of themes and analyse the most transient of emotions with an exactitude worthy of the great names in our literature.

SOURCE: unsigned review in *The Athenaeum* (8 January 1910), No. 4289

Times Literary Supplement (1914) on *Satires of Circumstance: Lyrics and Reveries, with Miscellaneous Pieces*

Poetry always tends to travel farther and farther away from prose; but while it remains a living art, there is always an effort made by some poets to bring it nearer to prose again. They are sick of the insipidity, the too easy music and emotion, of over-poetical poetry, just as some preachers react from the excessive unction of the ordinary pulpit orator. Meredith and Mr Hardy, coming at the end of the Romantic movement and contemporaries of that extreme poet Swinburne, have been prose writers who have tried to impart some of the virtues of prose to poetry. But both have known, too, that a poem has no right to exist if what it says could be better said in prose; and their verse, even when it seems crabbed or morose or tantalising, is still thoroughly poetic in form. It may be that Meredith is too intellectual in his verse, that reason rather than emotion gives it its continuity, that Mr Hardy is too

despondent, too conscious of the dullness of routine for a poet; but
neither of them makes us feel that he has mistaken his vocation. We
might say to Mr Hardy – why try to be a poet at all, when you think
what you do think of life? But he can answer to us that life, in spite of
what he thinks about it, does move him to write poetry, and a poetry
which has the unexpected beauty of winter upon it.

> While rain, with eve in partnership,
> Descended darkly, drip, drip, drip,
> Beyond the last lone lamp I passed
>   Walking slowly, whispering sadly,
>   Two linked loiterers, wan, downcast:
> Some heavy thought constrained each face,
> And blinded them to time and place.　　　　　[257*]

That is the first verse from a poem in this new volume; and it has a music
which seems to order the dull desponding words against their will. Or
here is another verse from the next poem:

> The travelled sun dropped
> To the north-west, low and lower,
> The pony's trot grew slower,
> And then we stopped.　　　　　[258]

A bare statement of fact; but still it makes its music and falls naturally
into the stanza, so that it is like something we remember vividly without
knowing why, except that it was part of the evening and we ourselves
were part of it.

But there is a section of this book, the fifteen 'Satires of Circumstance'
which give it its title, in which we feel that Mr Hardy would have done
better in prose. It is not that they are prosaic, but that he does not
manage to tell enough in verse. In each he gives us merely a situation,
an ugly situation, with all the emphasis of verse laid on the ugliness, as if
he had a brief against life; and in each case we feel that the whole truth is
not told and could not be told in this medium. There are some themes fit
only for prose because verse is too summary for them. They need
patience and a sense of justice and a boundless psychological curiosity to
expound them. Such are the themes which Mr Hardy has chosen for
these fifteen short poems; and he seems merely to throw them at us
impatiently, as if he wanted to destroy our foolish optimism, as if he
were determined to tell us ugly secrets about life in as few words as
possible. He has a mood about the universe in which he reminds us of
the extreme anti-patriot who is sick of fulsome compliments paid to his
own country. 'God's in his Heaven; all's right with the world.' Is it? says

Mr Hardy, and offers a few instances to the contrary. But he seems to waste himself in such telling of home-truths, especially as we are convinced that they are only half-truths. We want him to be more disinterested and not to be an *advocatus diaboli* because others have been too obsequious in justifying the ways of God to man.

But in another section, 'Poems of 1912–13', he is less argumentative and less irritable. Here, for instance, is the last verse of a Lament that seems to be written to an old tune to suit an old sadness:

> And we are here staying
> Amid those stale things
> Who care not for gaying,
> And those junketings
> That used so to joy her,
> And never to cloy her
> As us they cloy! . . . But
> She is shut, she is shut
> > From the cheer of them, dead
> > To all done and said
> > In her yew-arched bed.   [283*]

And in 'The Haunter' he gives us another tune, strange and alluring, as if he had heard some one playing it on a pipe out in the darkness and had fitted his own words to it:

> Yes, I accompany him to places
> > Only dreamers know,
> Where the shy hares show their faces,
> > Where the night rooks go;
> Into old aisles where the past is all to him,
> > Close as his shade can do,
> Always lacking the power to call to him,
> > Near as I reach thereto!   [284*]

It is curious how, at the end of a long practice in the art of prose, Mr Hardy turns more and more to poetry and writes as if he were a young poet still utterly unreconciled to life. You might call him a pagan, except that he cannot forget all the hopes which Christianity has offered in between and all the sense of the meaning of humanity with which it has enlarged our minds. He keeps that sense; but in him it is baffled. Men, he feels, deserve that immense hope which has traversed the world; but he is haunted by the fear that it is vain, that men have enriched their natures for a future that will never be. And yet he loves them for this enrichment; and that love, growing intenser with the years, has turned him from prose to poetry. It is useless to argue with him about this; we have only to note what has happened to him, and to be grateful for the art with which he expresses it. The last poem in the book is the 'Song of the Soldiers' [493][1] which was published only the other day. There is a faith in that and a rebuke to the faithless; and in all his poems, even those which seem bitterest with disappointment, there is perhaps a faith implied, though the author may not, because he cannot, put it into words; because so many things in life seem to contradict it, and with their incessant contradiction trouble the mind like an argument pertinaciously renewed.

SOURCE: unsigned review in the *Times Literary Supplement*, (19 November 1914).

NOTE

1. Subsequently retitled 'Men Who March Away (Song of the Soldiers)', and included in Hardy's next collection of verse, *Moments of Vision* (1917) [Eds].

Lytton Strachey (1914) on *Satires of Circumstance* . . .

Mr Hardy's new volume of poems is a very interesting, and in some ways a baffling book, which may be recommended particularly to aesthetic theorists and to those dogmatic persons who, ever since the days of Confucius, have laid down definitions upon the function and nature of poetry. The dictum of Confucius is less well known than it ought to be. 'Read poetry, oh my children!' he said, 'for it will teach you the divine truths of filial affection, patriotism, and natural history.' Here the Chinese sage expressed, with the engaging frankness of his nation, a view of poetry implicitly held by that long succession of earnest critics for whom the real justification of any work of art lies in the edifying nature of the lessons which it instils. Such generalisations upon poetry would be more satisfactory if it were not for the poets. One can never make sure of that inconvenient and unreliable race. The remark of Confucius, for instance, which, one feels, must have been written with a prophetic eye upon the works of Wordsworth, seems absurdly inapplicable to the works of Keats. Then there is Milton's famous 'simple, sensuous, and passionate' test – a test which serves admirably for Keats, but which seems in an odd way to exclude the

complicated style, the severe temper, and the remote imaginations of
Milton himself. Yet another school insists upon the necessity of a certain
technical accomplishment; beauty is for them, as it was – in a somewhat
different connection – for Herbert Spencer, a '*sine quâ non*'. Harmony of
sound, mastery of rhythm, the exact and exquisite employment of
words – in these things, they declare, lies the very soul of poetry, and
without them the noblest thoughts and the finest feelings will never rise
above the level of tolerable verse. This is the theory which Mr Hardy's
volume seems especially designed to disprove. It is full of poetry; and yet
it is also full of ugly and cumbrous expressions, clumsy metres, and flat,
prosaic turns of speech. To take a few random examples, in the second of
the following lines cacophony is incarnate:

> Dear ghost, in the past did you ever find
> Me one whom consequence influenced much?   [278*]

A curious mixture of the contorted and the jog-trot appears in such a
line as:

> And adumbrates too therewith our unexpected troublous case;[1]
> [263*]

while a line like:

> And the daytime talk of the Roman investigations   [308*]

rails along in the manner of an undistinguished phrase in prose. Even
Mr Hardy's grammar is not impeccable. He speaks of one,

> whom, anon,
> My great deeds done,
> Will be mine alway.   [253]

And his vocabulary, though in general it is rich and apt, has occasional
significant lapses, as, for instance, in the elegy on Swinburne, where, in
the middle of a passage deliberately tuned to a pitch of lyrical resonance
not to be found elsewhere in the volume, there occurs the horrid hybrid
'naïvely' – a neologism exactly calculated, one would suppose, to make
the classic author of *Atalanta* turn in his grave.

It is important to observe such characteristics, because, in Mr
Hardy's case, they are not merely superficial and occasional blemishes;
they are in reality an essential ingredient in the very essence of his work.
The originality of his poetry lies in the fact that it bears everywhere
upon it the impress of a master of prose fiction. Just as the great

seventeenth-century writers of prose, such as Sir Thomas Browne and
Jeremy Taylor, managed to fill their sentences with the splendour and
passion of poetry, while still preserving the texture of an essentially
prose style, so Mr Hardy, by a contrary process, has brought the realism
and sobriety of prose into the service of his poetry. The result is a
product of a kind very difficult to parallel in our literature. Browning,
no doubt, in his intimate and reflective moods – in 'By the Fireside' or
'Any Wife to Any Husband' – sometimes comes near it; but the full-
blooded and romantic optimism of Browning's temper offers a singular
contrast to the repressed melancholy of Mr Hardy's. Browning was too
adventurous to be content for long with the plain facts of ordinary
existence; he was far more at home with the curiosities and the
excitements of life; but what gives Mr Hardy's poems their unique
flavour is precisely their utter lack of romanticism, their common,
undecorated presentments of things. They are, in fact, modern as no
other poems are. The author of *Jude the Obscure* speaks in them, but with
the concentration, the intensity, the subtle disturbing force of poetry.
And he speaks; he does not sing. Or rather, he talks – in the quiet voice
of a modern man or woman, who finds it difficult, as modern men and
women do, to put into words exactly what is in the mind. He is
incorrect; but then how unreal and artificial a thing is correctness! He
fumbles; but it is that very fumbling that brings him so near to ourselves.
In that 'me one whom consequence influenced much', does not one
seem to catch the very accent of hesitating and half-ironical affection?
And in the drab rhythm of that 'daytime talk of the Roman
investigations', does not all the dreariness of long hours of boredom lie
compressed? And who does not feel the perplexity, the discomfort, and
the dim agitation in that clumsy collection of vocables – 'And adum-
brates too therewith our unexpected troublous case'? What a relief such
uncertainties and inexpressivenesses are after the delicate exactitudes of
our more polished poets! And how mysterious and potent are the forces
of inspiration and sincerity! All the taste, all the scholarship, all the art
of the Poet Laureate seem only to end in something that is admirable,
perhaps, something that is wonderful, but something that is irre-
mediably remote and cold; while the flat, undistinguished poetry of Mr
Hardy has found out the secret of touching our marrow-bones.

   It is not only in its style and feeling that this poetry reveals the
novelist; it is also in its subject-matter. Many of the poems – and in
particular the remarkable group of 'fifteen glimpses' which gives its title
to the volume – consist of compressed dramatic narratives, of central
episodes of passion and circumstance, depicted with extraordinary
vividness. A flashlight is turned for a moment upon some scene or upon
some character, and in that moment the tragedies of whole lives and the
long fatalities of human relationships seem to stand revealed:

My stick! he says, and turns in the lane
To the house just left, whence a vixen voice
Comes out with the firelight through the pane,
And he sees within that the girl of his choice
Stands rating her mother with eyes aglare
For something said while he was there.

'At last I behold her soul undraped!'
Thinks the man who had loved her more than himself . . .

[343]

It is easy to imagine the scene as the turning-point in a realistic psychological novel; and, indeed, a novelist in want of plots or incidents might well be tempted to appropriate some of the marvellously pregnant suggestions with which this book is crowded. Among these sketches the longest and most elaborate is the 'Conversation at Dawn' [305], which contains in its few pages the matter of an entire novel – a remorseless and terrible novel of modern life. Perhaps the most gruesome is 'At the Draper's', in which a dying man tells his wife how he saw her in a shop, unperceived:

You were viewing some lovely things. *'Soon required*
    For a widow, of latest fashion';
And I knew 'twould upset you to meet the man
    Who had to be cold and ashen

And screwed in a box before they could dress you
    'In the last new note of mourning,'
As they defined it. So, not to distress you,
    I left you to your adorning.   [348]

As these extracts indicate, the prevailing mood in this volume – as in Mr Hardy's later novels – is not a cheerful one. And, in the more reflective and personal pieces, the melancholy is if anything yet more intense. It is the melancholy of regretful recollection, of bitter speculation, of immortal longings unsatisfied; it is the melancholy of one who has suffered, in Gibbon's poignant phrase, 'the abridgement of hope'. Mortality, and the cruelties of time, and the ironic irrevocability of things – these are the themes upon which Mr Hardy has chosen to weave his grave and moving variations. If there is joy in these pages, it is joy that is long since dead; and if there are smiles, they are sardonical. The sentimentalist will find very little comfort among them. Some-times, perhaps, his hopes will rise a little – for the sentimentalist is a hopeful creature; but they will soon be dashed. 'Who is digging on my

grave?' asks the dead woman, who has been forgotten by her lover and
her kinsfolk and even her enemy; since it is none of these, who can it be?

> O it is I, my mistress dear,
> Your little dog, who still lives near,
> And much I hope my movements here
>   Have not disturbed your rest.

'Ah, yes!' murmurs the ghost:

> *You* dig upon my grave . . .
> Why flashed it not on me
> That one true heart was left behind?
> What feeling do we ever find
> To equal among human kind
>   A dog's fidelity?

And so, with this comforting conclusion, the poem might have ended.
But that is not Mr Hardy's way. 'Mistress,' comes the reply:

> I dug upon your grave
> To bury a bone, in case
> I should be hungry near this spot
> When passing on my daily trot,
> I am sorry, but I quite forgot
>   It was your resting-place.   [269]

That is all; the desolation is complete. And the gloom is not even
relieved by a little elegance of diction.

SOURCE: review in *New Statesman* (19 December 1914).

NOTE

1. Line 10 of poem, completely revised in later printings, probably as a result
of Strachey's criticism [Eds].

The Nation (1915) on Satires of Circumstance . . .

An intelligent person who knew Mr Hardy only from his fiction might be rather surprised at the sort of poetry he writes. There are two conspicuous elements in his novels which seem obviously likely to provide the right fuel for the intenser fires of poetry. They are, first, that metaphysical conception of the world as a whole which is more or less implied in the action of all his stories; and, secondly, the famous landscapes and the profound intimacy with the workings of Nature which surround the human events in the stories. These are the things which one would expect Mr Hardy would have disengaged from his prose art for the finer elaboration and concentration of poetry. For they are things which essentially belong to poetry; fiction has only borrowed them from poetry, and, although Mr Hardy's fiction is perhaps unequalled for the noble use it has made of the loan, the art of the novel can never hope to match itself with poetry in these matters. But what one may roughly call the humanity of Mr Hardy's fiction is, of course, the very thing for which the art primarily exists. Fiction consoles itself for having to fall behind poetry in some things by developing incomparably easier and more tempting ways of dealing with humanity; and this is what one would have expected Mr Hardy to leave behind when he decided to forsake fiction for poetry.

But our intelligent person, on taking up Mr Hardy's poetry, would find these plausible predictions pretty flatly contradicted. This is true, at least, of his lyrical poetry. Perhaps it is because, in *The Dynasts*, he disengaged so completely the metaphysic implicit in his novels, and worked it up into such a monumental shape – into, in fact, one of the greatest of modern poems; perhaps it is because of this that his lyrical poetry has shown so little tendency to essentialise and volatilise, in the way one might have expected, his characteristic philosophy. There are, to be sure, several early poems of his which attempt something like this; but they are of doubtful success, and the tendency has been more and more to take the philosophy for granted, to refer to it in subdued hints, which we might scarcely notice if we were not already familiar with Mr Hardy's attitude. And the same holds, too, for his feeling for landscape and the life of the earth. It is a feeling which often seems, in his novels, to be just on the point to fly off into poetry; and yet, when Mr Hardy comes to give his genius up to poetry, we find that this feeling – again with a few exceptions, mainly among the earlier poems – is much less important than it is in the novels. In fact, the elements in Mr Hardy's inspiration which seem most likely to demand poetic utterance are just those which he has made least use of in his poetry. Instead, he has fashioned for himself – not without noticeable hammering and difficult forging – a style of poetry for dealing in another way with the staple of his fiction; indeed, for distilling it down to sheer, unmixed essence of human character, will, and passion.

In his latest volume of poems, the tendency is about as completely successful as it could be. His metaphysic and his landscape (to use terms of convenience rather than of precision) could not, of course, be entirely eliminated; but *Satires of Circumstance* has less of these elements in it, and is more singly concerned with pure human nature (for the most part, tragic human nature) than any other of his poetry. The familiar metaphysic does, indeed, make one quite undisguised and quite magnificent appearance in 'The Convergence of the Twain,' a philosophic dirge for the loss of the *Titanic*. Both the mood and the phrasing of this unmistakably recall the spirit of *The Dynasts* and the later novels:

> Well: while was fashioning
> This creature of cleaving wing,
> The Immanent Will that stirs and urges everything

> Prepared a sinister mate
> For her – so gaily great –
> A Shape of Ice, for the time far and dissociate.

> And as the smart ship grew
> In stature, grace, and hue,
> In shadowy silent distance grew the Iceberg too.   [248*]

But that kind of poetry – which might be paralleled, though scarcely matched, among the earlier poems – is altogether the exception here. There is very little of this metaphysical mood, even in the diluted form of a comprehensive irony; though in this form it again makes one decidedly happy appearance – in 'Channel Firing.' The dead wake up at the sound of gun practice, which they mistake for Judgement Day; but the Deity assures them that the world is still a long way from Judgement Day, if, indeed, Judgement Day had not better be indefinitely postponed, since men show not the least sign of improvement:

> And many a skeleton shook his head.
> 'Instead of preaching forty year,'
> My neighbour Parson Thirdly said,
> 'I wish I had stuck to pipes and beer!'   [247*]

There is even, in the admirable 'Song of the Soldiers,'[1] which is perhaps the best poem the war has inspired, something which looks like a contradiction of Mr Hardy's customary philosophy:

> Is it a purblind prank, O think you,
>   Friend with the musing eye,
>   Who watch us stepping by
>   With doubt and dolorous sigh?
> Can much pondering so hoodwink you?
>
>   . . .
>
> In our heart of hearts believing
>   Victory crowns the just,
>   And that braggarts must
>   Surely bite the dust,
> Press we to the field, ungrieving.   [493]

It certainly seems, just there, as if 'Victory crowns the just' in Mr Hardy's heart of hearts, too; which is by no means what the mood of *The Dynasts* would assent to.

As for his profound faculty for realising landscape and the life of Nature, so dear to Mr Hardy's admirers, it is allowed to accomplish here nothing but a few decorative touches. These, to be sure, are on the whole extremely fine; for vividness and economy, nothing, for instance, could be better than this:

> She answered not, but lay listlessly
> With her dark, dry eyes on the coppery sea,
>   That now and then
> Flung its lazy flounce at the neighbouring quay.   [305]

Commonly, these allusions to Nature serve merely to enforce the special quality of some entirely human transaction, as in the poem which begins with a reference to

> the boom
> Of the ocean, *like a hammering in a hollow tomb;*   [301]

a phrase instinct with sinister imagination exactly right for the spectral tragedy which it introduces. But always in these poems the human event is the main thing; and, as a rule, sheer human nature is the only thing the poem is made of.

The chief quality in these poems is, more than ever before in Mr Hardy's poetry, their concentration. Nothing is too trival or too commonplace for their art. One feels that a hundred times a day one might be supplying subjects for Mr Hardy's Muse; it is a flattering delusion, though not so far from the truth. A single trait or a single incident is seized and compressed into strictest artistic form, and described in language which disguises, in a sort of nonchalance, an intense pre-occupation with essentials of motive and significance, though it does not always disguise (as Mr Gibson's[2] apparent carelessness invariably does) an exact sense of the poetic values in words. The series of short poems which gives the book its title, the 'Satires of Circumstance' themselves, are more characteristic than anything else of Mr Hardy's completed poetic method. [There] is one which may stand as a type; a Greek would have called it an epigram [quotes 'Outside the Window' (343)]. It seems almost casual; but there is not a single word that does not tell in the whole effect, and the effect is (in twelve lines) the quintessence of two human lives. It was, indeed, worth waiting for, this final poetic method of Mr Hardy's. It is a method entirely his own. Its limitations and oddities could not, perhaps, have been passed over during its composition by any other poet; but that is probably because of Mr Hardy's single-minded determination to perfect the virtue his poetry now seems always to have aimed at; to reveal in inescapable suggestion (scarcely ever deducing in open terms) the essential tragic significance of some moment of human nature through sheer intense, abrupt description, concentrated into rigorous formality, of some such event as a dog scratching on a woman's grave, a parson posturing before a mirror, or a woman concealing a gay hat under her crinoline. The kind of thing described is usually familiar, if not to experience, certainly to quite humdrum fancy. The result of the description is always astonishing; and to that result has gone a specialised skill unlike anything else in our literature.

SOURCE: unsigned review in *The Nation* (16 January 1915).

NOTES

1. See note 1, p. 62 above, on the retitling of this poem [Eds.].
2. Wilfrid Gibson, the poet.

Edward Thomas (1915)

There is a greater than Duck or Barnes still among us, a wide-ranging poet, who is always a countryman of a somewhat lonely heart, Mr Thomas Hardy. For I do notice something in his poetry which I hope I may with respect call rustic, and, what is much the same thing, old-fashioned. It enables him to mingle elements unexpectedly, so that, thinking of 1967 in the year 1867, he spoke not only of the new century having 'new minds, new modes, new fools, new wise', but concluded

> For I would only ask thereof,
> That thy worm should be my worm, Love   [167*]

– which is an antique as Donne's Flea that wedded the lovers by combining blood from both of them within its body. The same rusticity manifests itself elsewhere as Elizabethanism, and the poet is something of a 'liberal shepherd' in his willingness to give things their grosser names or to hint at them. He has a real taste for such comparisons as that made by a French officer looking at the English fleet at Trafalgar:

> Their overcrowded sails
> Bulge like blown bladders in a tripeman's shop
> The market-morning after slaughter-day. [*Dynasts*, pt 1:vi]

Then, how his illustrations to his own poems – such as the pair of spectacles lying right across the landscape, following 'In a Eweleaze near Weatherbury' [47] – remind us of a seventeenth-century book of emblems! Sometimes his excuse is that he is impersonating a man of an earlier age, as in the Sergeant's song [stanza 4 (19)] . . .

He has written songs and narratives which prove his descent from some ancient ballad-maker, perhaps the one who wrote 'A pleasant ballad of the merry miller's wooing of the baker's daughter of Manchester', or 'A new ballade, showing the cruel robberies and lewd life of Philip Collins, *alias* Osburne, commonly called Philip of the West, who was pressed to death at Newgate in London the third of December last past, 1597', to be sung to the tune of 'Paggington's round'. Some of the lyric stanzas to which he fits a narrative originated probably in some such tune.

And how often is he delighted to represent a peasant's view, a peasant's contribution to the irony of things, a capital instance being the Belgian who killed Grouchy to save his farm, and so lost Napoleon the battle of Waterloo [25*].[1]

With this rusticity, if that be the right name for it, I cannot help connecting that most tyrannous obsession of the blindness of Fate, the carelessness of Nature, and the insignificance of Man, crawling in multitudes like caterpillars, twitched by the Immanent Will hither and thither. Over and over again, from the earliest poems up to *The Dynasts*, he amplifies those words which he puts into the mouth of God:

> . . . 'My labours – logicless –
>   You may explain; not I:
> Sense-sealed I have wrought, without a guess
> That I evolved a Consciousness
>   To ask for reasons why.'   [231*]

And, referring to the earth:

> 'It lost my interest from the first,
> My aims therefore[2] succeeding ill;'   [87*]
>   . . .

[Thomas quotes the complete 5th stanza of 'God-Forgotten'.] 'Sportsman Time' and 'those purblind Doomsters' are characteristic phrases. The many things said by him of birth he sums up at the end of a death-bed poem:

> We see by littles now the deft achievement
> Whereby she has escaped the Wrongers all,
> In view of which our momentary bereavement
>   Outshapes but small.   [223*]

As gravely he descends to the ludicrous extreme of making a country girl planting a pine-tree sing:

> It will sigh in the morning,
>   Will sigh at noon,
> At the winter's warning,
>   In wafts of June;
> Grieving that never
>   Kind Fate decreed
> It should for ever
>   Remain a seed,
> And shun the welter
>   Of things without,
> Unneeding shelter
>   From storm and drought.   [225]

He puts into the mouths of field, flock and tree – because while he gazed at them at dawn they looked like chastened children sitting in school silently – the question:

> 'Has some Vast Imbecility,
>   Mighty to build and blend
>   But impotent to tend,
> Framed us in jest, and left us now to hazardry?'   [43*]

Napoleon, in *The Dynasts*, asks the question, 'Why am I here?' and answers it:

> By laws imposed on me inexorably
> History makes use of me to weave her web.

Twentieth-century superstition can no farther go than in that enormous poem, which is astonishing in many ways, not least in being readable. I call it superstition because truth, or a genuine attempt at truth, has been turned apparently by an isolated rustic imagination into an obsession so powerful that only a very great talent could have rescued anything uninjured from the weight of it. A hundred years ago, Mr Hardy would have seen 'real ghosts'. Today he has to invent them, and call his Spirits of the Years and of the Pities, Spirits Sinister and Ironic, Rumours and Recording Angels, who have the best seats at the human comedy, 'contrivances of the fancy merely'.

Even his use of irony verges on the superstitious. Artistically, at least in the shorter poems, it may be sound, and it is certainly effective, as where the old man laments on learning that his wife is to be in the same wing of the workhouse, instead of setting him 'free of his forty years' chain'. ['The Curate's Kindness: A Workhouse Irony' (159*).] But the frequent use and abuse of it change the reader's smile into a laugh at the perversity.

Mr Hardy must have discovered the blindness of Fate, the indifference of Nature, and the irony of Life, before he met them in books. They have been brooded over in solitude, until they afflict him as the wickedness of man afflicts a Puritan. The skull and crossbones, Death as the scythed skeleton, and the symbolic hour-glass have been as real to him as to some of those carvers of tombstones in country churchyards, or to the painter of that window at St Edmund's in Salisbury who represented 'God the Father . . . in blue and red vests, like a little old man, the head, feet and hands naked; in one place fixing a pair of compasses on the sun and moon'. If I were told that he had spent his days in a woodland hermitage, though I should not believe the story, I should suspect that it was founded on fact.

But the woodland, and the country in general, have given Mr Hardy some of his principal consolations. And one, at least, of these is almost superstitious. I mean the idea that 'the longlegs, the moth, and the dumbledore' know 'earth-secrets' that he knows not. ['An August Midnight' (113*).] In 'The Darkling Thrush' [119*] it is to be found in another stage, the bird's song in Winter impelling him to think that 'some blessed Hope' of which he was unaware was known to it. He compares town and country much as Meredith does. The country is paradise in the comparison; for he speaks of the Holiday Fund for City Children as temporarily 'changing their urban murk to paradise' [51]. Country life, paradise or not, he handles with a combination of power and exactness beyond that of any poet who could be compared to him, and for country women I should give the palm to his 'Julie-Jane' [(205*); Thomas quotes stanzas 1 and 8]

Such a woman has even made him merry like his fiddling ancestor, in the song of 'The Dark-Eyed Gentleman':

> And he came and tied up my garter for me.   [201]

And what with Nature and Beauty and Truth, he is really farther from surrender than might appear in some poems. His 'Let Me Enjoy' [(193); stanza 1 is quoted] is in the minor key, but by no means repudiates or makes little of Joy, and is at least as likely as

> Lord, with what care hast thou begirt us round[3]

to make a marching song.

> SOURCE: extract from *In Pursuit of Spring* (London: 1915), ch. V,
> pp. 180–98: a revised version of Thomas's article, 'Thomas Hardy
> of Dorchester', *Poetry and Drama*, I, 3 (June 1913). See also his *A
> Literary Pilgrim in England* (London, 1917), pp. 139–48, reprinted,
> along with the material reproduced here, in H. A. T. Johnson,
> 'Edward Thomas on Thomas Hardy', *Thomas Hardy Year Book*, IV
> (1976).

NOTES

1. In fact Hardy relates that it was Napoleon's messenger to Grouchy who was killed, after being misled, by the peasant [Eds].
2. For 'therefore' read 'therefor' [Eds].
3. A slightly misremembered quotation from George Herbert's 'Sin'. It should read 'Lord with what care hast Thou begirt us round' or, in some editions, 'Lord, with what care Thou hast begirt us round.' [Eds].

Harold Child (1916)

... To future generations Hardy will mean first and foremost the author of *The Dynasts* ... there is a sense in which *The Dynasts* is the perfect flower of Hardy the poet and of Hardy the novelist. His novels of themselves show his power of handling a great tragic argument with elevation,. dignity and passion. Through his lyric poems we have to learn his power over metre and rhyme, and his command of that intensity of measured utterance which, in the end, makes the difference between poetry and prose. As a writer of lyrics, Hardy is not among our greatest. The secret of lyric poetry is, after all, joy. It may be the simple Elizabethan joy in the spring and the eyes of a woman; it may be joy in a love that has flamed through flesh to spirit; it may be joy in a various and wonderful world; or joy in the Divine vision; or joy in the hope of a state of perfection on earth, and faith in man's power to reach it. It may even be the fine, heady joy of defiance flung in the face of fate. It is always a conscious gladness in power and vitality. We have seen enough of the bent of Hardy's mind to guess that in him the consciousness of power common to all great artists cannot jet out in pure exultation or hope, nor in defiance of a fate that neither hears nor cares. He cannot believe, like Shelley, that love is eternal and almighty; he is not just happy, like Browning; and he is not, like Meredith, aflame with the clear light of a reasonable faith. His own intensity of feeling is, in fact, at variance with his vision of the universe; and, thanks to his indomitable rectitude, so much of his feeling as can escape into expression is not ebullient joy. Always his intellect is at war with his emotions; he cannot give himself wholly and simply up. The result is extraordinarily interesting. There is nothing quite like Hardy's lyric poetry. It can hardly be said to sing. Indeed, on a first reading, it is easy to miss the music altogether, and to notice only that occasional stiffness which we have noticed in his prose, his compressed and sometimes clogged diction. Further study will show that, in spite of rare echoes of the manner of other poets, this poet has worked out for himself, with his masterly rectitude and self-reliance, a very varied, very individual music. Once more, he achieves nothing by accident. He has never trusted, one would say, words that forced themselves upon him, as other poets, and Wordsworth in particular, have trusted them, with effects miraculous. In Hardy's lyric poetry there is nothing miraculous. There are no flashing phrases, no single lines that seem to open windows to the infinite. It is hammered out; but it is hammered fine, and out of fine matter. It is never prose cut into lengths and rhymed. Its chief characteristics are simplicity and intensity. Like the prose it clings with minute fidelity to the author's precise meaning; and this, whether it is passionately searching the infinity of space and time or recording a slight incident of emotion or thought. It can be splendid, and it can be drab; it is always simple and intense.

If Hardy's place as lyric poet is not so much with the 'natural' singers as with the philosophical lyricists of the seventeenth century, his poetry is differentiated from theirs by the intensity of his feeling. We go, people tell us, to Wordsworth for consolation, to Browning for hope and energy, to Meredith for counsel and aspiration. It may be so. But first of all we go to poets for poetry, and Hardy is no less a poet because he cannot be discovered to prescribe for any disease of the mind. What his lyric poetry gives is the communication of intense feeling, and the sympathetic enlargement that must come of the contemplation of any soul deeply moved by the crosses and contradictions of life. Many of the poems, their author warns us, are 'dramatic or impersonative.' Well and good; but a mind reveals itself through its imaginings no less than through its deliberate beliefs and denials, and these imaginings must take their place among 'the unadjusted impressions' which, he holds, 'have their value.' And, to continue our quotation, 'the road to a true philosophy of life seems to be in humbly recording diverse readings of its phenomena as they are forced upon us by chance or change.' It is not, therefore, unfounded presumption that would find in Hardy's lyric poems the privilege of a closer intimacy with the mind that created the novels. The novels cannot be fully appreciated without a knowledge of the poems; but there is a sense in which the novels only lead up to the poems. For the poems offer an intenser and by some degrees a more personal expression of the ideas and experiences upon which the novels are built.

The volumes of minor poetry [i.e., at the date of Child's study – Eds] are four: *Wessex Poems* (1898), which is illustrated with some interesting drawings by the author; *Poems of the Past and the Present* (1901); *Time's Laughing-Stocks* (1909), and *Satires of Circumstance* (1914). The contents were composed at various times in Mr Hardy's working life and are various in subject and form. There are yarns of the Napoleonic wars, merry and tragic ballads, little stories of a bitter and sometimes a savage irony; grave and beautiful love poems; poems of a profound tenderness; speculations, spurts of anger; poems on the South African War, poems in dialect and poems august and high-sounding. Amid all this variety the reader, dipping where he will, will find always the unmistakable signs of the same strongly individual mind, seeing acutely, feeling intensely, and expressing itself powerfully. Perhaps the pleasantest, the most musically and suggestively beautiful poems that Hardy ever wrote are the 'Poems of 1912–13' in *Satires of Circumstance*. They are intimate, they are personal, they are gentle; they come like a fresh breeze on the fall of a summer evening. But I find myself going back again and again to the more definitely philosophical poems scattered throughout the four volumes: those in which the poet speaks most directly of his thoughts concerning the government of the world and the destiny of man.

And since he is, in effect, speaking here directly for himself, we may expect to find poems of a great sadness. We find, too, especially among the youthful poems, some of great bitterness. These are not pleasant. Were it not for this force of feeling and expression, they would make bad reading. But a man does not forgo palliatives and face a dark future in a mood of jollity; and some of the finest spirits – Shakespeare and Shelley among them – have cried out when they were hurt. If there were something to defy, one of Hardy's poems tells us, malignity would be easier to bear than the crass casualty of purblind doomsters; it is his sorrow, not his joy, says another, that he cannot comfortably acquiesce in the simple faith of his neighbours. Solace, a third poem tells us, is to be gained not from seeing, but from dreaming, when perhaps a fine morning may cheat the mind into imagining 'a benignant plan.' Very rarely do we find even so much of faith as Meredith expressed in his counsel to trust Nature, or Earth; and very rarely so much of hope as we find in the address to 'the unknown God' which closes the volume of *Poems of the Past and the Present* [151*]. The sweetest and bravest note of all is that which here and there sings of men

> In brotherhood bonded close and graced
> With loving-kindness fully blown,
> And visioned help unsought, unknown.   [266*]

Many of these lyric poems must inevitably pain those whose faith in the human spirit, whether within or without the pale of revealed religion, flames high; but for those who are seeking closer knowledge of the mind which gave us the novels and *The Dynasts*, they remain documents of profound interest. And they are more than that. They are intense and burning expressions of thoughts that must waylay all who are walking the path of truth alone. . . .

SOURCE: extract from *Thomas Hardy* (London: 1916; rev. ed. 1925), pp. 83–91 (1916 edition used here).

The Athenaeum (1918) on *Moments of Vision and Miscellaneous Verses*

Mr Hardy's poems have been written in an age which is in at least one sense fortunate. It may be an exaggeration to talk as though there had been a revival of poetry in the last few years, but there has certainly been a revival of the habit of reading poetry – especially of the habit of reading new poetry. Mr Hardy resembles some of the new poets in several respects. For one thing, he uses the verse-form with something of the gracelessness of a youth learning to skate. For another, he is intensely self-absorbed: his poems are, one after another, complaints of the self. He has obviously been greatly influenced by the dramatic lyrics of Browning, but, whereas Browning introduces us to all the sad and joyous households of life, Mr Hardy seldom takes us to any house that has not its blinds down on account either of a death or marital infidelity. His poems are written in a monotony of mournfulness; and even the genius of an imaginative man does not keep them from being, as the Scotsman said of mineral waters, very 'lowering,' as neither tragic literature nor any other sort of literature has the right to be.

There is nothing to separate Mr Hardy from the great poetic tradition in the fact that he sees man as a corpse temporarily permitted to walk upright on the surface of the earth. Other poets have meditated as darkly on death. Where Mr Hardy differs from the mass of tragic poets is that he sees so little grandeur in the gloom. His men and women are hapless and helpless beings, and have scarcely anything in common with the Plutarchian figures in the tragedies of Shakespeare. Mr Hardy's lovers, again, are seldom happy lovers. He dramatises their boredom and their unfaithfulness oftener than their joy. The history of love seems almost to be summed up for him in such a line as:

> We were irked by the scene, by our own selves; yes; [355*]

or in such a passage as:

> Wasted were two souls in their prime,
> And great was the waste, that July time
> When the rain came down. [355*]

His songs are songs of division. There is no triumphant daring in any of his lovers to enable them to face the world boldly either in honest love or in sin. In 'The Dolls' we find a little girl asking her mother why she always dresses up her dolls as soldiers (when she does not know any soldiers) instead of as

> . . . . gentle ladies
> With frills and frocks and curls,
> As people dress the dollies
> Of other little girls.

Mr Hardy unfolds the inevitable situation in a second verse:

> Ah – why did she not answer:
>   'Because your mammy's heed
> Is always gallant soldiers,
>   As well may be, indeed.
> One of them was your daddy,
>   His name I must not tell;
> He's not the dad who lives here,
>   But one I love too well.'   [443]

That is bad verse, but it is interesting as evidence of the extent to which Mr Hardy's vision of the world as a monotony of misfits has become an obsession with him. Love appears as a ruinous misfortune rather than a saving grace in most of his poems. It comes and goes with the wind, and man suffers through it rather than is exalted by it into secure godhead. Mr Hardy has never got beyond the doubting philosophy of love which he expresses in the fine poem 'The Wind's Prophecy' [440*] which begins:

> I travel on by barren farms,
> And gulls glint out like silver flecks
> Against a cloud that speaks of wrecks,
> And bellies down with black alarms.
> I say: 'Thus from my lady's arms
> I go; those arms I love the best!'
> The wind replies from dip and rise,
> 'Nay; toward her arms thou journeyest.'

In Mr Hardy's philosophy the lover, helpless in his inconstancy, is deceived even in the hour of his love.

'The Wind's Prophecy' is interesting, however, not only for the light it throws on Mr Hardy's vision of life, but because it reminds us that in his genius he is essentially an interpreter of the earth. One may be allowed to isolate the little passages of landscape in the poem from the rest in order to enable his gift as a painter and poet to reveal itself the better. Here is the world seen under the light of imagination, though unquestionably of pessimistic imagination:

A distant verge morosely gray
Appears, while clots of flying foam
Break from its muddy monochrome,
And a light blinks up far away.

. . .

From tides the lofty coastlands screen
Come smitings like the slam of doors,
Or hammerings on hollow floors,
As the swell cleaves through caves unseen.

. . .

The all-prevailing clouds exclude
The one quick timorous transient star;
The waves outside where breakers are
Huzza like a mad multitude.

. . .

Yonder the headland, vulturine,
Snores like a giant in his sleep,
And every chasm and every steep
Blackens as wakes each pharos-shine.
. . .

There, if anywhere in Mr Hardy's new book, is the mark of the brooding and imaginative vision of poetry. Almost can we believe that Mr Hardy's world, so passionately is it seen, is beautiful. While he writes of the scene of things he is impressionable as a child. Nature is still in a measure grand for him in a world of drab destinies. It is only when he turns to human beings and his philosophy about them that he can write such lines as:

> 'Where the sun ups it, mist-imbued,'
> I cry, 'there reigns the star for me!'
> The wind outshrieks from points and peaks:
> 'Here, westward, where it downs, mean ye!'   [440*]

Mr Hardy's philosophy, however, pessimistic though it is, casts a queer sort of spell over his poems. His book, we feel, is the truthful record of a man's soul. It is a statement of experience in terms of a philosophy of disaster. And even in the drear night of this philosophy, faith seems to peep out at moments like a star. Mr Hardy's war poems communicate the spirit of the fighter, though most of his work in prose and verse has communicated rather the spirit of the victim. His poem 'For Life I Had

Never Cared Greatly' ends in a refusal on the part of the poet to accept failure as his destiny:

> And so, the rough highway forgetting,
>   I face hill and dale,
>   Regarding the sky,
>   Regarding the vision on high,
> And thus re-illumed have no humour for letting
>   My pilgrimage fail.   [492]

Perhaps, after all, it is foolish to call any man a pessimist who takes the trouble to express his pessimism in works of art. If one were a real pessimist, one would hardly think it worth while to write books. While there is literature there is hope. To write is itself an act of faith. Apart from this, Mr Hardy, in that beautiful Christmas reverie 'The Oxen' [403*] comes as near faith, perhaps, as the average man of this unsettled hour. But the mood of 'The Oxen' is, unhappily, not characteristic of him.

SOURCE: unsigned review in *The Athenaeum* (January 1918), No. 4625.

J. Middleton Murry (1919)

One meets fairly often with the critical opinion that Mr Hardy's poetry is incidental. It is admitted on all sides that his poetry has curious merits of its own, but it is held to be completely subordinate to his novels, and those who maintain that it must be considered as having equal standing with his prose, are not seldom treated as guilty of paradox and preciousness.

We are inclined to wonder, as we review the situation, whether those of the contrary persuasion are not allowing themselves to be impressed primarily by mere bulk, and arguing that a man's chief work must necessarily be what he has done most of; and we feel that some such supposition is necessary to explain what appears to us as a visible reluctance to allow Mr Hardy's poetry a clean impact upon the critical consciousness. It is true that we have ranged against us critics of distinction, such as Mr Lascelles Abercrombie and Mr Robert Lynd, and that it may savour of impertinence to suggest that the case could have been unconsciously pre-judged in their minds when they addressed themselves to Mr Hardy's poetry. Nevertheless, we find some significance in the fact that both these critics are of such an age that

when they came to years of discretion the Wessex Novels were in
existence as a *corpus*. There, before their eyes, was a monument of
literary work having a unity unlike that of any contemporary author.
The poems became public only after they had laid the foundations of
their judgement. For them Mr Hardy's work was done. Whatever he
might subsequently produce was an interesting but, to their criticism,
an otiose appendix to his prose achievement.

It happens therefore that to a somewhat younger critic the perspective may be different. By the accident of years it would appear to
him that Mr Hardy's poetry was no less a *corpus* than his prose. They
would be extended equally and at the same moment before his eyes; he
would embark upon voyages of discovery into both at roughly the same
time; and he might find that the poetry would yield up to him a quality
of perfume not less essential than any that he could extract from the
prose.

This is, at any rate, the case with us. We discover all that our elders
discover in Mr Hardy's novels; we see more than they in his poetry. To
our mind it exists superbly in its own right; it is not lifted into
significance upon the glorious substructure of the novels. They also are
complete in themselves. We recognise the relation between the
achievements, and discern that they are the work of a single mind; but
they are separate works, having separate and unique excellences. The
one is only approximately explicable in terms of the other. We incline,
therefore, to attach a signal importance to what has always seemed to us
the most interesting sentence in *Who's Who?* – namely, that in which Mr
Hardy confesses that in 1868 he was 'compelled' – that is his own word –
to give up writing poetry for prose.

For Mr Hardy's poetic gift is not a late and freakish flowering. In the
volume[1] into which has been gathered all his poetical work with the
exception of *The Dynasts*, are pieces bearing the date 1866 which display
an astonishing mastery, not merely of technique but of the essential
content of great poetry. Nor are such pieces exceptional. Granted that
Mr Hardy has retained only the finest of his early poetry, still there are a
dozen poems of 1866–7 which belong either entirely or in part to the
category of major poetry. Take, for instance, 'Neutral Tones':

> We stood by a pond that winter day,
> And the sun was white, as though chidden of God,
> And a few leaves lay on the starving sod;
> – They had fallen from an ash, and were gray.
>
>
> Your eyes on me were as eyes that rove
> Over tedious riddles long ago;

And some words played between us to and fro
  On which lost the more by our love.

The smile on your mouth was the deadest thing
Alive enough to have strength to die;
And a grin of bitterness swept thereby
  Like an ominous bird a-wing. . . .

Since then, keen lessons that love deceives,
And wrings with wrong, have shaped to me
Your face, and the God-curst sun, and a tree
  And a pond edged with grayish leaves.   [9*]

That was written in 1867. The date of *Desperate Remedies*, Mr Hardy's
first novel, was 1871. *Desperate Remedies* may have been written some
years before. It makes no difference to the striking contrast between the
immaturity of the novel and the maturity of the poem. It is surely
impossible in the face of such a juxtaposition to deny that Mr Hardy's
poetry exists in its own individual right, and not as a curious
simulacrum of his prose.

These early poems have other points of deep interest, of which one of
the chief is in a sense technical. One can trace a quite definite influence
of Shakespeare's sonnets in his language and imagery. The four sonnets,
'She, to Him' (1866), are full of echoes, as:

Numb as a vane that cankers on its point,
True to the wind that kissed ere canker came.   [16]

or this from another sonnet of the same year:

As common chests encasing wares of price
Are borne with tenderness through halls of state.   [168]

Yet no one reading the sonnets of these years can fail to mark the
impress of an individual personality. The effect is, at times, curious and
impressive in the extreme. We almost feel that Mr Hardy is bringing
some physical compulsion to bear on Shakespeare and forcing him to
say something that he does not want to say. Of course, it is merely a
curious tweak of the fancy; but there comes to us in such lines as the
following an insistent vision of two youths of an age, the one masterful,
the other indulgent, and carrying out his companion's firm suggestion:

Remembering mine the loss is, not the blame
That Sportsman Time rears but his brood to kill,

> Knowing me in my soul the very same –
> One who would die to spare you touch of ill! –
> Will you not grant to old affection's claim
> The hand of friendship down Life's sunless hill?   [14]

But, fancies aside, the effect of these early poems is two-fold. Their attitude is definite:

> Crass Casualty obstructs the sun and rain,
> And dicing Time for gladness calls a moan . . .
> These purblind Doomsters had as readily thrown
> Blisses about my pilgrimage as pain.   [4*]

and the technique has the mark of mastery, a complete economy of statement which produces the conviction that the words are saying only what poet ordained they should say, neither less nor more.

The early years were followed by the long period of the novels, in which, we are prepared to admit, poetry was actually if not in intention incidental. It is the grim truth that poetry cannot be written in between times; and, though we have hardly any dates on which to rely, we are willing to believe that few of Mr Hardy's characteristic poems were written between the appearance of *Desperate Remedies* and his farewell to the activity of novel-writing with *The Well-Beloved* (1897). But the few dates which we have tell us that 'Thoughts of Phena,' the beautiful poem beginning:

> Not a line of her writing have I,
> Not a thread of her hair. . . .   [38*]

which reaches forward to the love poems of 1912–13, was written in 1890.

Whether the development of Mr Hardy's poetry was concealed or visible during the period of the novels, development there was into a maturity so manifest that by its touchstone the poetical work of his famous contemporaries appears singularly jejune and false. But, though by the accident of social conditions – for that Mr Hardy waited till 1898 to publish his first volume of poems is more a social than an artistic fact – it is impossible to follow out the phases of his poetical progress in the detail we would desire, it is impossible not to recognise that the mature poet, Mr Hardy, is of the same poetical substance as the young poet of the 'sixties. The attitude is unchanged; the modifications of the theme of 'crass Casualty' leave its central asseveration unchanged. There are restatements, enlargements of perspective, a slow and forceful expansion of the personal into the universal, but the truth once recognised is never suffered for a moment to be hidden or mollified. Only a superficial logic would point, for instance, to his

> Wonder if Man's consciousness
> Was a mistake of God's,

as a denial of 'Casualty.' To envisage an accepted truth from a new angle, to turn it over and over again in the mind in the hope of finding some aspect which might accord with a large and general view is the inevitable movement of any mind that is alive and not dead. To say that Mr Hardy has finally discovered unity may be paradoxical; but it is true. The harmony of the artist is not as the harmony of the preacher or the philosopher. Neither would grant, neither would understand the profound acquiescence that lies behind 'Adonais' or the 'Ode to the Grecian Urn.' Such acquiescence has no moral quality, as morality is even now understood, nor any logical compulsion. It does not stifle anger nor deny anguish; it turns no smiling face upon unsmiling things; it is not puffed up with the resonance of futile heroics. It accepts the things that are as the necessary basis of artistic creation. This unity which comes of the instinctive refusal in the great poet to deny experience, and subdues the self into the whole as part of that which is not denied, is to be found in every corner of Mr Hardy's mature poetry. It gives, as it alone can really give, to personal emotion what is called the impersonality of great poetry. We feel it as a sense of background, a conviction that a given poem is not the record, but the consummation of an experience, and that the experience of which it is the consummation is larger and more profound than the one which it seems to record.

At the basis of great poetry lies an all-embracing realism, an adequacy to all experience, a refusal of the merely personal in exultation or dismay. Take the contrast between Rupert Brooke's deservedly famous lines: 'There is some corner of a foreign field . . .' and Mr Hardy's 'Drummer Hodge':

> Yet portion of that unknown plain
>   Will Hodge for ever be;
> His homely Northern heart and brain
>   Grow to some Southern tree,
> And strange-eyed constellations reign
>   His stars eternally.   [60*]

We know which is the truer. Which is the more beautiful? Is it not Mr Hardy? And which (strange question) is the more consoling, the more satisfying, the more acceptable? Is it not Mr Hardy? There is sorrow, but it is the sorrow of the spheres. And this, not the apparent anger and dismay of a self's discomfiture, is the quality of greatness in Mr Hardy's poetry. The Mr Hardy of the love poems of 1912–13 is not a man giving way to memory in poetry; he is a great poet uttering the cry of the universe. A vast range of acknowledged experience returns to weight each syllable; it is the quality of life that is vocal, gathered into a moment of time with a vista of years:

> Ignorant of what there is flitting here to see,
>   The waked birds preen and the seals flop lazily;
> Soon you will have, Dear, to vanish from me,
>   For the stars close their shutters and the dawn whitens hazily.
> Trust me, I mind not, though Life lours,
>   The bringing me here; nay, bring me here again!
>   I am just the same as when
> Our days were a joy, and our paths through flowers.   [289*]

We have read these poems of Thomas Hardy, read them not once, but many times. Many of them have already become part of our being; they have given shape to dumb and striving elements in our soul; they have set free and purged mute, heart-devouring regrets. And yet, though this is so, the reading of them in a single volume, the submission to their movement with a like unbroken motion of the mind, gathers their greatness, their poignancy and passion, into one stream, submerging us and leaving us patient and purified.

There have been many poets among us in the last fifty years, poets of sure talent, and it may be even of genius, but no other of them has this compulsive power. The secret is not hard to find. We have in our hearts a new touchstone of poetic greatness. We have learned too much to be wholly responsive to less than an adamantine honesty of soul and a complete acknowledgment of experience. 'Give us the whole,' we cry, 'give us the truth.' Unless we can catch the undertone of this acknowledgement, a poet's voice is in our ears hardly more than sounding brass or a tinkling cymbal.

Therefore we turn – some by instinct and some by deliberate choice – to the greatest; therefore we deliberately set Mr Hardy among these. What they have, he has, and has in their degree – a plenary vision of life. He is the master of the fundamental theme; it enters into, echoes in, modulates and modifies all his particular emotions, and the individual poems of which they are the substance. Each work of his is a fragment of a whole – not a detached and arbitrarily severed fragment, but a unity which implies, calls for and in a profound sense creates a vaster and complete comprehensive whole. His reaction to an episode has behind and within it a reaction to the universe. An overwhelming endorsement descends upon his words: he traces them with a pencil, and straightway they are graven in stone.

Thus his short poems have a weight and validity which sets them apart in kind from even the very finest work of his contemporaries. These may be perfect in and for themselves; but a short poem by Mr Hardy is often perfect in a higher sense. As the lines of a diagram may be produced in imagination to contain within themselves all space, one of Mr Hardy's most characteristic poems may expand and embrace all human experience. In it we may hear the sombre, ruthless rhythm of life itself – the dominant theme that gives individuation to the ripple of fragmentary joys and sorrows. Take 'A Broken Appointment':

> You did not come,
> And marching Time drew on, and wore me numb. –
> Yet less for loss of your dear presence there
> Than that I thus found lacking in your make
> That high compassion which can overbear
> Reluctance for pure lovingkindness' sake
> Grieved I, when, as the hope-hour stroked its sum,
> You did not come.
>
> You love not me,
> And love alone can lend you loyalty;
> – I know and knew it. But, unto the store
> Of human deeds divine in all but name,
> Was it not worth a little hour or more
> To add yet this: Once you, a woman, came
> To soothe a time-torn man; even though it be
> You love not me?   [99*]

On such a seeming fragment of personal experience lies the visible endorsement of the universe. The hopes not of a lover but of humanity are crushed beneath its rhythm. The ruthlessness of the event is intensified in the motion of the poem till one can hear the even pad of destiny; and a moment comes when to a sense made eager by the strain of intense attention it seems to have been written by the destiny it records.

What is the secret of poetic power like this? We do not look for it in technique, though the technique of this poem is masterly. But the technique of 'as the hope-hour stroked its sum' is of such a kind that we know as we read that it proceeds from a sheer compulsive force. For a moment it startles; a moment more and the echo of those very words is reverberant with accumulated purpose. They are pitiless as the poem; the sign of an ultimate obedience is upon them. Whence came the power that compelled it? Can the source be defined or indicated? We believe it can be indicated, though not defined. We can show where to look for the mystery, that in spite of our regard remains a mystery still. We are persuaded that almost on the instant that it was felt the original emotion of the poem was endorsed. Perhaps it came to the poet as the pain of a particular and personal experience; but in a little or a long while – creative time is not measured by days or years – it became, for him, a part of the texture of the general life. It became a manifestation of life, almost, nay wholly, in the sacramental sense, a veritable epiphany. The manifold and inexhaustible quality of life was focused into a single revelation. A critic's words do not lend themselves to the necessary precision. The word 'revelation' is fertile in false suggestion; the creative act of power which seeks to elucidate is an act of plenary apprehension, by which one manifestation, one form of life, one experience is seen in its rigorous relation to all other and to all possible manifestations, forms, and experiences. It is, we believe, the act which Mr Hardy himself has tried to formulate in the phrase which is the title of one of his books of poems – *Moments of Vision.*

Only those who do not read Mr Hardy could make the mistake of supposing that on his lips such a phrase had a mystical implication. Between belief and logic lies a third kingdom, which the mystics and the philosophers alike are too eager to forget – the kingdom of art, no less the residence of truth than the two other realms, and to some, perhaps, more authentic even than they. Therefore when we expand the word 'vision' in the phrase to 'æsthetic vision' we mean, not the perception of beauty, at least in the ordinary sense of that ill-used word, but the apprehension of truth, the recognition of a complete system of valid relations incapable of logical statement. Such are the acts of unique apprehension which Mr Hardy, we believe, implied by his title. In a 'moment of vision' the poet recognises in a single separate incident of life, life's essential quality. The uniqueness of the whole, the infinite multiplicity and variety of its elements, are manifested and apprehended in a part. Since we are here at work on the confines of intelligible statement, it is better, even at the cost of brutalising a poem, to choose an example from the book that bears the mysterious name. The verses that follow come from 'Near Lanivet, 1872.' We choose them as an example of Mr Hardy's method at less than its best, at a point at which the scaffolding of his process is just visible.

There was a stunted hand-post just on the crest,
    Only a few feet high:
She was tired, and we stopped in the twilight-time for her rest,
    At the crossways close thereby.

She leant back, being so weary, against its stem,
  And laid her arms on its own,
Each open palm stretched out to each end of them,
  Her sad face sideways thrown.

Her white-clothed form at this dim-lit cease of day
  Made her look as one crucified
In my gaze at her from the midst of the dusty way,
  And hurriedly 'Don't,' I cried.

I do not think she heard. Loosing thence she said,
  As she stepped forth ready to go,
'I am rested now. – Something strange came into my head;
  I wish I had not leant so!'

. . .

And we dragged on and on, while we seemed to see
  In the running of Time's far glass
Her crucified, as she had wondered if she might be
  Some day. – Alas, alas!   [366*]

Superstition and symbolism, some may say; but they mistakenly invert the order of the creative process. The poet's act of apprehension is wholly different from the lover's fear; and of this apprehension the chance-shaped crucifix is the symbol and not the cause. The concentration of life's vicissitude upon that white-clothed form was first recognised by a sovereign act of æsthetic understanding or intuition; the seeming crucifix supplied a scaffolding for its expression; it afforded a clue to the method of transposition into words which might convey the truth thus apprehended; it suggested an equivalence. The distinction may appear to be hair-drawn, but we believe that it is vital to the theory as a whole, and to an understanding of Mr Hardy's poetry in particular. Indeed, in it must be sought the meaning of another of his titles, *Satires of Circumstance*, where the particular circumstance is neither typical nor fortuitous, but a symbol necessary to communicate to others the sense of a quality in life more largely and variously apprehended by the poet.

At the risk of appearing fantastic we will endeavour still further to elucidate our meaning. The poetic process is, we believe, twofold. The one part, the discovery of symbol, the establishment of an equivalence, is what we may call poetic method. It is concerned with the transposition and communication of emotion, no matter what the emotion may be, for to poetic method the emotional material is, strictly, indifferent. The other part is an æsthetic apprehension of significance, the recognition of the all in the one. This is a specifically poetic act, or rather the supreme poetic act. Yet it may be absent from poetry. For there is no necessary connection between poetic apprehension and poetic method. Poetic method frequently exists without poetic apprehension; and there is no reason to suppose that the reverse is not also true, for the recognition of greatness in poetry is probably not the peculiar privilege of great poets. We have here, at least a principle of division between major and minor poetry.

Mr Hardy is a major poet; and we are impelled to seek further and ask what it is that enables such a poet to perform this sovereign act of apprehension and to recognise the quality of the all in the quality of the one. We believe that the answer is simple. The great poet knows what he is looking for. Once more we speak too precisely, and so falsely, being compelled to use the language of the kingdom of logic to describe what is being done in the kingdom of art. The poet, we say, knows the quality for which he seeks; but this knowledge is rather a condition than a possession of soul. It is a state of responsiveness rather than a knowledge of that to which he will respond. But it is knowledge inasmuch as the choice of that to which he will respond is determined by the condition of his soul. On the purity of that condition depends his greatness as a poet, and that purity in its turn depends upon his denying no element of his profound experience. If he denies or forgets, the synthesis – again the word is a metaphor – which must establish itself within him is fragmentary and false. The new event can wake but partial echoes in his soul or none at all; it can neither be received into, nor can it create a complete relation, and so it passes incommensurable from limbo into forgetfulness.

Mr Hardy stands high above all other modern poets by the deliberate purity of his responsiveness. The contagion of the world's slow stain has not touched him; from the first he held aloof from the general conspiracy to forget in which not only those who are professional optimists take a part. Therefore his simplest words have a vehemence and strangeness of their own:

> It will have been:
> Nor God nor Demon can undo the done,
> Unsight the seen,
> Make muted music be as unbegun
> Though things terrene
> Groan in their bondage till oblivion supervene.   [251]

What neither God nor Demon can do, men are incessantly at work to accomplish. Life itself rewards them for their assiduity, for she scatters her roses chiefly on the paths of those who forget her thorns. But the great poet remembers both rose and thorn; and it is beyond his power to remember them otherwise than together.

It was fitting, then, and to some senses inevitable, that Mr Hardy should have crowned his work as a poet in his old age by a series of love poems that are unique for power and passion in even the English language. This late and wonderful flowering has no tinge of miracle; it has sprung straight from the main stem of Mr Hardy's poetic growth. Into 'Veteris Vestigia Flammæ'² is distilled the quintessence of the power that created the Wessex Novels and *The Dynasts*; all that Mr Hardy has to tell us of life, the whole of the truth that he has apprehended, is in these poems, and no poet since poetry began has apprehended or told us more. *Sunt lacrimæ rerum.*

SOURCE: essay on 'The Poetry of Mr Hardy', *The Athenaeum* (November 1919); reprinted in *Aspects of Literature* (London: 1920), pp. 125–51.

NOTES

1. Murry refers to the first version of *Collected Poems* (embracing the five separate volumes of poetry issued up to 1917), published in 1919 [Eds].
2. Hardy's epigraph to 'Poems of 1912–13' in *Satires of Circumstance . . .* [Eds].

Walter de la Mare (1919)

If devotion and love are the happiest flowers that can intertwine a poet's laurels, then the wreath upon Mr Hardy's brows is indeed burdened with sweetness. It is impossible to read him with indifference or in mere admiration. We blow either hot or cold; a fact that may in part explain why, years ago, he was compelled to surrender verse for prose, and long afterwards to forswear the writing of fiction. That dead past has now prudently buried its dead. Today our proud affection may even veil his rarest qualities. In heart as well as in time we stand too close to his work to appraise its complete achievement, to see it in true perspective and in relation to that of the great masters.

In reading again, and in reading steadily through, his lyrical poems we can realise, at any rate, the abundance and variety of his work, its homogeneousness and originality. No other English novelist has, in a chosen context, written prose that in effect, in feeling and atmosphere is nearer to poetry. No other English dramatist has written an historical play which more closely resembles than does *The Dynasts* a vast

panoramic fiction, wherein real men and women so strangely reflect the
idiosyncrasies of a distinct personality and imagination. So with these
poems. They are, one and all, haunted with the presence of their writer.
Every line of them – best and worst – is sealed with his own hand. We
share an intense solitude of the spirit. We are as close to actual
experience as words can bring us.

But even the most lyrical and individual of them is touched with the
dramatic. A score of diverse disguises conceal (and betray) the one
wearer; and ever to and fro glides the shuttle of wizardry, weaving
make-believe out of the actual. More than once Mr Hardy has warned
us that his lyrics are dramatic or impersonative in conception, even
when not obviously so. He has bidden us make allowance for widely
differing moods and circumstances. He deprecates, that is, an arraign-
ment of himself as A for what another self utters as Z. None the less –
Alpha to Omega – all here is his, and all is himself. Nor should the
inherent apparent contradictions be cancelled out as in a sum in
arithmetic. They are light and colour from the facets of one multi-
angled consciousness, that makes a various and chequered beauty of the
white ray that is the infinite reality.

The simplest of poets may, it is true, drape himself in more than one
domino. Herrick is Ariel in his songs, Caliban in his epigrams; the
bacchanalian of the Mermaid and of the Triple Tun at one moment,
the pious vicar of Dean Prior the next. But Mr Hardy in his lyrics not
only plays countless parts (from Prospero's to Trinculo's), and will
squander on three brief stanzas the nucleus of a novel, but he is
untrammelled by the incapacity to make poetry of the commonplace.
In the Sala delle Muse, in Rome, he once kept tryst with one (surely a
distant cousin of Sue Bridehead's) who was 'an essence of the Nine' – 'a
pensive smile on her sweet, small, marvellous face'. He lamented his
fickleness, his inconstant love for Form also, and Tune, Story, Dance,
and Hymn. She consoled him:

> Nay, wight, thou sway'st not. These are but phases of one;
>
> And that one is I; and I am projected from thee,
> One that out of thy brain and heart thou causest to be –
> Extern to thee nothing. Grieve not, nor thyself becall,
> Woo where thou wilt; and rejoice thou canst love at all!   [70*]

So well has he obeyed her that anywhen, anywhere that ghostly face
may smile on him in still regard, and make of every working day exactly
four-and-twenty timeless hours. Certain themes may recur again and
again; but he is not confined to any particular region of thought,

experience, or of the imagination. Self-forgotten, he lives in the created. Absorbed in characters of his own making, he none the less fashions them in his own protean image. Never was the tinder of the mind more hospitable to the feeblest of actuality's sparks. The merest glimpse – a boy in a railway carriage with a key hung round his neck, a skeleton parasol, a tapping moth, a cheval glass, a fly bestraddling his midnight manuscript, a candle-lit face, a tottering tombstone, a church clock, a gargoyle, a fiddle, the wind in the chimney, dying daylight – and the poet in him answers as to a decoy. It may be convenient to call him a realist – though what poet, if reality is the habitation of the spirit as well as of the body, can be anything else is a nice question. A more precise term would be realisationist.

But if, apart from mask and domino, his scope, his multifarious range of theme, differentiates Mr Hardy's lyrical poetry, no less does his treatment of it, the thought with which he complicates and deepens it, and the intensity, less of impulse than of elaboration, with which he constrains it to his will. The poet whose nut-tree bears silver nutmegs and gold pears would only scare his Spanish princess if he plucked for her also crab-apples and sloes. Fruits as tart and acrid abound in Mr Hardy's orchard; and however gladly we may feast our eyes upon their vivid and sombre clusters, they are as bitter to some stomachs as was the honey-flavoured book to St John. Lyrical poetry in general makes its own lovely paradise, fresh and sweet with dews of Lethe. Its airs blow rare from the intense inane. Much of Mr Hardy's poetry limes our wings and tethers us close indeed to a God-forgotten 'tainted ball'. Mutes attired in dead black, their eyes submissive though preternaturally active, their ears exquisitely 'on the *qui vive*', stand on either side of the portals of its philosophy. Poem after poem reiterates that this poor scene of our earthly life is 'a show God ought surely to shut up soon', the 'unweeting dream-work' of some vast Imbecility, that spends eternity in passive reverie or remorse, that framed this planet in jest and abandoned it to hazardry: 'That I made Earth, and life, and man It still repenteth me.' As for Nature –she is nought more pitiful than a sleep-walker. 'Busy in her handsome house known as Space', she has fallen a-drowse; and man's only sure reward for all his hopes and aspirations is that 'storm-tight roof' which 'earth grants all her kind'; his only comfort that, though he must at last fall a prey to the 'iron daggers of distress', twice he cannot die. If this, and scores of kindred maledictions, were the final, unalleviated message to humanity of 'One who, past doubtings all, Waits in Unhope', then the poet in Mr Hardy would have died in the arms of the philosopher, as might have Heine in those of Schopenhauer. But Mr Hardy is too imaginative a philosopher to venture a final answer to the great riddle. He asks and asks:

Thy shadow, Earth, from Pole to Central Sea,
Now steals along upon the Moon's meek shine
In even monochrome and curving line
Of imperturbable serenity.

How shall I link such sun-cast symmetry
With the torn troubled form I know as thine,
That profile, placid as a brow divine,
With continents of moil and misery?

And can immense Mortality but throw
So small a shade . . .   [79*]

No God, it is true, could loom more phantasmal and remote from our
trivial and agonising affairs than the 'all-Immanent Will' that drives us
into the world in 'rabble rout', mutters in slumber, or mocks, or sighs
out of his tenebrous abiding-place in consciousness, at 'the monotonous
moil of strained hard-run Humanity'. But anthropomorphic deities are
usually flattering reflections of their creators. This deity is infinitely less
compassionate, tender, magnanimous, and faithful than the poet whose
workmanship he is, and who in every word he writes is present with us.
Wherefore relenting and tenderness often steal into the limning of this
Divine conception, and pity smiles from the eye-holes of the cold mask
of the ironic:

'Thou shouldst have learnt that *Not to Mend*
For Me could mean but *Not to Know. . . .*'   [87*]

It takes two to make either a quarrel or a friendship. 'Dazed and
puzzled 'twixt the gleam and gloom', the only human hope is honesty.

Yet would men look at true things,
And unilluded view things,
And count to bear undue things,

The real might mend the seeming,
Facts better their foredeeming,
And Life its disesteeming.   [233]

And in 'The Spell of the Rose', another story is told to us:

But I was called from earth – yea, called
Before my rose-bush grew;
And would that now I knew
What feels he of the tree I planted,

And whether, after I was called
To be a ghost, he, as of old,
    Gave me his heart anew!

Perhaps now blooms that queen of trees
    I set but saw not grow,
    And he, beside its glow –
Eyes couched of the mis-vision that blurred me –
    Ay, there beside that queen of trees
    He sees me as I was, though sees
        Too late to tell me so!   [295*]

That rose-bush is love – 'long-suffering, brave . . . sweet, prompt,
precious', even though 'cruel as the grave'. Not ours the arrogance to
reconcile on his behalf a poet's contradictions. Yet there is a bloom
upon this Dead Sea fruit that is more inviting and even more sustaining
than the milky juices of that of the mere optimist. Beyond this, simply
because the faithful and unflinching presentation of a philosophy,
however Spartan, darkened or forlorn it may be, is poetic, it confers
light, energy, and even peace on us. *Worse* tidings cannot reach us, nor
can Truth wear a colder, harsher, more sardonic grin (and assuredly in
the 'Fifteen Glimpses' she displays her dog teeth to some purpose). But
we have fallen in love with her ambassador; and like ambassador, the
heart argues, like Queen.
    Beneath this heaven, indifferent or hostile, Mr Hardy sets up his
stage, the panorama of mortal existence, calls up his characters, peoples
his solitude:

            Listen: I'll tell the tale,
            It may bring faint relief.

Our company, it must be admitted, is not that of 'the winged seraphs':
or of alien divinities as lovely as they are inexacting; or of a society
urbane, at ease, immune in its Palace of Art. There are not many
'ladies' in this volume – the majority of them are haplessly jilted, or
helplessly wed. There are far fewer perfect gentlemen. One such buys
an enemy's portrait intent on the joy (of which he is cheated) of
destroying it; another is the husband of the unfortunate bride in 'A
Conversation at Dawn:'

            'I'm a practical man, and want no tears;
            You've made a fool of me, it appears;
                That you don't again
            Is a lesson I'll teach you in future years.'

> She answered not, lying listlessly
> With her dark dry eyes on the coppery sea,
>   That now and then
> Flung its lazy flounce at the neighbouring quay.   [305]

A third 'gentleman' affrighted even a wagtail.

In a world indeed wherein, if closely examined, the guise of life is less 'fell' only when it is realised that cold, sickness, gloom, death are but 'subalterns', passively subject to the higher command, class distinctions seem of trivial import, and 'the courtesies of the bland' a mere veneer. It is little wonder then that poor Mrs Grundy cuts a sorry figure in it; that the conventions and conformities are left to take care of themselves, as they very well can; and that 'Order-keeping's rigorous control' resembles that of a foolish and embittered nurse in a rebellious nursery. Moonshine or noonday, and whether its stage be thronged or deserted, this is a world also, whose borders are astir with the spectral. How could it be otherwise, seeing that of any man's friends so large a number are in the grave? It is here, if anywhere, that literary company looks in on Mr Hardy, and come to sup with him Emily Brontë and the author of *The Duchess of Malfi*. Barham, too, when the port is on the table, will rap at the door; and neighbour Burton lug in a folio on the Pleasures of Melancholy. His phantoms and revenants are for the most part the wistful evocations of misgiving or regret. Some of them are more lovely, and all are more understandable, even when inclined to the satirical, than when in the real. Many are earthily jovial, 'clay-cadavers', with their mugs and pipes, their lutes and viols, touched by lights of midnight, under willow and yew. And amid their revelries from among the deeper shadows leers out the sinister-grotesque.

Thus freed from the artificial, thus haunted, thus aroused, we share the company of Mr. Hardy's wayfaring men and women, intent on their all-absorbing share in the egregious drama, and part-perfect. Entangled in the webs of circumstance, the majority of them are the prey of their desires, their aspirations or their folly, racked, cheated by mischance, victims of age or affliction, or of a tender and lively charm and innocence that is but a mockery in its transitoriness. Their happiest stories are overcast with the precarious (and at the mercy of an ironic appendix!); but even the most tragic are such as our own experience can ratify, however hastily a self-defensive memory may have strown her poppy.

Like the figure which we discern in the poems that are not obviously impersonative or dramatic, these characters are mysterious, and touched with a kind of strangeness or romance, as indeed all humanity is mysterious when, viewed searchingly, it is off its guard, or when the scales of habit or prejudice have dropped from our eyes. Unobserved, we watch them as closely as in mind we can watch the faces of friends with whom long ago we were in intimate and earnest colloquy; but seldom, indeed, as watches Peeping Tom when the vivisectionist is busy. So passionately intent is Mr Hardy's 'visionary power' on the naked truth of things in their changing aspects that he seems designedly to reject in his record of them the refinements of art and beauty.

But since beauty and significance are debts which no living imagination can evade paying to reality, his poetry is drenched with them. Even if these figments of humanity were absent from his pages, we might almost guess his portraits from their frames. No other poetry is richer in scene, within doors or without; in landscape – its times and lights and seasons; in Englishness. To present a true account, debit and credit, between Mr Hardy and his Wessex would make the fame of a literary accountant. But what of that further west of the most passionate of his poems, where 'in chasmal beauty' roars the Atlantic, and swing the surges over sunken Lyonesse?

Yet, for pure melody, the music of this verse is unlikely to redden with envy the cheeks of the Sirens. The style is often crustacean. Occasionally it is 'an irk no local hope beguiles', and as if 'smitten by years-long wryness born of misprision'. The thought, too, may be as densely burdened in its expression as the scar of a tree by the healing saps that have enwarted its surface. But what rare and wondrous clumps of mistletoe bedeck the branches. Stubborn the medium may be, but with what mastery is it compelled to do this craftsman's bidding. Let the practised poet borrow but a score of Mr Hardy's latinities and vernaculars – hodiernal, receptivity, deicide, a senior-soul-flame, his mindsight, naysaying, eyesome, potent appraisements, smugger, years-haired, forefolk, and the rest—and then invoke his own Muse! Difficulty, seeming impossibility, is the breath of Mr Hardy's nostrils as a craftsman. He makes our English so much his own that a single quoted line, lifted at random, betrays his workmanship. He forces, hammers poetry into his words; not, like most poets, charms it out of them. He disdains the 'poetical', yet will redeem the veriest commonplace; and will so encrust his chosen theme that it shines the brighter for the roughness and uncouthness of its setting. His argument winds in and out of his congested, complex stanzas, keeping a low pitch, and, by emphasising rather than by suddenly escaping its monotony, wins his effect.

When indeed life and energy pour their visionings of truth and reality into the mould of form, poetry cannot but be their reward. This imagination, accepting the world even while renouncing the 'Impercipient' that set it in the void, redeems its mischances, and of the sorriest disaster makes a memory for our comfort and understanding. Charm, grace, delicacy seem idle terms in the presence of this genius. Bare, uncompromising, mocking, pitiful, and utterly human. Mr Hardy has gone his way, aloof, impassioned, watching life, living it, sharing it with man and nature; and, above all, loving its seared, suffering, heroic face that smiles on at grief, and is indomitable in happiness in a world that seemingly cheats to destroy.

A poem entitled 'In the Seventies,' having for motto '*Qui deridetur ab amico suo sicut ego*', tells, in retrospect, of the starry thoughts that in those far days shed their magic light on this poet's 'worktimes' and his 'soundless hours of rest'; tells, too, of 'the vision';

> In the seventies nought could darken or destroy it,
> > Locked in me,
> Though as delicate as lamp-worm's lucency;
> Neither mist not murk could weaken or alloy it
> In the seventies! – could not darken or destroy it,
> > Locked in me.   [389]

Upwards of forty years have passed since that day, and all but a fraction of the work in this volume is of the last two or three decades. Mr Hardy, once and for all, set up as a poet, then, at an age when Shakespeare left our mortal stage. This book, for that reason alone, is an unprecedented achievement. Apart from that, to read steadily through it – and what severer test of lyrical poetry could be devised? – is to win to the consciousness, not of any superficial consistency, but assuredly of a 'harmony of colouring'; not, however keen the joy manifest 'in the making', of an art become habitual, but of a shadowy unity and design. In the seventies Mr Hardy could not have foreseen that full design, nor can he have consciously traced it out. But laborious days and an unfaltering constancy have set free those starry thoughts, that secret wondrous vision, and have thrown open one of the most hospitable doors in English literature in welcome to all.

SOURCE: 'Thomas Hardy's Lyrics', review of *Collected Poems* (1919 edition), *Times Literary Supplement* (27 November 1919); reprinted in *Private View* (London: 1953), pp. 95–103.

R. W. King (1925)

There is probably no parallel in English, and perhaps in all European, literature to the vigour and persistency of Mr Hardy's creative activity. His career as a writer covers without a break from 1865 to the present day – sixty years. He has outlived not only every member of his family, but almost all his contemporaries in literature. When he began to write, during what he has called 'Victoria's formal middle time,' Tennyson and Browning, Ruskin and Carlyle, were in full career; R. L. Stevenson, Oscar Wilde, Bernard Shaw, Yeats and Kipling were small boys; and Germany was not yet an Empire. Hardy has lived through the last European War to compose a striking poem on the Armistice of 1918.

Not less impressive are the range and bulk of Hardy's achievements in the field of letters. In the novel and the drama as well as in the lyric he has done work of the first importance both for quantity and for quality. He is still, of course, much more widely famous for his novels than for any other part of his work; yet even before his poems began to appear only the most superficial criticism could fail to discern that he is by nature poet rather than story-teller or playwright. We may express this more exactly by saying that Hardy is primarily a lyrist, a strongly subjective artist, present in all his work in his own personality if not actually in his own person, and never, like Homer or Shakespeare, completely veiled by his own creations. This will go some way to explain why in *Tess of the D'Urbervilles* and *The Dynasts* for example, Hardy has created what are virtually new forms of the novel and the drama; while in his lyrics – which he has himself described as 'the more individual part of my literary fruitage' – he has not needed to go outside the traditional forms, much as he has extended them in certain directions. And so the lyrics, standing so to speak in the centre, as his most characteristic mode of expression, may with some excuse be examined separately.

It may be admitted that an adequate presentation of Hardy's philosophical and sociological ideas could not safely pass over the plays or the greater novels; but it is not intended, in the present article, to describe Hardy's 'universe' or to paraphrase his 'message' – aspects of his work which have, I think, had somewhat more than their due share of attention. A more specifically æsthetic account of the lyrics is surely worth attempting; for both in variety of subject-matter and in mastery of a highly individual technique they are among the most interesting in the language.

We encounter at the outset a curious problem of chronology. Hardy published his first novel at thirty-one; but very little of his poetry saw the light until he was nearly sixty years old. All his lyrics have appeared during the second half of his long career, in the seven volumes from

Wessex Poems (1898) to *Human Shows* (1925). Yet we know, of course, that Hardy was a poet from the first;[1] and of the eight hundred or so short poems which have been printed [i.e., up to 1925 – Eds] at least a third must have been composed a generation or more before their publication. It is, therefore, impossible with the data at our disposal to trace chronologically the development of his poetic style to maturity. Some few poems are dated, but many of these have been retouched later. Still, making what comparisons and allowances we can, we may plausibly guess that as a poet Hardy matured comparatively soon. It is remarkable how uniform a quality we find alike in poems of the earliest and of the most recent date. Already in the group of a dozen love-lyrics belonging to 1865–7 (though not printed till 1898) there is no mistaking the note of the real Hardy. The best of these, 'Neutral Tones' [9*] has a theme – the 'bitter-sweet jest' of love – which he was to make all his own [quotes stanzas 1, 2 and 4]. It has a touch of the crudity of youth; but it has, too, most of the qualities we find in the later lyrics. There is the simple, almost colloquially plain-spoken diction, the flicks of alliteration which give emphasis rather than adornment, the indifference to bright colouring in description—tending therefore, in Hardy's own phrase, to an effect of 'even monochrome and curving line'. And in sum there is a kind of acrid clarity in both thought and style. One detects precisely the same flavour in a much later lyric like 'The Darkling Thrush' [119*], written in 1900, and even in the most recent work, like the one-act lyrical play, *The Famous History of the Queen of Cornwall*, begun in 1916 and finished in 1923.

Clearly, in this instance to ignore chronology is not seriously to falsify the perspective of criticism. But does this unity of spirit and steadiness of style, maintained over a period of more than half a century, necessarily imply a lack of variety? Such an opinion is, I think, implicit in the hasty remark sometimes ventured, that Hardy's work is 'monotonous' and 'depressing'. Let us set aside the question of his alleged 'pessimism'; for I think we shall find, at any rate, that this view is not supported by a survey of his themes, moods, and range of technique in lyrical forms.

A rough grouping by subject-matter is perhaps the simplest way of dealing with the whole mass of Hardy's lyrics. Starting, as is convenient, with the poems having the most obvious connection with the novels, we find a large group of short narrative pieces embodying legends or recollections of Wessex. Such are 'The Alarm' [26], 'San Sebastian' [21*], and other tales in verse of Wessex men and the Napoleonic Wars; tragic ballads like 'At Shag's Heath' [719*], which tells of the Wessex woman who betrayed the ill-fated Duke of Monmouth to his pursuers in 1685; and such sad or ironical or whimsical love-tales as 'The Burghers' [23*] or 'The Inscription' [642], which are the verse counterparts of the stories in *Life's Little Ironies* and *A Group of Noble Dames*. The Mellstock

Church Quire, well-known from *Under the Greenwood Tree*, appears in several of the best tales, including 'The Rash Bride' [212] and 'The Paphian Ball' [796*]. Though the rendering of a mood or an atmosphere is the aim of these pieces quite as much as a purely narrative interest, they stand really on the borderline of strictly lyrical poetry; and only occasionally, as in 'Her Death and After' [27], one of the most moving, do they 'surprise by a fine excess' of feeling and imagery.

More intense, and more truly characteristic, are the elegiac or meditative poems of Wessex life. The best-known elegy is 'Friends Beyond', in which the shades of Mellstock worthies . . . who lie in the churchyard 'murmur mildly' to the poet of their godlike indifference to the chances and changes of mortal life:

'Curious not the least are we if our intents you make or mar,
  If you quire to our old tune,
If the City stage still passes, if the weirs still roar afar.' [36*]

In a companion poem, 'Voices from Things Growing in a Churchyard', Hardy adds an eerie touch to his rendering of that air of remoteness from the concerns of the living which one feels in any quiet churchyard. The flowers and leaves seem to the poet to whisper with the voices of the humans whose death has given them birth:

These flowers are I, poor Fanny Hurd,
  Sir or Madam,
A little girl here sepultured.
Once I flitted like a bird
Above the grass, as now I wave
In daisy shapes above my grave,
  All day cheerily,
  All night eerily! [580*]

There is a grave irony in this, but it would be unjust to call it cynical.

These two poems present an odd and interesting contrast to Gray's famous *Elegy*, with its speculations on 'mute inglorious Miltons' and its elaborate, gem-like descriptions. Hardy in general shows no love of pictorial description for its own sake; and so what in one sense would be called his nature poems – and he has painted the Wessex countryside, in verse as in prose, in all seasons and weathers – in another sense might just as well be described as elegiac or meditative; for human feeling, individual or general, is always the primary interest. Such are 'The Darkling Thrush' [119*] and 'Yell'ham Wood's Story' [244*] – both of which, by the way, Ruskin might have taken to illustrate his rather silly theory of the 'pathetic fallacy'; or 'The Pine-Planters' [225], a poetic rendering of a famous scene in *The Woodlanders*; or another striking poem on trees called 'In a Wood'. Here the poet, wearied and 'city-opprest', seeks consolation among the trees; but he finds that struggle is the law of life there also:

> Touches from ash, O wych,
>   Sting you like scorn!
> You, too, brave hollies, twitch
>   Sideways from thorn.
> Even the rank poplars bear
> Illy a rival's air,
> Cankering in black despair
>   If overborne.

and he turns back to human fellowship:

> There at least smiles abound,
>   There discourse trills around,
> There, now and then, are found
>   Life-loyalties.   [40]

If faithfulness to the facts of science is vital to poetry—it is a moot question—then this would come off best in a comparison with Wordsworth's poems on the 'education of nature', in which 'one impulse from a vernal wood' is claimed as a better teacher of moral good and evil than 'all the sages'.

We may pass lightly over what may be called Hardy's poems of social satire, for with a few exceptions they are among his weakest work. That an artist who has elsewhere made such masterly incidental and subsidiary use of irony should fail in this particular application of it is itself a pretty piece of irony. Most of the poems in the two series called 'Satires of Circumstance' and 'Time's Laughingstocks' [in the eponymous volumes – Eds] fall flat from overstatement. A sick man overhears his wife ordering her widow's weeds by anticipation [348], or women quarrel over their children's graves, not knowing that they have all been dug up 'because the main drain had to cross' [342*]: situations rather grotesque than truly ironical, and spoiled in the handling by a sort of inverted sentimentalism. Yet in pure satire of a lighter kind Hardy is occasionally very successful. Nothing could be more refreshing than the almost Shavian wit of 'The Ruined Maid' [128*] or the insouciant banter of 'The Respectable Burgher on the Higher Criticism', in which a worthy citizen, shocked at the disintegration of his Bible, exclaims indignantly:

> All churchgoing will I forswear,
> And sit on Sundays in my chair,
> And read that moderate man Voltaire.   [129*]

On the whole, however, it is true that on social, theological or philosophical themes Hardy is more in his element when both his mood and his manner of presentation – whether tinged with irony, sad or bitter, or not – is deeply serious. This group has occasioned more comment and controversy than the rest of his poems put together. In spite of – or should we say because of? – the dignified but not over-conciliatory 'Apology' printed in 1922 with *Late Lyrics and Earlier*, there seems still to be those who think that all Hardy's poems are of the type of, say, 'To the Moon' [368] or 'To Life' [81], or that other poem on the moon, written during the late war and printed at the end of *Moments of Vision*, in which the poet looks up from his writing to find 'the moon's full gaze' fixed on him. His involuntary question, 'What are you doing there?' is thus answered:

> 'Oh, I've been scanning pond and hole
>   And waterway hereabout
> For the body of one with a sunken soul
>   Who has put his life-light out.
>
> 'Did you hear his frenzied tattle?
>   It was sorrow for his son
> Who is slain in brutish battle,
>   Though he has injured none.
>
> 'And now I am curious to look
>   Into the blinkered mind
> Of one who wants to write a book
>   In a world of such a kind.'
>
> Her temper overwrought me,
>   And I edged to shun her view,
> For I felt assured she thought me
>   One who should drown him too.   [509*]

The passionate pity in this really speaks for itself, and at any rate this and the other examples should make clear, by a sort of *reductio ad absurdum*, that fatuousness of taking such poems as a final and settled expression of opinion or 'criticism of life'. Plainly, if they were so, the poet *should* drown himself. But do not many of us – did we not during the War – have such moods? And may not the imaginative expression of them have the value of a kind of emotional catharsis? 'Give sorrow words', says Malcolm in *Macbeth*:

> the grief that does not speak
> Whispers the o'er fraught heart and bids it break.

The poems just mentioned represent, of course, only one type of mood out of many. Elsewhere the almost limitless variety of form goes with an equally striking variation of mood. We have flippant cynicism in the neatness of 'A Young Man's Epigram on Existence', written just sixty years ago:

> A senseless school, where we must give
> Our lives that we may learn to live!
> A dolt is he who memorizes
> Lessons that leave no time for prizes.   [245*];

while Matthew Arnold himself must have acclaimed the 'high serious-ness' of such great philosophical poems as 'The Absolute Explains' [722*], 'Xenophanes the Monist' [697] and many of the choruses in *The Dynasts*. It is, no doubt, in the great final 'Chorus of the Years and Pities' that the poet proclaims the essentials of his creed; in the prose 'Apology' to which I have alluded he gives it the ugly but accurate name of 'evolutionary meliorism'. We find it again in 'To the Unknown God':

> Perhaps Thy ancient rote-restricted ways
>   Thy ripening rule transcends;
>   That listless effort tends
> To grow percipient with advance of days,
>   And with percipience mends.
>
> For, in unwonted purlieus, far and nigh,
>   At whiles or short or long,
>   May be discerned a wrong
> Dying as of self-slaughter; whereat I
>   Would raise my voice in song.   [151*]

And indeed there is abundant evidence of an active zeal for reform in numerous occasional poems like 'Compassion: An Ode' [805*], written in 1924 for the centenary of the RSPCA. Most appealing of all, perhaps, is the wistful tenderness and pity for human faiths and failings which breathes alike in 'The Oxen' [403*], a Christmas poem, and in the remarkable lines (1923) on 'On the Portrait of a Woman about to be Hanged' [748].

On a distinct though related group of poems, which might be labelled
'commemorative' or 'memorial' lyrics, only a word or two can here be
said. It includes numerous personal elegies, on relatives of the poet and
on famous English men of letters, friends or favourite poets of Hardy's;
prominent among them are Keats, Shelley, Swinburne and George
Meredith. There are, besides, two small but notable sheaves of 'Lyrics of
War and Patriotism' – inspired respectively by the South African War
and the European War of 1914–18. Among these are some of Hardy's
best-known and most moving pieces. In 'Drummer Hodge' [60*]
Hardy is for a moment not very unlike A. E. Housman, while 'The Man
He Killed' [236*] oddly touches (though from above) the Kipling of
Barrack-Room Ballads; but 'Men Who March Away' [493] and 'In Time
of "The Breaking of Nations"' [500*] could come from no other hand
than that which wrote the chorus 'On the Eve of Waterloo' in *The
Dynasts* [Pt 3 VI viii].

Lastly we come to Hardy's love lyrics–probably the largest group, and
certainly including the majority of his finest and most carefully
elaborated poems. To say that on the whole Hardy expresses more
profoundly the griefs than the joys of love is to utter the obvious half-
truth which misleads more than falsehood. The same thing might be
plausibly argued of almost any English love-poet; at any rate it is
doubtful whether we have any poems of the opposite mood as intense in
feeling as Donne's 'The Expiration', Wordsworth's 'A Slumber did my
spirit seal', Burns's 'Ae fond kiss' or Keats's 'In a drear-nighted
December', to name a few at random. Why this is so would be a delicate
and difficult enquiry upon which I do not propose to enter. The real
significance of Hardy's achievement lies in his expression of the grief of
love remembered when it has gone by—whether through estrangement, disillusionment or bereavement. It is a lover who, in the *Inferno*,
speaks those famous words:

> Nessun maggior dolore
> Che ricordarsi del tempo felice
> Nella miseria[2]

and this bitter-sweet recollection of the joys of past love runs through
dozens of Hardy's lyrics. Most frequently—even in the briefest lyrics—
the framework is narrative, and actual. Living scenes or events of the
'days when love was new' are recalled with an exact and pictorial
particularity. Hardy is supremely the poet of memories, of individual
recollections, carried in the mind often for many years before being
recorded, with undiminished vividness and with a sort of added
perspective which enhances their significance. Usually, though not
invariably, it is the happy moments that are thus recalled at a time of

grief or loneliness; and the contrast between the two moods seen
together, as it were, in a single moment of time, sharpens the poignancy
of both. Examples might be given either from poems more or less
dramatic or 'personative' (Hardy's own word), or from those in which
the experience and the emotion are direct and subjective. It is, not
unnaturally, in the latter that the method is seen at its most striking –
above all in that wonderful series, the 'Poems of 1912–13', printed in
Satires of Circumstance. They are headed with the phrase *Veteris Vestigia
Flammae*, and were of course occasioned by the death of Hardy's first
wife. . . . Several poems in the series refer to the same month, March
1870; 'The Phantom Horsewoman' speaks, it would seem, of the very
same vision 'of heretofore':

> A ghost-girl-rider. And though, toil-tried,
>> He withers daily,
>> Time touches her not,
>> But she still rides gaily
>> In his rapt thought
>> On that shagged and shaly
>> Atlantic spot,
>> And as when first eyed
> Draws rein and sings to the swing of the tide.   [294*]

More recent memories are enshrined in 'Your Last Drive' [278*], 'The
Going' [277*] and 'Where the Picnic Was' [297*]; but though the
interval is smaller, the method of contrasted moments of time is
precisely similar. The 'Poems of 1912–13' contains only twenty-one
lyrics, but many more clearly belonging to the same series are scattered
throughout the [later] volumes. A few of the most beautiful, which must
be named if not quoted, are 'The Last Performance' [430*], 'On a
Discovered Curl of Hair' [630], 'The Last Time' [651], 'Ten Years
Since' [691], 'A Second Attempt' [720] and 'Days to Recollect' [792].
Of all these the keynote is a truly astonishing simplicity. To Hardy the
commonest object – a garden seat, a 'little old table', a signpost or an
almanack – may have tremendous significance, may carry memories
and associations of a lifetime's love, with all its joys and sorrows. He says
truly of himself: 'I only need the homeliest of heartstirrings.'

I have examined only one division of the love-poems, and that the
most personal and passionate; but what has already been said applies
also, in essential, to the other varieties – meditative, whimsical, tragic or
bitterly ironical. We must, however, notice one very significant
limitation to the range of feelings expressed. There is, I think, no
instance of the recording of a moment of thoughtless or light-hearted
pleasure simply in and for itself. Hardy has given us nothing

comparable with Herrick's 'Cherry-ripe' or 'Whenas in silks my Julia goes', or with similar pieces by Campion and other Elizabethans. In Hardy – and this is true whether the theme is love or something else – the perspective of human life is always present; the sense of time passed or passing is always strong, and this precludes any attempt to communicate a merely momentary sensation. It is here, I believe, that we shall find the key to Hardy's lyric method. Just as most of the love-poems express the sweet and bitter feelings of love as a unity in memory, so very many of the lyrics in general embody at once a brief incident and a long process, a momentary action and an enduring state of feeling. They therefore tend to take shape as a *significant anecdote*, chosen, or invented, not merely for its own sake, but for its value as a symbol, as a 'moment of vision', which gathers up the emotional experience of years. 'Beeny Cliff' [291*], for instance, not only renders the radiance of that March day in 1870, but suggests the whole course of the poet's life since then. So with even so early a poem as 'Neutral Tones' [9*] the scene depicted is viewed, as it were, down a long tunnel of time. A closely similar process may be seen at work in the ostensibly narrative form of many poems on other themes – 'The Darkling Thrush' [119*], 'In a Wood' [40] and 'The Oxen' [403*], for example. Commemorative poems like those on Keats and Shelley or on the poet's father and mother are mostly 'biographical' rather than 'exclamatory'; and even philosophical themes are frequently handled by means of the symbolic or illustrative anecdote.

I do not know any other English poet who has worked out this particular method with anything like Hardy's thoroughness. Words-worth approaches the 'anecdotic' form sometimes, as in 'Simon Lee' and 'The Leech Gatherer'; but the sense of a long experience gathered up in a moment is stronger, and so the resemblance to Hardy is closer, in one or two of the 'Lucy' poems, notably 'Strange fits of passion have I known'. We may notice also a curious and unexpected likeness between Hardy's method and that of Browning's 'dramatic lyrics', which are more often than not based on a single striking incident. In both poets, too, the lyric is often an imaginary dialogue or monologue as well as an anecdote. The chief differences are that in Browning the perspective of memory is generally much less noticeable, and the main interest – for example, in 'The Last Ride Together' or in 'Porphyria's Lover' – rests on the strange or startling nature of the incident itself. Hence the term 'dramatic' is more obviously appropriate to Browning's work; and in Hardy dialogue, when used, is little more than a means to compactness and conversational simplicity. That Browning had a certain limited influence on Hardy in the latter's early days is, I think, undeniable; but it can never have struck very deep – for in spirit and outlook on life the two are poles asunder – and even on the side of technique, in such

matters as stanza-forms, metres, and the use of a semi-conversational
diction, the resemblances, though obvious up to a certain point, are not
close. . . .

It would be a task far beyond the scope of the present article to
examine Hardy's technique in detail; little even can be said on the not
unimportant question of diction. It is chiefly his peculiarities in this
direction which are responsible for the casual remark sometimes made,
that Hardy is a careless, rugged, uncouth songster, too intent on his
mood or his message to trouble about grace or harmony of word or line.
What has already been said will, I hope, have made it obvious that
'careless' is the last form of censure which can justly be applied to him. If
he is rough and rugged it is wilfully, of set purpose. Now it is true that
though Hardy's themes are often homely and simple enough, he
handles them, as a rule, in a style which is certainly not homely, and
which, unlike that of the traditional ballads, attains simplicity through
effort and not instinctively. He stands, therefore, among the deliberate
artists, but at the opposite extreme to such poets as Spenser or
Tennyson; he seeks to avoid the immediately smooth and flowing, and
to make an equally subtle but more surprising melody out of rougher
and more unpromising material. 'Picnics', 'unhope', 'undecrease', 'the
pyrotechnic art', 'the yon world's clamorous clutch', 'chartered
armipotents lust-led' – such ungainly and apparently prosaic words and
phrases as these he will drag into poetry by main force, like a man
strenuously wrestling with his thoughts rather than effortlessly weaving
word-patterns.

It is a mistake to suppose that either general type of artistry deserves a
monopoly of our respect or admiration. The proof of the puddings is in
the eating; there are moods for the smoothness of *The Faerie Queene*, of
songs like 'Go to bed, sweet Muse' and 'Sweet and Low'; and there are
moods for the abruptness of Donne's 'For God's sake hold your tongue,
and let me love', of Vaughan's 'I saw eternity the other night', and of
this of Hardy's, from a love-poem entitled 'To Meet, or Otherwise':

> By briefest meeting something sure is won;
>   It will have been:
> Nor God nor Demon can undo the done,
>   Unsight the seen,
> Make muted music be as unbegun,
>   Though things terrene
> Groan in their bondage till oblivion supervene.   [251]

Hardy, then, justly claims a place in the traditions of the greatest
English lyric poetry. Donne and Wordsworth are often as surprisingly
direct and sincere, but their range in lyric verse is slighter; Shelley and

Swinburne are perhaps his equals in metrical inventiveness, but they cannot combine this, as Hardy does, with a conversational simplicity which comes nearer to carrying out Wordsworth's famous theory of poetic diction than any of that poet's own works. And lastly Browning, with all his wide interests and vigorous poetic activity, is far inferior to Hardy in the more essential virtues of sincerity, steadiness and self-restraint. This is visible both in technique, where Browning shows almost invariably a wilful imperfection of form which reflects a kind of unsteadiness or violence in the emotion, and in substance or 'matter', in the way in which opinions are expressed rather than in the opinions themselves. Browning's poems, as Mr George Santayana has well said, 'not only portray passion, which is admirable – they betray passion, which is odious'. To phrase it more simply, he seems to be forever shouting at us:

> God's in his heaven –
> All's right with the world

or

> He at least believed in Soul, was very sure of God.

This is asseveration rather than expression or communication of feeling. It is the optimistic counterpart of the declamatory 'pessimism' of a good deal of Swinburne and of such minor verse as Thomson's 'The City of Dreadful Night'. Hardy addresses us in a quieter tone:

> O sweet sincerity! –
> Where modern methods be
> What scope for thine and thee?
>
> . . .
>
> – Yet, would men look at true things,
> And unilluded view things,
> And count to bear undue things,
>
> The real might mend the seeming,
> Facts better their foredeeming,
> And Life its disesteeming.   [233]

SOURCE: extracts from 'The Lyrical Poems of Thomas Hardy', *The London Mercury* (December, 1925), 157–64, 164–6, 169–70. See also R. W. King's 'Verse and Prose Parallels in the Work of Thomas Hardy', *Review of English Studies* (February 1962.)

NOTES

1. I am afraid however that the absurd notion that Hardy 'took up' verse in his old age as a kind of hobby is not quite dead yet; and, partly as another result of the curious delay in publishing his verse, he seems still to be known in France and elsewhere on the Continent only as a novelist. In 1920, for instance, the University of Aix-en-Provence prescribed *Jude the Obscure* for study by candidates for the 'Agrégation d'Anglais'; yet its library did not then possess a single volume of Hardy's poetry. See the curious and interesting correspondence on this subject in *The Athenaeum* (26 Nov., 3, 17 and 31 Dec. 1920).

2. 'No greater grief than to remember days
Of joy, when misery is at hand'   (Cary's translation)

I. A. Richards (1926)

. . . It is time to turn to those living poets through study of whose work these reflections [on science and poetry] have arisen. Mr Hardy is for every reason the poet with whom it is most natural to begin. Not only does his work span the whole period in which what I have called the neutralisation of nature was finally effected, but it has throughout definitely reflected that change. Short essays in verse are fairly frequent among his *Collected Poems*, essays almost always dealing with this very topic; but these, however suggestive, are not the ground for singling him out as the poet who has most fully and courageously accepted the contemporary background; nor are the poems which are most definitely *about* the neutrality of nature the ground for the assertion. There is an opportunity for a misunderstanding at this point. The ground is the tone, the handling and the rhythm of poems which treat other subjects: for example, 'The Self Unseeing' [135*], 'The Voice' [285*], 'A Broken Appointment' [99*], and pre-eminently 'After a Journey' [289*]. A poem does not necessarily accept the situation because it gives it explicit recognition, but only through the precise mutation of the attitudes of which it is composed. Mr Middleton Murry, against whose recent positions parts of this essay may be suspected by the reader to be aimed, has best pointed out, in his *Aspects of Literature*, how peculiarly 'adequate to what we know and have suffered' Mr Hardy's poetry is. 'His reaction to an episode has behind it and within it a reaction to the universe.' This is not as I should put it were I making a statement; but read as a pseudo-statement, emotively, it is excellent; it makes us remember how we felt. Actually, it describes just what Hardy, at his best, does not do. He makes no reaction to the universe, recognising it as something to which no reaction is more relevant than another. Mr Murry is again well inspired, this time both emotively and scientifically, when he says: 'Mr Hardy stands high above all other modern poets by the deliberate purity of his responsiveness. The contagion of the world's slow stain has not touched him; from the first he held aloof from the general conspiracy to forget in which not only those who are professional optimists take a part.' These extracts (from a writer more agonisingly aware than others that some strange change has befallen man in this generation, though his diagnosis is, I believe, mistaken) indicates very well Mr Hardy's place and rank in English poetry. He is the poet who has most steadily refused to be comforted. The comfort of forgetfulness, the comfort of beliefs, he has put both these away. Hence his singular preoccupation with death; because it is in the contemplation of death that the necessity for human attitudes, in the face of an indifferent universe, to become self-supporting is felt most poignantly. Only the greatest tragic poets have achieved an equally self-reliant and immitigable acceptance. . . .

SOURCE: extract from *Science and Poetry* (London: 1926), p. 68.

Arthur S. MacDowall (1928)

To most of its readers the poetry of Thomas Hardy has stood for so long in a relation of friendship, if the word may be allowed of poetry, that it is hard to disbelieve now in the living presence of the singer. In the scale of distances along which poetry is strung his place was among the nearest. There are poets who seem to belong so little to the earth that to enjoy them we must seclude ourselves and break with the habitual rhythm of our lives. We do not feel that it was so with Hardy. To whatever remote horizons he might carry us, there was no hour so brief or place so unpropitious that one could not turn to his lyrics or narratives. The feeling or thought in them rose like a continuation of our own experience – an experience often transposed and sharpened to dramatic issues, but not less often pausing on the most familiar or casual things that happen. With a voice that hardly seemed to concern itself whether it were poetical or not, he began speaking of matters which might have belonged to the insignificant prose of life until he touched them.

So a pale, empty, rain-swept day would yield up its burden in a lyric. We sit quiet in a room, and one of its small mysterious sounds shapes a memory or a symbol. We go out into the fields, noting how a tree or a fence has weathered; or with a rustic *pietas* we are drawn to the graves of the dead, and under the churchyard yews we are among their histories. For such quiet is but the background or aftermath of the tumultuous lives of men. 'With a tale, forsooth, he cometh unto you.' He places us before a house, spectators of a drama that has clothed itself in acts there; since he was a poet by Wordsworth's definition of the term, more sensitive than most men to the passions and volitions in the universe, and impelled to create them where he did not find them. So he was a teller of tales, and in all his verse or prose *The Dynasts* was the greatest story. An imagination like Hardy's is the last in which a line can be drawn between memory and invention. *The Dynasts* grew out of memories in a native soil that were drawn into the national story; and then, like a stone dropped into a pool, the drama of events widened its circles till they passed out of sight in an element of spiritual significances.

Poetry like this has a strong, continuous idiosyncrasy. The earliest of his published poems are divided from the last by sixty years, but the likeness of style in them is marked, and just as observable is his grasp of the nearness of life and poetry. He had already begun to see the world as he would continue to see it; and he might also seem to have divined that poetry would be not only (as he, at any rate, believed) his most individual form of expression, but that it was the vehicle for a last, concentrated truth of things. The art and the truth in it would not be severed. As an art, it was the one which he delighted in most, which he turned to at first and spent the last thirty years of his life in exercising. Its practice might be suspended by the novels, but was never really broken; and the half-hidden growth with its late, full harvest was surely one of the felicities of literary history. But he also described poetry as an exploration of reality. In this light all the miscellany of his shorter poems – which taken together more than equal *The Dynasts* in bulk – are like a large and intimate journal in which he noted down his enterprise. It was an adventure of imagination and at the same time a running commentary on experience. And it was characteristic of his mind, which might seem so strongly and even narrowly set within his own vision, that he turned still to the workings and incidents of life, with an almost Balzacian ambition of embracing all its cardinal situations in his verse. In this there was a sign of what is, perhaps, the most instinctive trait in his poetry – the contrast and comprehension of opposites. Just as when one thinks of him as intent on a startling or dramatic thing he brings us back to an affection for the usual, so – if they could momentarily be taken apart – the outward and inward movements of his poetry would appear as one rhythm. The way in which his mind dwells in memory, that inmost medium of the mental life, suggests one unbroken inner vision. No poet since Wordsworth has depicted memories more constantly and vividly; and Hardy was to show once more that no lapse of time is a bar to the passionate imagination of a remembered thing by poetry. But the recollected life abated nothing of his susceptibility to fresh impressions. One would rather say that it added strength, threading them on a chain of experience; in fact, many of his dramatic poems are vivid just because they have the air of being not so much imagined as actually remembered.

But the fresh response was vital – so much so that he would say that while he knew his verses might have been polished more smoothly, it was more important to write down the impression while its vividness still lasted. There is no real contradiction in this either to the memories or the later retouchings; the two things represent simply two moods or moments in the life of a poet. But it brings us face to face with the qualities of this poetry, which was so unlike most other poetry. It was both individual and uneven – uneven partly by intention, because there were so many changes of tone and varying degrees of form in that imagined 'journal,' and partly because Hardy's poetry had the defects of his qualities. We should seek him almost in vain for that natural magic, that seemingly effortless colour and flowering of words, which has been a charm and glory of English poetry. His utterance will often appear dry and halting by comparison. Many a poem seems a curious mixture of the formal and the casual or prosaic; there is no entire certainty that his expression will rise and no security that it may not fall. And then some of the fullness and richness of Nature which makes a poetry of delight in his novels has certainly been thinned away in his verse – in obedience, as we may think, to that greater brevity of essence which he noted as a trait of poetry. Yet when he bids us

> see the nightfall shades subtrude,
> And hear the monotonous hours clang negligently by [30*]

we recognise not only the mark of the same hand which wrote the chapter on Egdon Heath, but a new power and music in the words with their sonorous vowel-sounds: the unusual word 'subtrude' adding the mystery of vision to the resonance.

The unusual was not forced on him. He could achieve his readiest effect with a sheer simplicity, as in the tiny poem called 'The Walk' [279*], a wonder of pathos; he could also, as in the fine sonnet on a lunar eclipse [79*], write with all the stateliness of tradition. He was loyal, again, to the inherited tradition in his love of metres and rhythms, and the hand of a master rather than a servant comes out in the variations which were never mere experiments but always effects of feeling. The old country tunes ran in his mind and added their echo in his verses. But that second language of his – as the new-coined, unfamiliar words may be called – is his own, with its own weight and colour. The suggestion of distance or strangeness which such words convey finds its climax in *The Dynasts*. Queer, ugly, or magnificent – for they can be all three – they have a rough-hewn strength in natural kinship with a style that seems trained to all weathers, like the tough and knotted growth of a heath-plant.

In a sense all technical comments on Hardy's poetry are rather unimportant. They may show its texture, but they are a clue to its comparative rather than its absolute value. What may be called its absolute value is implied in our recognising that he has the feeling and thought of a major poet; a human perception of the smallest things, an imaginative vision of the smallest and the greatest. The vision might come and go, but it was his very often, and there is an imaginative quality in his poems which provides a setting for it. We may be absorbed in the human import of some lyric or narrative; but sooner or later we also feel that we are 'at this point of time, at this point in space,' and the lines which have converged stretch far away into vastness. It is a physical, or rather metaphysical, impression of the contrast between the fleeting and the permanent, the present and the unseen, which inspired so much of his poetry. Nearness and remoteness, with Hardy, seem to call up one another, and so in a Christmas poem he would imagine the feelings of the Elgin Marbles [917*]. It is his sense of the unseen but imminent limits set by fate, and the rare persistence with which he probed them, that we usually think of when we call him a philosophic poet. The feelings accumulate, the thoughts return so steadily, that his attitude has a more philosophic cast than is common in poetry. Not directly, but by tragic implication, he unflinchingly explored man's predicament in the universe which modern science has made known. We may say, of course, that the view which coloured his imaginings – the view of a closed, monistic universe – is already passing out of date. Yet this would not affect the poetic quality of his vision; and it does not affect the truth in his delineation of passions and aspirations at strife with each other and with the limits set by Nature. The ultimate question lies behind this, and will steal in at the close of one of the most lightly flitting movements in his verse [quotes last four stanzas of 'After the Visit', concluding]:

> The eternal question of what Life was,
> And why we were there, and by whose strange laws
> That which mattered most could not be.   [250*]

That question, implied or avowed, is never long absent from his poetry.

The world has been described as a comedy to those who think and a tragedy to those who feel. Hardy's mingling of passion and detachment bridges the smart antithesis; his manner as a tragic poet is so often that of a tragic ironist. The subtler element in his irony appears in the way in which he makes chaos itself into a pattern. At times, as in those pieces which gave their name to *Satires of Circumstance*, he is more curtly sardonic, and then it is as if the countryman in him leapt to the surface and delivered a word like a blow. As the blow is clean the wound seldom festers, and when Parson Thirdly or his fellow-shades speak it is just with a grimly irresistible humour [247*]. Yet throughout his verse there are moments when its statement seems too biased for truth because it is too bald for poetry. We see him best as a poet of love. Like Browning he has left us here a gallery of scenes and figures; and like Browning's it is constantly dramatic. Hardy's is less rich, if only because his full-length figures are in his novels; but his notation of moods is perhaps subtler in the poems than in the novels, and the feeling is as poignant. He is really closer here to the hearts of men and women. So one lyric after another can breathe the passion or wistfulness of love. Joy as well as suspense and disillusion has found a voice there; but what has most impressed him is the inexorable limit of things. We feel that with Hardy love can be the whole of happiness, but never, as with Browning, that happiness might make the whole of life. He knew, too, that love has its own bitterness:

> Love is long-suffering, brave,
> Sweet, prompt, precious as a jewel;
> But O, too, Love is cruel,
>   Cruel as the grave.   [258]

But with that his sense of the worth of it, as of all human charities and loyalties, does not falter; in pity, as in passion, he is most human. And this compassion – and indeed certitude of a larger understanding – would move through a great lyric [quotes 'A Broken Appointment' (99*)]. A poet who could sing of 'human deeds divine in all but name' can hardly be charged with an indifference to values. And so it is that the singer of so many thwartings and errancies of love is also, in a peculiar degree, the poet of fidelity. No one who reads him attentively can miss that deepest instinct of his, which breathes even where it is apparently denied, and was the source of those 'Poems of 1912–13,' where memory lives with the vividness of passion.

Musing as he did over the limits of things, it was natural that some of his most wistful questionings and tersest repudiations should be found in speculative poems. More than once his poems of Nature are philosophic pieces, where, in 'a sad-coloured landscape,' the protagonists are shadowy figures of unconscious Will or Fate. With all their interest we may miss the full tragic beauty and splendour with which he invested his landscape elsewhere. But just as the old country tunes stole into his mind, so, with this lover of them, the country sights and sounds could not be kept out of his poetry; and it is a very intimate, if restricted, 'Nature' that he paints in his verse – mainly the streams, hills and meadows close to his door, and the western coast-line of his own romance. There, too, were the lives of the creatures and the changes of time which he sums up in 'Afterwards.' The question which the poem asks has been answered; but there is a lasting beauty in the self-portrait, the subtle touches of perception and the rhythm, which hovers so delicately up to the brusque last line in each verse. . . .

The imaginative energy which embraced all these things is at once an outer and an inner vision. With Hardy we can never forget that inner vision or focus of his view, which sets its own print on all that he sees and feels. He called those impressions unadjusted; he never advanced them as a system; yet to us they appear as a whole, and feeling acquires the force of thought in them. An absolute sincerity to his feelings and thoughts was the first quality of the truth in his poetry. His tragic emphasis also has its truth, for those sad or ruthless elements which it reflected are themselves a part of life. But his exploration of reality lies in the use that he made of them. Without that grave harmony of his, without the pity and the strength of mind which can make beauty out of harshness, we may feel now that there would have been a vacant place in English poetry. But the human range of his poetry has, perhaps, something else to tell us; and it is that a poet who sees deeply enough may also – such is the relatedness of things – see widely. So Hardy's poetry, turning from the vastness of Nature, would come back as with a balance-stroke to what is universal in the heart of man. There was nothing so obscure or small that it might not reflect some greatness. He renewed a magic in the prose of life, and his far vistas gave it the strangeness of adventure. We read his poetry, and whatever it may lack it has had the power to make the world look different. By contrasts and by instancy of feeling it brings reality nearer and quickens our awareness of life.

SOURCE: leading article (unsigned) in *Times Literary Supplement* (26 January 1928).

PART THREE

Critical Comment Since 1928

Arthur S. MacDowall 'An Explorer of Reality' (1931)

. . . There is something . . . in the poems that brings them extraordinarily near to us. We begin to read them, and are in a world where life has been certainly transposed. But it joins our experience without a break and we are there with scarcely the sense of a transition. Most poetry demands at first some seclusion of the mind, a suspension of the usual rhythm of our lives; a reversal, even, when it is winged for an unearthly flight. Hardy's poetry, though it can stretch into remoteness, is so close to life that to read it seems a simple act of living. It is, itself, a reading of existences and a recurring story, in which men and women, with their moods and fates, seem often to be much nearer to us than they are in the novels. They are nearer to Hardy; he is, for the time, living in their lives, and only in the poems can one really measure his zest for humanity. Human feelings and ways have all the foreground; Nature, though vivid at a touch, has thinned away and is most often the image of a mood; the lines and shapes of destiny are the real, if intangible, landscape of the poems. It is as though some urgency of truth, or poetic concentration, had pared off all but the essential.

The nearness of the poems, in a vital sense, comes from this direct sincerity; and Hardy's way of communicating it is half the matter. Here, again, we are scarcely aware of a transition. There is the movement of rhythm or song, but no hint of singing-robes put on for the occasion. Hardy seems indifferent whether he is poetical or not, and in fact achieves much of his poetry with a prose language. Emotional or poetical words are not lacking – it is a mixed language, like his prose – but the natural magic, the seemingly effortless colour and flowering of words are not to be found there. It is singularly bare of verbal image and metaphor. If we compare it with his prose, we may doubt if it is quite true to assume that he wrote as he did only because he could not write otherwise. Partly, at least, it may have been because he would not. A note of his,[1] making an odd little calculus of emotion and expression as components of poetry, suggests not only that he could separate the two, but that – if they can be separated – emotion would be the dominant in most of his own verse. And it is easy to see in his poetry a recoil, voluntary or involuntary, from the melodious Tennysonian expressiveness, and still more from the decoration and embroidery that crept later over a poetry which had nothing very convincing to say. Nothing could have been further from his impulse than to woo the graces or try to capture beauty directly for its own sake. It would only come, if it did come, as a reward of the truth in his verse. Neither in substance nor manner could he be a prophet of smooth things, and nature and his art

united to lead him away from them. He loves a tune and can sing the
simplest of songs. But, as in his prose, there are the marks of a struggle
with language, the defects of sureness; and there are the intentional
roughnesses and irregularities of rhythm which he believed in and
practised as an artist. Both are present – and his own thoughts on poetry
show that he knew what he was doing much more than is usually
supposed.

But the touch is not secure and the inspiration may desert him.
Again, as in the novels, there is a mixture of the poetic and prosaic: a
precision that drops away, for whole poems at a time, into the casual or
conventional. It is a sign of Hardy's power that he shapes this amalgam
with so much individuality that it is difficult not to call it a style; and,
still more remarkably, that he makes it transparent to his thought. One
feels, in spite of all lapses, that he has said what he meant to say. But in
what poetry says there is a transmutation. It is not 'life', however closely
it may mirror life; its essence and texture belong to imagination. There
is a process and change; and the question, with Hardy's verse, is how far
this has been carried. There is nothing he will disdain as matter for a
poem; but as regards manner, he seems often bent on showing how
much poetry can do without, and yet be poetry. What remains then, as
its quality? If we can slip into it with scarcely a feeling that we have been
carried out of life and prose, is it because, perhaps, the verse itself has
stayed there? As a test case, take a little poem which is perhaps nearer
than any other to being an unchanged life-emotion; and uncommonly
close, as expression, to a statement in prose. This is the simplicity of 'The
Walk':

> You did not walk with me
> Of late to the hill-top tree
>   By the gated ways,
>   As in earlier days;
>   You were weak and lame,
>   So you never came,
> And I went alone, and I did not mind,
> Not thinking of you as left behind.
>
> I walked up there to-day
> Just in the former way:
>   Surveyed around
>   The familiar ground
>   By myself again:
>   What difference, then?
> Only that underlying sense
> Of the look of a room on returning thence.   [279*]

If a criticism of this atom of sincerity were not rather like beating the air, two possible exceptions might be taken to it. One might be that the pathos of the first stanza is too artlessly poignant; too intimate, in its 'life', for us to hear. The other is that even the feeling and the metre have barely changed either the sequence or the words from prose; the simplicity fails to keep out a line like 'surveyed around'; and the thought comes, in the last couplet, with something of the emphasis of a moral. But then, restore the whole impression; can there be a doubt that neither the feeling nor the thought has failed? It is true that the tiny lyric has the extreme intimacy, almost the privacy, which it is meant to have. 'Eloquence is heard, poetry is overheard . . . is feeling confessing itself to itself' – those unexpected words of Mill's are peculiarly and constantly true of Hardy, and nowhere more than in the intensely personal set of poems to which this one belongs. But, just as its soliloquy gives us a relation of two people, so merely by the contrast of his two moods and walks Hardy's feeling has detached itself and comprehended both in a poem. Both moods are riveted by the thought at the end, which was the source of the lyric and is also its symbol; and if it comes with that clinching directness one need only ask, as the poem does, 'what difference, then?' The difference of result here is that he appears to have told us once for all, in a way to be remembered, what 'the look of a room' may mean.

He did not always make his point like that, but, if the term can be used of poetry at all, it was a thing he seldom or never missed. It might be the sort of perception that can be really called a thought, as in the sonnet 'At a Lunar Eclipse': his one great poem in a genre which was not his, and perhaps the only one he ever wrote in the grand style. [79*]. There it is the small, smooth shadow of the earth which rouses wonder that the anguishes and glories of man, and 'Heaven's human scheme' itself, should be summed in this placid profile. The thought, here too, is at the same time an imaginative perception. And in the poems of irony and, of course, in all the consciously reflective poems, there is – implicit or explicit – something that must be called a thought or at least an apprehension. But thought and feeling, in Hardy's case, can least of all be separated. His feeling is shadowed and coloured by the whole of his outlook on the world, and this mental attitude is made of emotional intuitions. In almost all of his poems that are conclusively poetry it is the feeling that speaks to us; and even the ironies are inverted feeling. It finds its way through the hazards of his expression with a sincerity that will not be denied, and a melody, at times, which recalls his own saying that there is a natural music in the sincere language of emotion. Even that colloquial measure in 'The Walk' [279*], with its little flow and staccato, had its just-heard cadence that accented each turn of the mood. Here, in 'A Night in November', there is not so much a spoken emphasis as the quietest softness, suffusing the feeling and the tune:

> I marked when the weather changed,
> And the panes began to quake,
> And the winds rose up and ranged,
> That night, lying half-awake.
>
> Dead leaves blew into my room,
> And alighted upon my bed,
> And a tree declared to the gloom
> Its sorrow that they were shed.
>
> One leaf of them touched my hand,
> And I thought that it was you
> There stood as you used to stand,
> And saying at last you knew!   [542*]

The last line recalls a motif which comes more than once in the poems. It is the burden of the unforeseen; the germ of tragedy is that consciousness, with all its capacity to feel, still does not *know*. From this, certainly, one might draw the opposite moral which Horace drew, and Hardy himself sounds that note, of taking the present as it comes, in a poem called, characteristically, 'The Musical Box'. All, indeed, of this slowly moving lyric, precise in its evocation, is in his manner; the man returning on a dusky evening when the road still flings back heat; the woman waiting in the doorway; 'the thin mechanic air' gently chiming inside the house:

> At whiles would flit
> Swart bats, whose wings, be-webbed and tanned,
> Whirred like the wheels of ancient clocks:
> She laughed a hailing as she scanned
> Me in the gloom, the tuneful box
>   Intoning it.
>
>   Lifelong to be
> I thought it. That there watched hard by
> A spirit who sang to the indoor tune,
> 'O make the most of what is nigh!'
> I did not hear in my dull soul-swoon –
>   I did not see.   [425*]

Yet how futile the sage advice looks in the shadow of the poem – which, none the less, holds out its moment's fascination; and marks it all the more exactly against what looms behind. The actor's ignorance is a theme of classic irony, and Hardy used it often in shrewdly caustic verse. But where his emphasis falls most on the unawareness, as here or in other lyrics like 'Unknowing' [35] and 'If You Had Known' [292], a purely tragic or wistful tone maintains itself. One begins to feel the invisible background. In a bare, but extremely potent, way it gradually lets itself be seen, and becomes a kind of mental scenery. Sometimes this gathers into a phantasmal shape –

> Then we looked closelier at Time
> And saw his ghostly arms revolving   [528]

– for Hardy, who could imagine himself a ghost, has a subtle sense of hauntings. But with all nature behind them chances, destinies become lines traced upon an abstract vastness, converging 'at this point of time, at this point in space' and radiating again to immeasurable distances. With a silence, almost, Hardy will thus evoke the nature of things behind the tangible thing; as though, with him, nearness and remoteness called up each other. The suggestion is of non-human and really inhuman spaces; the rigidity which he caught from the science of his time barred him from more plastic images. So his verse, for all its detail and variety, tends to fall into monochrome. But the dread which comes to the surface in some poems does not cover it as a whole; what appears is a meditative acceptance and a kind of essential loneliness that the poet knows in himself and discerns everywhere. The figures in his poems are lonely souls drawn all the more passionately to each other.

That is why the near scene easily unfolds those vistas. The invocation, or rather invitation, in 'After the Visit' glides from touches of colour and memory up to its end:

> Through the dark corridors
> Your walk was so soundless I did not know
> Your form from a phantom's of long ago
> Said to pass on the ancient floors,
>
> Till you drew from the shade,
> And I saw the large luminous living eyes
> Regard me in fixed inquiring-wise
> As those of a soul that weighed,
>
> Scarce consciously,
> The eternal question of what Life was,
> And why we were there, and by whose strange laws
> That which mattered most could not be.   [250*]

The question is not always, or often, as explicit as that, but it is never far away. Hardy makes the contact between this metaphysical infinite and the other 'universal' in human hearts and ways. The small, near thing can become an actual symbol of the distant; it was by just such a stroke of imagination that the tune of the musical box was identified with the ominous spirit's song. A significant vision makes the image something more than a fancy and the object more than a toy. Hardy's perceptions of the simplest things are linked and deepened by a sense of what lies behind them: ultimately, perhaps, a sense that 'all aspects are within us' and nothing is intrinsically great or small. It is this deeper comprehension and connectedness that takes him beyond the genuine but minor poets, such as William Barnes or John Clare. Both of these can equal him in pure feeling and natural perceptions; and Barnes, of whose art Hardy wrote with perfect insight, is a more audibly musical singer. But there is a difference in Hardy which, at first sight, is merely the difference of a more powerful range and brain. The sign of it is that, for all the local touches in his verse, he passes clean outside the sphere and interests of a country poet.

The final difference, however, might be shown like this. The other two poets each wrote one of their most moving poems on the vanishing of joy; Barnes's lyric looks back to a time when one happiness followed another and ends by asking what has concluded them:

> Was it when once I missed a call
> To rise, and thenceforth seem'd to fall;
> Or when my wife to my hands left
> Her few bright keys, a doleful heft;
> Or when before the door I stood
> To watch a child away for good;
> > Or where some crowd
> > In mirth was loud;
> Or where I saw a mourner sigh;
> Where did my joy all pass me by?

That is, in itself, on Hardy's level. And Clare's 'Remembrances', though centred round boyish things, is poignant in the same sense of change and lost delight. Each acts on us like a reminder that the spell of Clare and Barnes is a spirit of joy, or a pathos in the main so simple (except in some of the later verses where Clare looks into his abyss) that it seems to be only the same spirit wearing another colour. Hardy, too, can return now and then to the mood of those first feelings; and whatever else may have vanished, it is obvious that his absorbed interest in life is left. But the primal joy does seem to have 'passed him by'; something different is there instead of it. And this is, of course, the experience which in one way or another befalls the greater poets. Wordsworth describes the same aspect of it in the ode on immortality. What ruled, in Hardy, afterwards was a profoundly tragic sense of life. It exceeds the pathos of a minor poet because he had thought, and felt his thought, more deeply and connected all that he thought and felt and saw. The tragic sense was also a fulfilment of his nature; it was, as he said, to this side of things that his expressive instinct responded most. It became, therefore, the spirit of his art, and because it was the stimulus of his expression one may suppose that in place of the 'first fine, careless rapture' he felt a creator's joy. For, although creative art must have its own pains as well as pleasures and, when it is tragic, must bear the weight of the pains and miseries of the world, there is a detachment in the mastery of them and a satisfaction in their shaping; indeed, such art, in so far as it is creative, obeys the same impulse in nature which called out the earlier joy.

One reads the signs of that enjoyment, artistic and innocent, in the very 'queerness' of a Hardy poem, the unexpected thought or odd conjuncture; as when he imagines what might be, at Christmas time, the feelings of the Elgin Marbles. The tragic and the ironic shade into each other with a readiness that implies it; for all irony presupposes, on the ironist's part at least, some enjoyment. There is the pleasing deftness of the stroke and, in Hardy's case, it weaves the chaos of things into a pattern. His irony expresses the drily shrewd reserves of his mind, a realism set free to play a little and indulge its humours. In essence it is always a reflection of the inexplicable irony of facts. But that it comes very naturally to him one can see from the way it brings out different sides of his nature. When 'Channel Firing', for instance, with its splendidly resonant beginning:

> That night your great guns, unawares,
> Shook all our coffins as we lay,

leads on to the penultimate verse –

> And many a skeleton shook his head.
> 'Instead of preaching forty year,'
> My neighbour Parson Thirdly said,
> 'I wish I had stuck to pipes and beer.' [247*]

– his simplicity speaks again, this time with a downright humour. And so it is more than once in the set of poems which give the volume called *Satires of Circumstance* its name, particularly in a remorseless one about the unwitting mothers weeping in a cemetery, which ends with the thrust

'And as well cry over a new-laid drain
As anything else, to ease your pain!'   [342*]

One feels as if the countryman had risen up in him, delivering his word
like a blow. Straight as it is, one does not mind it; he has intended
something cheerfully ghoulish, very likely prompted by an observation
of his own, and has succeeded. The other pieces of the set lack this
convincingness; they have a rather unpleasantly forced or trivial note
that one can scarcely accept as significant. Hardy does best when his
realism is frank or when his thought becomes piercing, and both outlets
show his affinity with a kind of verse very different from that of the poets
last mentioned. This caustic-dryness, with its realism and its innuendo,
joins the line that leads back to Swift. Some of his most whimsically
characteristic side-glances are in this kind of vein. The seeker after a *sors
Hardiana* who happened, for example, to open *Late Lyrics and Earlier*
about the middle, where two poems called 'The Collector' and 'The
Wood Fire' are to be found, would come on singularly mordant
evocations. The first [573] describes how a hard-worked parson, whose
one saving relaxation is to hunt for old canvasses on the chance of
finding a hidden masterpiece, sets to cleaning his last acquisition.
Features emerge, with the suggestion of a Venus that has an overpower-
ing effect on the lonely man; until after a night's work the dawn shows a
hag pointing her finger 'towards a bosom Eaten away of a rot from the
lusts of a life time'. He sits horror-struck and stunned till the Sunday
bells, with a clear note, arouse him. After this bizarre variation on an
old idea comes a better one, in shrewd colloquial phrasing. A log fire has
kindled to a bright blaze on a bleak spring evening in Palestine, and the
man of the house explains that he bought the wood cheap from the
executioners. There is a glimpse of what was the Crucifixion; and this is,
indeed, the Cross:

I heard the noise from my garden. This piece is the one he was on . . .
Yes, it blazes up well if lit with a few dry chips and shroff;
And it's worthless for much else, what with cuts and stains thereon.

[574]

Quotation may do wrong to this fragment, which, as a whole, and 'in
character', could not offend. But both are curious poems, especially this
second and cynical side-leap of a mind that elsewhere utters the
nostalgia of a lost faith so simply. We are reminded again of its different
sides. It is the thinking mind that declares itself in the subtler irony of
'God-Forgotten', where an imagined speaker lays the plaints of earth
before its creator [quotes first three stanzas, and then]:

'It lost my interest from the first.
My aims therefor succeeding ill;
Haply it died of doing as it durst?' –
'Lord, it existeth still.' –   [87*]

The deadly precision of the last of these stanzas could scarcely be improved on. It compares with the only other poet of his time – a Victorian, born earlier than Hardy – who, as has been said, even went farther in her unshrinking divinations: the American poet, Emily Dickinson. She could be subtler and more ruthless in her intuitions, which at their best have a strangely transparent exactness; but, apart from the fact that she often stumbles and he is always clear, her nature, after tragic disappointment, renounces where he accepts. There is a difference of kind between her searching introspection and the inner vision which, with Hardy, still drew its substance from the movement of life. He, therefore, seems as universal as she seems confined, and by the end of the poem which began with those stanzas his irony has vanished into the feeling which it really is. The feeling, which brings nearness with it, is an immediate response to life.

His responsiveness is uncommon among poets by its mere extent and quantity: by the amount of life he brings into his poetry. On its obvious side, it appeals through the oldest of mediums. 'With a tale, forsooth, he cometh unto you.' Terser than Crabbe and plainer than Browning, in the number of stories he tells or suggests he yields – if he does yield – only to them among his modern predecessors. At first this was accounted for by the short and easy way of saying that he was a novelist who went on writing stories in verse; of which many were, so to speak, abortive novels. But, although one is probably not a novelist for twenty-five years without retaining traces of it, all this objective, 'impersonative' side of his verse must surely have been native to him. It was there in germ from the beginning. He had an attentive mind for fact; a love for passion and action, and for a strange story. And the interest of human beings and their predicaments was inexhaustible. The outcome of all this looks so spontaneous that it is half a surprise to find he had the almost Balzacian ambition of including 'most of the cardinal situations which occur in social and public life' in his narrative and dramatic poems.

The ballads, at any rate, have the impulse of their kind. They are the most vigorous, because Hardy reveals a kind of primitive strength in them, and it concentrates in their pictures of human nature and passion. He likes the spirit of a ballad, the tune and refrains in it; outside the ballads, a refrain sounds often in his lyrical songs. But ballads themselves are lyrical in their music and passion; and perhaps it was because there is so much of this quality in 'A Trampwoman's Tragedy' [153*] that he thought it, as he seems to have done, the most successful of his poems. The best of his in this kind, it is, with its throbbing lilt and sense of open country; as his best *poem* one can hardly accept it, because many of the lyrics have a more essential poetry. Most of the ballads, being aspects of passion, belong to his love poetry . . . But it is characteristic of them, as Mr Abercrombie has observed, that Hardy gives a thoroughly modern and actualised air to an old form and there, too, finds a place for irony as well as passion.

In fact, the distinctions in his poetry begin to vanish as soon as one marks them. All of it is the work of one hand, which takes whatever elements it chooses. There was scarcely anything he would not take; none of the poets, it might seem, has lived more in the spirit of Flaubert's dictum that any subject is as good as another. It does not mean that the subject disappears. On the contrary, the criticisms of his verse might almost reduce to this, that there is too much subject and too little poetry. What is left, it may be asked, when one has taken the 'prose meaning'; what remembered magic of words is there, or what music in the cadences that are so secretive except when they frankly sing a tune; what fusion of emotion with all these into something that is greater than any of them? And it may be answered that in many of the pieces in this large miscellany not much appears to be left except the metre, as a frame; while the 'moments of vision' themselves scarcely carry us to the topmost heights of imagination. Yet Hardy's baldest verses manage to exist in themselves, and suggest connections that they do not always show. It may be that one reads into a fragment the accumulated sense of all the rest. But, allowing for this, the verse, as a medium, is like a background of his own where

> . . . the blank lack of any charm
>   Of landscape did no harm.
> The bald steep cutting, rigid, rough,
>   And moon-lit, was enough
> For poetry of place: its weathered face
> Formed a convenient sheet whereon
> The visions of his mind were drawn.   [599]

And in his lyrics there is a completer harmony than this. They are not states of ecstasy, because their sense of the actual is too strong; they seem to imply a fact within their feeling. Indeed the narrative lyric, if one takes it in the broadest sense, conveying often no more than the hint of an experience or a story, is the chief and intimate delight in Hardy's poetry; he did not invent it, but he renews and extends it by his blend of the poetic forms and the actuality he gathers into them. There is always a contact with life, and a moment comes when it unlocks an instant and deeper reality.

So his poetry brings a sense that the familiarity of things has been changed into a curious adventure. As we read it we seem to be entering an experience that is astonishingly full and yet half-hidden; it repeats that experience of life which Hazlitt likened to a narrow path with a thin curtain drawn around it. Hardy's path is narrow because his vision is intensely concentrated and focused on the passing and the doom of things. And few have made us feel more sharply than he did that the invisible hangs behind it. But the variety of life goes into his verse, as well as the monotony of disaster, and the curtain is not lifeless or opaque. It flutters at the touch of ghostly hauntings; grows transparent, at other times, to a light of intellectual imagination; and when it darkens, the emotional perceptions gain a delicacy as the colours of flowers do against a sombre sky.

In that reality and instancy of feeling, in his touch on common things and his loyalty to the heart's affections, he has affinities with a much greater poet. His poetry, like Wordsworth's, swings back from the vastness of nature to the heart of man. But he, too, has the power to make the world look different; and so, though he is much closer to tradition than he seems to be, those differences which make the uniqueness of a poet come out in him with a sort of double strength. There was nothing clamant in them. The quietness of his verse is a sign that its originality was true, and there is another in the way it seems now to have filled a place that was vacant in English poetry. For it shows that a poet who sees deeply enough may also – such is the relatedness of things – see widely. The strength of mind that could face harsh truths united with his breadth of compassion. What they achieved, most of all, was to reclaim the bitterness and ugliness in life and convert it into beauty. So it is not a mere figure of speech to call him an explorer of reality. He is one of the poets who have quickened and altered our awareness of life and enlarged the field of experience.

SOURCE: extract from *Thomas Hardy: A Critical Study* (London: 1931), pp. 203–19

NOTE

1. F. E. Hardy, *The Later Years of TH* (London: 1930), p. 92. [Later combined, with the *Early Life* (1978), into one volume, *The Life of TH* (London: 1962) – Eds.]

F. L. Lucas 'Truth and Compassion' (1940)

. . . The architect is of all artists the least able to indulge in airy dreams. Bricks and mortar, strains and stresses, the relentless drag of the earth and the buffets of the stormy sky are no playthings. . . . Further, of all the arts, no other is so desperately at war as the architect's with Time. . . . Now two of the fundamental things in Hardy are his stern sense of Reality and his saddened sense of Time. . . .

From architecture he turned to fiction. With that he won his fame. For a quarter of a century he wrote it, until in 1895 the British Public had another of its spasms of outraged morality over *Jude the Obscure*. . . . Howled down as a novelist, Hardy turned back to poetry; he had always loved verse better than prose; now for the first time he began to publish it. But even on his poetry the novelist in him, as well as the architect, has left its mark. . . . For the novelist must understand others; and it is this power of subtle sympathy that makes so poignant much of Hardy's verse.

Such, then, is the personality behind it – an architect who has struggled with solid earth and masonry, a novelist who has lived and suffered in hearts outside his own; and, underneath, a Wessex countryman seeing life with the mingled grimness and tenderness, irony and pity of those who see life at its hardest. There lies the contrast between him and Meredith; who looked on the world less steadily, and less compassionately also. There was less of the woman in him than in Hardy; and he was the smaller man in consequence. In Meredith the head outgrew the heart; he tended to prefer cleverness to wisdom, brilliance to truth.

But how does this truthfulness show itself in Hardy's work? Partly in his sincerity, the sense he gives of never having written a line he did not feel; but still more in his intellectual honesty. With most people there is an incorrigible tendency to believe what they want to believe, because it would be so pleasant if only it were true. The wish with them is father to the thought; and the thought is generally a bastard and deceptive thought in consequence. There are poets like Tennyson who think of Beauty before Truth; they tend to produce poetry that is perfect rather than great: and there are poets like Hardy who have a feeling for Truth even before Beauty; these tend to produce poetry that is great rather than perfect.

> Between us now and here
> Two thrown together
>
> . . .
>
> Let there be truth at last,
> Even if despair.   [100*]

Those last two lines might make the motto of all Hardy's work.

As Reuben the Tranter says: 'Well, now, that coarseness that's so upsetting to Ann's feelings, is to my mind a recommendation; for it do always prove a story to be true. And for the same reason, I like a story with a bad moral. My sonnies, all true stories have a coarseness or a bad moral, depend on't. If the story-tellers could have got decency and good morals from stories, who'd ha' troubled to invent parables?' The logic is not flawless; Reuben is not Hardy; but a family likeness is there – the same hatred of cant. 'Write a list', runs an entry in Hardy's Journal for 1883, 'of things which everybody thinks and nobody says; and a list of things that everybody says and nobody thinks.' If a particular instance of this passion for truth is needed, we may contrast his view of Nature with Wordsworth's. The two poets have much in common. Both turned back from the sophistication of great cities to the simplicity and sincerity of the countryside:

> Love had *they* found in huts where poor men lie.

But for Wordsworth Nature could do no wrong: for Hardy all her beauty could not hide her witless cruelty. In a vernal wood Wordsworth found more lessons of moral good and evil than in all the sages put together; there is a certain truth in that, no doubt, but not truth enough – less than in Hardy's vision of the death-struggle for a place in the sun that rages there between tree and tree, between plant and parasite, none the less grimly because it is too silent for us to hear, too slow for us to see. Nature is radiantly beautiful – let us feast our eyes; but she is also a blind fiend – let us face that too. In the twentieth century the human herd tends more to turn its heads rather than its tails to the storm of life; so that Wordsworth's caressing hand now rubs us the wrong way. If it is a question of 'goodness', give us men with all their faults, not trees. [quotes stanza 4 of 'In a Wood', and then]:

> Since, then, no grace I find
>   Taught me of trees,
> Turn I back to my kind,
>   Worthy as these.
> There at least smiles abound,
> There discourse trills around,
> There, now and then, are found
>   Life-loyalties.   [40]

'Funny man, Browning!' – said Hardy once (so a friend has told me), 'all that optimism! He must have put it in to please the public. He *can't* have believed it.' This is not a judgement to be taken too seriously; but it is characteristic, I think.

This lifelong refusal to shut his eyes to the unwelcome or hide his head in the sand makes much of Hardy's writing inevitably sad. Existence trailed for him no clouds of glory.

> 'I do not promise overmuch,
>   Child, overmuch.
> Just neutral-tinted haps and such,'
>   You said to minds like mine.   [873*]

But it is not sad poetry that is depressing; it is bad poetry. Truth about life calmly faced kills no one not sick already. The snake that was once found curled harmlessly asleep on the little Hardy's chest in childhood, might serve for a symbol of that. And he had his own consolations, lasting ones, in a sense of life's tragic beauty, and also of its tragic irony. Because he was haunted by Time and transience, because he never saw the commonest thing without a vision of what it once had been, of what it one day would be, in return even the commonest things were lit for him with a gleam of tragic poetry. He saw things as instinctively in three tenses as in three dimensions. In this way he widened the domain of poetry till it became for him as wide as life itself, a life intensely sad and yet intensely real. The comfort that religion failed to give, he found and thought that others might find, not necessarily in writing poetry about this world, but in seeing this world poetically, as anyone with an imagination can. Philosophy, as I have said elsewhere, demands that we take her dreams for truth; poetry, more wisely, offers her dreams as dreams alone. And Hardy found her in the simplest things – a milestone by a rabbit-burrow, or an old log upon the fire, raindrops on a door-step, or green tiles high up a roof; no subject was too minute for that vast vision of his which had yet in *The Dynasts* seen Napoleon's Grande Armée as a creeping caterpillar and had versified even the curving space of Einstein in the last volume of his old age. Hardy did not simply make poetry out of life; he made life into poetry.

Hence yet another source of his truthfulness; he never needed to employ the fantastic passions, the remotely strained psychology of more romantic writers. He deliberately took for his subjects the commonest and most natural feelings; but by an unfamiliar side, and with that insight which only sensitiveness and sympathy can possess. This sympathy is important; for, as I have said, if truthfulness is one main feature of Hardy's work, its compassion is another. Without that, the bitter truth in his pages might seem too bitter, the irony too sardonic; but that pity which he found so wanting in the Universe, crowns his own work with perfect things like 'Tess's Lament'

> I would that folk forgot me quite,
>   Forgot me quite!
> I would that I could shrink from sight,
>   And no more see the sun.
> Would it were time to say farewell,
> To claim my nook, to need my knell,
> Time for them all to stand and tell
>   Of my day's work as done.
>
> . . .
>
> It wears me out to think of it,
>   To think of it;
> I cannot bear my fate as writ,
>   I'd have my life unbe;
> Would turn my memory to a blot,
> Make every relic of me rot,
> My doings be as they were not,
>   And gone all trace of me!   [141]

One day Anatole France, being baited by an American professor as to the ultimate essence of literary genius, answered – 'Pity'. It was the exclamation of a moment, lightly thrown off in repartee. But, however inadequate, it is less wild than at first might seem: pity – nobility – personality – those three, as Anatole France explained, do indeed go together; not always, but often. There are modern critics who harp without ceasing on the theme that the writer must efface his personality; in their own case such abstinence may be easy; it may even be well-advised: but in the supreme authors of the world their personality is an ineffaceable and essential part of their work. It need not be obtruded; as a rule, it is better not obtruded; but between every two lines of the greatest it is there – the footprint of the lion. Even in Stendhal it is present, even in Flaubert, behind all their impassivity. And without it, all the brains in Christendom are profitless. Which is one reason why poets are born, not made; since personality is not to be taught. It rings clear in all that Hardy wrote; and a dominant note in it is this sense of compassion. Throughout his lyrics, as through *The Dynasts*, the Spirits of the Pities and the Spirits Ironic sing alternately; but in both the Pities have the last word. He never forgave the world the red streak of cruelty that runs through all its beauty: and the divine he found, not in Heaven, but in the cage of the blinded bird that sings on still with unembittered gaiety though man with a red-hot needle has burnt out both its eyes [375].

Hardy's own eyes were too clear for him to sing without a note of bitterness; but sing he also could. Of all the critical imbecilities bandied about at the present day, none is sillier than the notion that Hardy is always harsh. If 'Tess's Lament' be harsh, what is music? Hardy when he chose could be as liquid as Tennyson, as elaborate as Swinburne, with a simple brevity that Swinburne lacked:

> Upon a poet's page I wrote
> Of old two letters of her name;
> Part seemed she of the effulgent thought
> Whence that high singer's rapture came.
> —When now I turn the leaf the same
> Immortal light illumes the lay,
> But from the letters of her name
> The radiance has waned away!   [11]

This poet who is talked of as a sort of unshaven, guttural rustic of genius, really delighted in the elaborate delicacy of triolets like 'At a Hasty Wedding':

> If hours be years the twain are blest,
> For now they solace swift desire
> By bonds of every bond the best,
> If hours be years. The twain are blest
> Do eastern stars slope never west,
> Nor pallid ashes follow fire:
> If hours be years the twain are blest,
> For now they solace swift desire.   [107]

or would set himself such difficulties as this piece of octuple masculine and, more arduous still, octuple feminine rhymes:

> Never a careworn wife but shows,
>   If a joy suffuse her,
> Something beautiful to those
>   Patient to peruse her,
> Some one charm the world unknows
>   Precious to a muser,
> Haply what, ere years were foes,
>   Moved her mate to choose her.
>
> But, be it a hint of rose
>   That an instant hues her,
> Or some early light or pose
>   Wherewith thought renews her –
> Seen by him at full, ere woes

> Practised to abuse her –
> Sparely comes it, swiftly goes,
> Time again subdues her.   [111]

But the excellence of Hardy's eloquence does not lie simply in this
power of executing technical *tours de force* so naturally that they are not
even noticed: it lies in the purity and sincerity, as of a perfect voice
speaking quietly, that echoes through his moods of gentle, hopeless
irony, as in these lines on a dead mistress:

> I need not go
> Through sleet and snow
> To where I know
> She waits for me;
> She will wait me there
> Till I find it fair,
> And have time to spare
> From company.
>
> . . .
>
> What – not upbraid me
> That I delayed me,
> Nor ask what stayed me
> So long? Ah no! –
> New cares may claim me,
> New loves inflame me,
> She will not blame me,
> But suffer it so.   [102]

If he is at other times rough, the roughness is deliberate; for he held that
Art should hide her artifice. But I doubt if any English poet has more
studied the craft of verse, or invented more new metrical forms and
variations. The roughness of *The Dynasts* is indeed, I think, at times
excessive; though even there a certain gnarled grandeur suits the
vastness of Hardy's theme. I know no work which combines such
impressiveness as a whole with such rudeness in detail. But you do not
polish the Pyramids, or manicure the Sphinx.

> Ha, ha, that's good! Thou'lt pray to It:
> But where do Its Companions sit?
> Yea, where abides the heart of It?
>
> Is it where sky-fires flame and flit,
> Or solar craters spew and spit,

> Or ultra-stellar night-webs knit?
>
> What is Its shape? Man's counterfeit?
> That turns in some far sphere unlit
> The Wheel which drives the Infinite?
>
> [Dynasts Pt 2 VI v]

With Hardy an epoch ended; he outlived the passing of Queen Victoria, and the War which left the spirit of her age buried for ever beneath the mountains of its dead. He had been already a boy of ten when Wordsworth died; he had seen Victorianism growl even at Tennyson, its chosen Laureate, and ignore complacently the saturnine irony of Arnold, and bait Rossetti, and howl at Swinburne; he had felt its teeth himself. Tess of the d'Urbervilles had been called a harlot; *Jude the Obscure* enjoyed the consecration of being burnt by a bishop, who wrote proudly to the papers to proclaim his exploit, and privately to Smith's Library to suppress the book. But at least Hardy lived to see justice done.

. . . The Victorian Age . . . is a strange age to look back on, in its mixture of baseness and greatness. The storm of loathing and derision hurled at it by the generation which grew up in time to inherit the War, has been too undiscriminating; but not unjustified. It was no ordinary reaction of one age against its predecessor. There is only one parallel to its violence and bitterness – the reaction that followed the Age of the Puritans. The true forerunner of , Mr Lytton Strachey's *Eminent Victorians* is Samuel Butler's *Hudibras*. In either case the reason is the same – the revulsion of the healthy human instincts for freedom and honesty against tyranny and cant. The great Victorians were the first to rebel; perhaps being rebels helped to make them great – knight-errants need dragons; at all events it is not easy for us to defend their own age against them. The social atmosphere which the English middle class created in their century of supremacy is nauseous to breathe to-day. On the other hand, we who in our own time have done more to defile and befoul the face of the English countryside than all the generations before us since Julius Caesar came, shall need in our turn all the indulgence of posterity. We shall be fortunate indeed, if we are judged to have added half as much as the Victorians to the beauty of English literature. For there were giants in those days; and their farewell has been finely uttered by one of the greatest and the last and most lovable of them all, Thomas Hardy himself.

> The bower we shrined to Tennyson,
>   Gentlemen,
> Is roof-wrecked; damps there drip upon

Sagged seats, the creeper nails are rust,
The spider is sole denizen;
Even she who read those rhymes is dust,
    Gentlemen.

. . .

And ye, red-lipped and smooth-browed; list,
    Gentlemen;
Much there is waits you we have missed;
Much lore we leave you worth the knowing,
Much, much has lain outside our ken:
Nay, rush not: time serves: we are going
    Gentlemen.   [660*]

SOURCE: extract from *Ten Victorian Poets* (London: 1940), pp.
187–99.

Howard Baker   Hardy's Poetic Certitude (1940)

Few minds will come to this.
The poet's only bliss
Is in cold certitude –
Laurel, archaic, rude.

YVOR WINTERS

This is the simplest but also the most necessary discovery to make: all
poetry which yields lasting enjoyment partakes of one complex but
distinguishable quality. All good poetry is essentially alike. It sets forth
its portion of palpable humanity with understanding, always with
understanding though the attributes of understanding are exceedingly
various. For if the palpably human stuffs of the poem are at fantastic
variance with the sum of the author's best experience, the poem is
humorous or ironic; if the human tangent violates his best convictions,
the poem must be a judgement; if the human instance bears out his
hopes or fears, the poem will show that painful tenderness which the
exegesis of all hoping or fearing is bound to bring home to us. The
human is the common denominator in poems, and its coherences are
unchanging. All good poems are alike in their humanity. Indeed the
mark of the lesser poem is that it is more special or more general than it is
human, more obtuse or more brilliant, more fortuitous or more logical;
it does not share, in short, in the likeness which it should share in.

These ought to be the most familiar of axioms. Indeed they may be platitudes; but if they are, I insist upon them nevertheless, for in the normal pursuit of freshness and originality in poetry, they can easily be lost sight of. Moreover they are Protean qualities. They come from empirical experience; they do not rest on a postulate of 'humanity' as an absolute essence; they are extensive only so far as experience with literature and humanity is extensive. Within this range they indicate, since all understanding of palpable humanity rests on judgement, how poetry is a criticism of life, and similarly, since such understanding is always finally of a piece, how poetry and morality are related. They also suggest extensions to other arts and to other processes of living. In the powerful little sentences of Robert Frost, the contemplative mind should find somewhat more than a nine days' wonder: 'The figure a poem makes. It begins in delight and ends in wisdom. The figure is the same as for love.'

From delight to wisdom, from experience to significance, written in the immutable characters of the heart: these should be familiar axioms, they are perhaps the only thing really worth talking about. Thomas Hardy must have heard them talked about only too infrequently. For in his lifetime Hardy had too little occasion to qualify his pronouncement on the critics of his poetry: ' . . . poetry is not at bottom criticised as such,' he wrote, ' . . . but with a secret eye on its theological and political propriety.' His critics, apart as he said from a few brilliant exceptions, were intent upon guarding the proprieties, those exhausted properties of theirs, which regularly included small infertile lawns of versification as well as religious and social boundaries. Meanwhile the magnificent humanity of Hardy flourished practically undiscerned. Because of shortsighted criticism he had given up the novel with *Jude the Obscure* in 1895; the wonder is that into the poems the delight and the wisdom continued to flow. But flow they did. And they are what is most worth talking about.

The difficulty is that the delight and wisdom, the humanity of Hardy, cannot be isolated from the structures in which they appear. All good poetry is essentially alike; but every good poem is physically different from every other. For every poem must have a pungent and rugged difference that plays against the tender pervasiveness of human emotion (which is always various, always the same); the pungent and rugged surface should be properly awkward, it may be Gothic in effect. For it must be concrete. It must bear clearly the stamp of the particular material, the mode of the thinking, the individual speech of the poet. . . .

The external variety and difficulty of Hardy's lyrics need special attention; otherwise the reader is caught in a hedge before he is fairly started. But in order to get at least a rough view of Hardy's fundamental quality, we may single out a simple early poem and fix ourselves in relation to it.

HER INITIALS

Upon a poet's page I wrote
Of old two letters of her name;
Part seemed she of the effulgent thought
Whence that high singer's rapture came.
— When now I turn the leaf the same
Immortal light illumes the lay,
But from the letters of her name
The radiance has waned away! [11]

Hardy wrote this when he was twenty-nine, which, for him, was still a youthful age, and the poem shows it. The lines are assembled fairly unimaginatively, like a house in a new subdivision. In the decorative blur of the high poet's rapturous lay, the particular dramatic situation floats undefined. Rugged concreteness has not yet come to dominate the verse. But even in these deficiencies a staunch humanity asserts itself. Hardy tells the truth. For though he seems to have loaded himself with the common baggage of sentimentality, he carries it where he wants to go, which is, not to the sentimental celebration of the woman in perhaps a new relation to the initialed page, but to the transience of a passion. Not that in another context the celebration of a woman remembered would also have been wrong; in many other contexts it is right, as in the much more beautiful 'Clock-Winder' [471*]. But in the example above the true lineaments of Hardy's large comprehension come out of the sad and happy clash in the anti-sentimental completion of the poem.

Just so, in many of the early lyrics, Hardy seems often to have been looking at the stock poetry of his times and to have bent it into the rich and rough and credible vision of life as he knew life. In 'Hap,' for instance, he appropriates, probably from Swinburne, the familiar lurid effusion about the gods' mockery at man's misery, and he criticises this very deliberately, with a coherence which is, I say, large and credible whether we agree with his conclusions or not. If the gods mock, his first rejoinder is this:

Then would I bear it, clench myself, and die,
Steeled by the sense of ire unmerited;
Half-eased in that a Powerfuller than I
Had willed and meted me the tears I shed.

'But not so,' he says, as if impatient with the pretentious Swinburnean alternatives; and he retreats to the solid, unflattering and unpromising construction which he found himself forced most often to see in things:

> –Crass Casualty obstructs the sun and rain,
> And dicing Time for gladness casts a moan. . . .
> These purblind Doomsters had as readily strown
> Blisses about my pilgrimage as pain.   [4*]

The progression here again is towards a truth which for him was inevitable. This settling down to truth, which runs through the early lyrics, is always accompanied by the entrance of such homely concreteness of metaphor as the sun and rain above. The direction is towards better poetry; and the better poetry puts a greater tax upon the reader. How the reader is taxed we shall try to describe now; but meanwhile, as a preliminary observation, we may give the man credit for the way he shakes himself free from familiar half-truths and settles himself upon his own hard truth. This in itself is a mark of the best sort of humanity. . . .

The problem of Hardy's mechanistic determinism still rests largely obscured in the not disinterested commentary of the religious critics. Hardy, of course, conjectured severely about a primary being whom he called indifferently God, Jahveh, the Willer, and also about human misery, which he thought was enormous, and possibly a cruelty inflicted upon men by one form or another of the primary being. These were conjectures, dramatic inquiries, not final pronouncements. But they inspired final pronouncements: even T. S. Eliot has found a diabolic strain in Hardy's work. Such judgements should be allowed perhaps to settle in silence on their own foundations. The theme of human misery, however, is so predominant in Hardy's work that a forthright attitude towards it cannot be avoided. It is each reader's individual problem; for me, this is true: even the bitterest of the writing, when it is genuinely motivated, serves only to show the insecurity of the world, its transitoriness, its defectiveness; and thus to bring about that chastening of the spirit which is not unlike the effect of religious literature itself. What it leads to further than this humbling effect, is another problem; I think that it is moral and wholesome and good in the way that any tragic art is moral and wholesome and good.

Not all of Hardy's pessimistic utterances are motivated, let there be no doubt about that: all the work of any writer is not always good. In 'A Meeting with Despair,' for instance [34], the hideous, hopeless, croaking Thing that he could feel rather than behold, is a melodramatic contrivance used to obliterate whatever solace one may think he finds in a sunset; but then, we are not in the habit of taking melodrama very seriously. And on the other hand a grotesque and beautiful and jarring poem such as 'Ah, Are You Digging on My Grave?' [269] is an example of Hardy's peculiar capacity for an irony that both shakes and strengthens the feelings. It takes fine discrimination to decide for or against each of the extreme conjectures. But if Hardy is blasphemous or diabolic he must be so in about the way indicated in these lines from his journal: 'September 8 [1896] . . . . There are certain questions which are made unimportant by their very magnitude. For example, the question whether we are moving in Space this way or that; the existence of a God, etc.' Perhaps there is pride in a humble recognition of human limitations. More often Hardy seems to suffer acutely in his awareness of 'Le silence éternal de ces espaces infinis . . . .' Only he did not leap with Pascal from terror to faith. Not everyone can.

The extreme conjecture is a sort of utterance *de contemptu mundi*. This, in itself, should not offend the religious critics. But it has: that which offended most was Hardy's inability always to appreciate, with G. K. Chesterton, the beef and beer of the world, and to share in Joyce Kilmer's shallow generalisation that made the philosophy of the Middle Ages joyous. As a matter of fact there is a strain of just such appreciation and joy in Hardy's work. Probably the root of his inspiration is much like that which brought forth Elizabethan tragedy – a conflict between the love of life and a contempt for the world, each component of which was modified for him by time and circumstance.

For the dark picture of the world always admits other possibilities. One predominant one in the poems is the simple enjoyment of the pleasurable sides of human life. In 'Night in the Old Home,' for instance, Hardy in the guise of the ghosts of his ancestors makes a counterstatement against his tendency to be 'a thinker of crooked thoughts':

'Take of Life what it grants, without question!' they answer me
    seemingly.
'Enjoy, suffer, wait: spread the table here freely like us,
And, satisfied, placid, unfretting, watch Time away beamingly!'
                                                              [222*]

Then there is always the possibility that, beyond the range of human vision, may be justice, reason, beneficence: there may be even a supreme being beyond the chief dramatis personae invented by a limited intelligence. The superb lyric 'The Darkling Thrush' is doubtless the best example of such conjecture, though it is only one among many. In all this Hardy opens the door to religious belief, just as in the preface to *Late Lyrics and Earlier* (1922) he opened the door, on intellectual grounds, to the Church. The doors had to close again, because 'evidence that the Church,' he wrote in a later footnote, 'will go far in the removal of "things that are shaken" has not been encouraging.' So too, most readers, I imagine, will have to stop just about where Hardy stopped in his pursuit of both theological and mystical solutions. As for the latter, most readers ought in all reasonableness to prefer the bleakest mechanism to the sweet mystical possibility that may be informing the song of the thrush:

> . . . I could think there trembled through
>   His happy good-night air
> Some blessed Hope, whereof he knew
>   And I was unaware.   [119*]

'The Darkling Thrush' is a splendid poem; but fortunately, because of the formlessness of its mysticism, its 'philosophy' is only a tangent from Hardy's philosophy.

His philosophy is concrete, rough, workable; it has a few more than ordinary limitations; it has somewhat more than ordinary powers because of its rude honesty. It is richly and rightly human. Perhaps Hardy's search for a faith, his rejection of the inhuman, and his return to the human, is symbolised in the last stanza of 'In a Wood' [40]. . . . Central in any estimate of Thomas Hardy must be an appreciation of his tendency to find greatest values in the homely relationships of people, finally in the 'life-loyalties' which 'now and then' appear. His insistence on the phrase 'now and then' is a mark of his particular temperament, evidence of a concretion of experience, which to some readers seems repellent. But whether loyalties appear now and then or more often, we can agree that they are to be praised, the breaches of them are to be regretted, and their infinitely complex natures are worth long study. These concerns provide Hardy with his principal materials.

More than any other poet he found substance for poems in the everyday histories of simple people. His method is to begin with a spare, sinewy account of a situation and to project from it his moment of vision. In comparison with Wordsworth he is more realistic; he is not so much interested in tracing from the beginning 'the primary laws of our nature' in the 'incidents and situations from common life,' not so much interested immediately in theme, but preoccupied with savoring the incident itself and then inducing the theme from it. The procedure is the same even when the personages are supernatural – ghosts or per-sonifications. This explains why Hardy's work is specially dramatic, why his lyrics are numerous, why many are occasional, why selection from them is difficult: begin with everyday life, and everything is a possible subject. There are other, conceivably better, ways of writing poetry; the lyric cannot be restricted to so essentially dramatic a pattern. But this, nevertheless, is Hardy's way.

To illustrate the bent towards the dramatic lyric, I shall set down here two short poems. The concreteness of the situations, of the point of view and of the language, will be observable; I hope that the simple humanity of Hardy, which finally must make all the difference in any account of him, will not be missed.

A CHURCH ROMANCE

She turned in the high pew, until her sight
Swept the west gallery, and caught its row
Of music-men with viol, book, and bow
Against the sinking sad tower-window light.

She turned again; and in her pride's despite
One strenuous viol's inspirer seemed to throw
A message from his string to her below,
Which said: 'I claim thee as my own forthright!'

Thus their hearts' bond began, in due time signed.
And long years thence, when Age had scared Romance,
At some old attitude of his or glance
That gallery-scene would break upon her mind,
With him as minstrel, ardent, young, and trim,
Bowing 'New Sabbath' or 'Mount Ephraim'.   [211*]

AFTER THE LAST BREATH

There's no more to be done, or feared, or hoped;
None now need watch, speak low, and list, and tire;
No irksome crease outsmoothed, no pillow sloped
     Does she require.

Blankly we gaze. We are free to go or stay;
Our morrow's anxious plans have missed their aim;
Whether we leave to-night or wait till day
     Counts as the same.

The lettered vessels of medicaments
Seem asking wherefore we have set them here;
Each palliative its silly face presents
     As useless gear.

And yet we feel that something savours well;
We note a numb relief withheld before;
Our well-beloved is prisoner in the cell
    Of Time no more.

We see by littles now the deft achievement
Whereby she has escaped the Wrongers all,
In view of which our momentary bereavement
    Outshapes but small.   [223*]

Both poems, I should say, are warm in their sad and happy blending of
emotion. The first puts positive value upon a life-loyalty which grows
out of an individual dramatic vision; the second expresses a not
uncommon mode of reconciliation with death, the sense of reconciliation being given character and indeed reality by the specific
situation.

Both poems are special, individual and concrete, and demand
therefore certain adjustments on the part of the reader. The language
needs only a few notations. To call dying a 'deft achievement' when all
other ways of relieving suffering have failed, is a mark of normal poetic
excellence. The phrase 'outshapes but small' is a sample, however, of
Hardy's peculiar ability to build up a perfectly concrete word when
there is need for it: in effect, Hardy seems with his two hands to be
weighing and balancing the benefit of death against the pain of
bereavement, and as he weighs them they take on another aspect of
concreteness – they become visible masses shaping themselves out
before the eyes. This has an emotional effect too: such weighing and
balancing is the opposite of egoistic; it gives largeness of vision,
comprehensiveness without damage to personal feeling.

'A Church Romance' is notable for its success in presenting a very
complicated scene and then in moving easily to the later recapitulation
of it. In such a recapitulation the sheer evocatory power that comes
from naming the old music is apparent. The transition, however, could
never have been accomplished without the compression achieved in the
one line:

Thus their hearts' bond began, in due time signed.

Similar compression also appears in the next line, in the phrase 'when
Age had scared Romance.' And this indicates the probable reason for
another of Hardy's stylistic peculiarities. His personifications as a rule
are the condensed expression of what he could have said in conventional
language if he had wanted to go the long way around. The personifications in these two poems – Age, Romance, Time, Wrongers –

are implements which keep dramatic treatment within very strict bounds. They doubtless should not be considered as having an existence outside the margins of the poem, for the context of the poem is necessary to define their meaning: the Wrongers, for instance, seem to have a dramatic significance relative to the sympathy with the suffering of a dying woman, rather than a metaphysical significance. These personifications are wholly satisfactory when they are given character by the dramatic situation in which they appear; I am not sure that they are so interesting when the process is reversed, as in *The Dynasts*, and they become principal characters in drama. . . .

A few notes in the way of definition by antithesis will have to round out the present sketch. In comparison with such a modern as D. H. Lawrence, Hardy's manner is dry. He had no traffic with the sensuous urgent psychology of Lawrence, not with 'misty cows,' but only with the psychology manifested in folk habit, in the bearing and gesture, the art and wisdom of the people, and in their conventional ghosts and witches. Lawrence, in his greater sensuousness, is egoistic and muddy; Hardy is limited and clear, at once sympathetic and detached, in his dryness. The comparison with Housman would be similar: the lyrical grace of the one ending in a swooning attitude, the dramatic terseness of the other leading to a gnarled wisdom.

To put side by side what the coming of the World War meant to Henry James and to Hardy seems perfectly to describe two kinds of wisdom, their powers and their limitations. James, for all his enormous comprehension of the moral complexity of any human being, had no way of foreseeing so obvious an event as the War, and the coming of war left him with no wisdom upon which to proceed. On August 5, 1914, he wrote in a letter:

The plunge of civilisation into this abyss of blood and darkness by the wanton feat of those two infamous autocrats is the thing that so gives away the whole long age during which we have supposed the world to be, with whatever abatement, gradually bettering, that to have to take it now for what the treacherous years were all the while really making for and *meaning* is too tragic for any words.

James had known and loved 'civilisation' in ways that were never open to Hardy; but he was unconsciously pledged to an airy meliorism that Hardy consciously claimed and unconsciously denied. James was wise and subtle and sensitive, and he was the one that was damned, not Hardy. For in the grotesquely beautiful 'Channel Firing' [247*] Hardy had foreseen what the years were meaning. He was too unsubtle to

conceive of the War as a treachery, and also too wisely aware of the
basic contours of life itself. And he had a faith which, though it alone is
not a sufficient faith, still has its merits in that it is an indestructible base
to return to.

> Only a man harrowing clods
>
> . . .
>
> Only thin smoke without flame
>   From the heaps of couch-grass;
> Yet this will go onward the same
>   Though Dynasties pass.   [500*]

Finally, in order not to seem to stress the modest certitude of Hardy at
the expense of his amazing artistry, I ask the reader to examine a less
familiar lyric than most of those quoted so far. The following could be
compared with Arnold's 'Dover Beach,' antithetically in regard to its
dramatic compactness, and equivalently in regard to its general
argument and significance; but the concreteness of its language is, as it
should be, unique, and so are the hoarse metaphors and the echoes of
the locality from which it came.

ONCE AT SWANAGE

> The spray sprang up across the cusps of the moon,
>   And all its light loomed green
>   As a witch-flame's weirdsome sheen
> At the minute of an incantation scene;
> And it greened our gaze – that night at demilune.
>
> Roaring high and roaring low was the sea
>   Behind the headland shores:
>   It symboled the slamming of doors,
> Or a regiment hurrying over hollow floors. . . .
> And there we too stood, hands clasped; I and she!   [753]

SOURCE: extracts from 'Hardy's Poetic Certitude', *The Southern
Review*, VI (Summer 1940), 49–51, 51–3, 55–61, 62–3.

C. Day Lewis The Lyrical Poetry (1951)

It is related of Thomas Hardy's infancy that, one hot afternoon, his mother returned to the cottage at Higher Bockhampton to find the baby asleep in his cradle, with 'a large snake curled up upon his breast, comfortably asleep like himself'. It had come in, no doubt, from the wild country near by, which he would immortalise one day as Egdon Heath. To strangle snakes in his cradle is a very proper symbol for the future hero of action. For one destined to be a hero of another kind – a contemplative who saw less good than evil in the human condition, but, by taking that evil to heart, by accepting it into his poetry, disarmed or purified it a little; a man of great compassion, a man who preserved through journey-work, fame, obloquy, and disillusionment a singular innocence – for such a hero the image of the sleeping snake on the infant's breast is strangely fitting. Was it perhaps only a blind-worm? Well, the fancy still holds, for Hardy believed that the forces which move men, nations, and the universe are blind.

Personalities as a rule should be kept out of the criticism of poetry. But it is extraordinarily difficult, and possibly undesirable, to dissociate Hardy's poetry from his character. Those who knew him best have all borne witness to his patience and modesty, his tenderness, and the magnanimity which gave grandeur to a sombre cast of mind. We know about the moral courage without which a mind so sensitive as his might well have closed up against experience in despair, and the integrity which insisted that what seemed true of life, however terrible, should not be excluded from art. We have, as I say, human witnesses to these qualities: but we do not need them; for they are manifest in the poems themselves. But in other respects we may misinterpret or undervalue the poems unless we realise the complicated nature, so oddly compounded of naiveté and erudition, ardour and melancholy, which produced them. For example, if we ignore the inherited peasant streak in Hardy, we shall fail to catch the countryman's raw humour and his love of a story for its own sake – fail to realise how many of Hardy's subjects, trivial, melodramatic, or absurd as they may seem to us, were chosen because they possessed for him the force and fascination of gossip.

There is another reason why personality must enter any discussion of Hardy's verse. Almost all his finest poems are deeply, nakedly personal: the love poems of 1912–13, for example, or the meditations in old age – 'Surview' [662], 'Afterwards' [511*], 'An Ancient to Ancients' [660*]. It is the tone of such poems which, more perhaps than any other facet of his genius, awakes in the reader a feeling of affectionate veneration[1] for the man who wrote them – the feeling of Marty South for Giles Winterborne: 'You was a good man and did good things.' Mr T. S. Eliot, however, is very differently affected. In *After*

Strange Gods, he allowed himself the following strictures: 'The work of the late Thomas Hardy represents an interesting example of a powerful personality uncurbed by any institutional attachment or by submission to any objective beliefs; unhampered by any ideas, or even by what sometimes acts as a partial restraint upon inferior writers, the desire to please a large public.'

Mr J. I. M. Stewart has shown that the only words in that passage which correspond to the truth about its subject are 'the late Thomas Hardy'.[2] But Mr Eliot continues: 'He seems to me to have written as nearly for the sake of "self expression" as a man well can; and the self which he had to express does not strike me as a particularly wholesome or edifying matter of communication.'

What are we to make of these frigid and unctuous phrases? It is true that Mr Eliot is discussing here the novels, not the poetry. But the 'self' which went into Hardy's verse was the same as that which went into his prose. If we are to use words like 'edifying' and 'wholesome', however, let us apply them to Hardy at his best and most characteristic, and see how he stands the test: here are the last two stanzas of his poem 'To An Unborn Pauper Child':

> Fain would I, dear, find some shut plot
> Of earth's wide wold for thee, where not
> One tear, one qualm,
> Should break the calm.
> But I am weak as thou and bare;
> No man can change the common lot to rare.
>
> Must come and bide. And such are we–
> Unreasoning, sanguine, visionary–
> That I can hope
> Health, love, friends, scope
> In full for thee; can dream thou'lt find
> Joys seldom yet attained by humankind!   [91*]

If the self which Hardy communicates here is unwholesome and unedifying, then words have lost all meaning. In this poem, as in so many others, we are struck by the note of true sincerity: Hardy will not force his feelings beyond the limit which his reason has fixed, will not let himself be carried away by pity, to make the poem more hopeful or more 'poetical'. None of his best poems bears out the charges of sadism, morbidity, and over-emotionalism which Mr Eliot brings against him as a novelist.

Nevertheless, Mr Eliot's criticism is suggestive in so far as it throws light upon the basic difference between two kinds of poet. His own poetry is, one feels, as impersonal as he can make it; the self he puts into it has gone through such a severe screening that the very minimum of human personality emerges; or we might venture to put it that he achieves poetry only by excluding large areas of personal experience. He has, indeed, roundly declared the need for dissociating the man who suffers from the mind that creates. Hardy, on the other hand, put everything he felt, everything he noticed, everything he was, into his poetry. As a result he wrote a great many bad poems – far more than Mr Eliot will ever have written: but also, because what he gave so unreservedly was the impressions of a magnanimous heart, the thoughts of a mind closely engaged in the problems of its own time and possessed of a strong historical sense, the experience of a man thoroughly versed in human suffering, his poetry has that breadth of matter and manner which only a major poet can compass.[3]

We must not, however, be led by the importance of the personal in Hardy's verse to judge him as a sort of well-meaning, ham-handed titan who somehow blundered into poetry now and then by sheer force of personality. This is a superficial judgement, though a common one still. Dr Leavis, for instance, speaks of his 'innocent awkwardness'; says that 'Hardy's great poetry is a triumph of character', and 'his rank as a major poet rests upon a dozen poems'. Dr Leavis does not tell us how he arrived at this round number, or which poems these are, or whether *The Dynasts* should be included amongst them – points one would have thought worth making by an exponent of 'practical' criticism. Though I sympathise with Dr Leavis's feelings of dismay at Hardy's gaucherie, compounded of the literary, the colloquial, the baldly prosaic, the conventionally poetical, the pedantic and the rustic', I believe that, in common with other critics who do not write verse, he has failed to notice the great technical skill which Hardy commanded and the amount of experiment in versification he undertook. Often, it is true, Hardy seems to lose all touch with his medium, and will dress up his subjects in the shoddiest, reach-me-down verse. But it is of the utmost significance that, whenever he comes to write of something near to his heart, of personal experience, he finds his touch again and his technique becomes masterly. Consider this enchanting picture of his childhood home:

> Here is the ancient floor,
> Footworn and hollowed and thin,
> Here was the former door
> Where the dead feet walked in.
>
> She sat here in her chair,
> Smiling into the fire;
> He who played stood there,
> Bowing it higher and higher.

> Childlike, I danced in a dream;
> Blessings emblazoned that day;
> Everything glowed with a gleam;
> Yet we were looking away!   [135*]

This lilting, serious, elegant poem, so notably lacking in the awkward-ness and uncouthness which some critics hold to be an essential trait of Hardy's style, well illustrates several of the salient qualities in his lyrical poetry. We see here, for example, what has been justly termed his 'natural piety' – the 'he' and the 'she' are, of course, his father and mother. We notice how the subject of beloved things in retrospect calls out here, as it seldom failed to do, the poet's lyrical tenderness. The poem illustrates, too, that love of music and the dance which affected Hardy from an early age, and clearly influenced his style. It shows his delicate skill in suffusing pathos with gaiety, his sense of the transient haunting all scenes of present happiness. And, although it is not strongly marked by his well-known idiosyncrasies of manner, it could not be mistaken for any other poet's writing – 'Blessings emblazoned that day; Everything glowed with a gleam' has the authentic Hardy ring.

I would like now to examine this last quality in more detail. The first thing we notice about Hardy's manner is that he seems to have been born with it. It can be detected in his earliest surviving poem, 'Domicilium' [1]: it is already full blown in

> I marked her ruined hues,
> Her custom-straitened views,
> And asked, 'Can there indwell
> My Amabel?'   [3]

That is the first stanza of a very early poem, written in 1865. Hardy wrote a fair number of poems during his young manhood, very few in his middle novel-writing period, and returned happily to verse – the medium he had always preferred – after the publication of *Jude the Obscure* and *The Well-Beloved*: it was during the last thirty years of his life that the bulk of his verse, including *The Dynasts*, was written. His first volume of verse, *Wessex Poems*, was not published till 1898. Here, as in each subsequent volume, he included a number of earlier poems with poems composed at much more recent dates. The former he sometimes, but not always, dated. His development would therefore have to be traced by internal evidence for the most part: luckily for the critic, there was no development, in the sense of a change from one style to another or from one field of subject-matter to another. Throughout, he was chiefly concerned with love, transience, death, and what the news-papers would call 'human-interest stories'. If we compare the poems dated between 1865 and 1875 with those of later provenance, we find little alteration in manner: what we do notice is that most of the earlier ones are in the iambic ten-syllable metre, and many of them sonnets. It seems that Hardy did not experiment widely in the complex stanza forms and flexible rhythms which represent his greatest technical achievement until he returned to poetry in his late fifties. To what extent this was due to the exigencies of novel-writing, or how far it may be attributed to his self-confessed slow development as a man, I am unable to judge.

Not only in idiosyncrasy, but in more general aspects of style Hardy's poetry shows little alteration through the years. Influence-spotters don't have a very happy time with him. We know he read Virgil young, admired Crabbe, Shelley, Keats, Scott, and, of his contemporaries, Barnes, Swinburne, Meredith, and Browning. But it is extremely difficult to detect any stylistic influence these writers had upon him, other than his use of certain of Barnes's stanza forms and his affinity with Browning. Browning is the only poet whose idiom is strongly echoed from Hardy's own verse; for example, the famous lines, which also sum up Hardy's attitude to life:

Let him in whose ears the low-voiced Best is killed by the clash of the
    First,
Who holds that if way to the Better there be, it exacts a full look at the
    Worst,
Who feels that delight is a delicate growth cramped by crookedness,
    custom, and fear,
Get him up and be gone as one shaped awry; he disturbs the order here.
                                                                [137*]

A more subtle comparison might be made between the opening sixteen lines of Hardy's 'Under the Waterfall' [276*] and certain stanzas of Browning's 'By The Fireside'. The shyness that prevented Hardy from meeting Browning and other contemporaries, during his young days in London may well have contributed to the persistence of his own early idiom: certainly, had he met them, he might have become a more self-critical poet. But I believe he gained more than he lost by not being thrown, so young and immature as he was then, into the deep end of literary society.

For Hardy's is a classic example, if ever there was one, of the self-made manner: not just a manner made largely out of his self, and in that sense full of character, full of flavour; but also as it were a self-taught manner, with the roughness, the *naïveté*, the vigour, the uncertainty of taste, which we might infer from the term 'self-made'. Mr Edmund Blunden has said that Hardy's faults 'are those of a zealous experimenter, whose materials do not always obey the purpose or yield a restful completeness'. We shall glance at these materials presently. But it would be unwise to over-emphasise Hardy's lack of critical sense. Much has been made of his remark to T. E. Lawrence, 'Oh, but I admire the *Iliad* greatly. Why, it's in the *Marmion* class!' I strongly suspect this was a leg-pull. Hardy was a countryman through and through; and anyone who knows the English countryman knows the quiet glee he gets from making himself out to be more dense than he is, from deliberately overacting the yokel part when he is in the presence of urban and sophisticated types. It is a form of poker-faced humorous self-protection which I suspect Hardy to have relished a good deal. Further, he was not altogether uncritical about his own work: for instance, when his first wife died, he wrote a considerable number of poems about their past: of these he selected twenty-one to appear in *Satires of Circumstance* as 'Poems of 1912–13': the remainder we find scattered about in later publications. If we compare these with the original twenty-one, we find that the latter are noticeably superior: his first choice was, in fact, a sound one; and to have chosen so well from a body of poems so intimately personal as these surely argues a genuine critical detachment.

We learn something about his attitude to poetry from Mrs Hardy's *Life of Thomas Hardy*. He approved Leslie Stephen's judgement that 'the ultimate aim of the poet should be to touch our hearts by showing his own; and not to exhibit his learning, or his fine taste, or his skill in mimicking the notes of his predecessors'. Elsewhere he says, 'To find beauty in ugliness is the province of the poet'. He made 'quantities of notes on rhyme and metre: with outlines and experiments in innumerable original measures', his tendency being always against too regular a beat. Again, writing of his prose method, he says, 'The whole secret of a living style and the difference between it and a dead style, lies in not having too much style – being, in fact, a little careless, or rather seeming to be, here and there . . . . It is, of course, simply a carrying into prose the knowledge I have acquired in poetry – that inexact rhymes and rhythms now and then are far more pleasing than correct ones.'

This is an appropriate moment for a few words about Hardy's poems in relation to his novels. We must notice first how very seldom his lyrics display that fresh, attentive and detailed description of natural objects which we find in the novels: the following stanza is one of the rare exceptions:

> And the wind flapped the moon in its float on the pool,
>   And stretched it to oval form;
> Then corkscrewed it like a wriggling worm;
>   Then wanned it weariful.   [680]

Nor does Hardy attempt in verse those brilliant, sustained image-passages which stand out so memorably from his novels – the swordplay of Sergeant Troy around Bathsheba Everdene; Wildeve and Venn gambling on the Heath by the light of glow-worms. Nor again, except in the stage-directions of *The Dynasts*, do we get the cinematic technique, frequently used in his fiction, by which some vast panorama is shown from a distance, is lovingly dwelt upon, and then the reader's eye so to speak pans up slowly to some human figure which before had been dwarfed in the immensity of the scene. These are perhaps the three qualities which most incline us to feel his novels as 'poetic'. But, except for the first-mentioned, they need more room for successful deployment than a lyric poem could offer, and Hardy's instinct to forgo them was sound. In another respect, however, the novelist and the poet were one. Nothing was too small to escape Hardy's notice, or too great to daunt his powers, whether it was a hedgehog crossing a lawn at night or Europe's armies on the march. And, in his poetry no less than in his novels, he showed a genius for focusing together the great and the small, for feeling and revealing 'infinite passion, and the pain of finite hearts that yearn', through some little glimpse or brief episode which, prosaic or trivial on the surface, he transmuted into a moment of vision. 'The Frozen Greenhouse' [706] is a typical example [quotes Blunden on Hardy].

Hardy's verse seldom strayed far from this 'vaster threne of decline', and is informed throughout by his belief that the 'law of all life' is but poorly adapted to mankind's creeds or needs. His greatness, Dr Leavis has well said, 'lies in the integrity with which he accepted the conclusion, enforced, he believed, by science, that nature is indifferent to human values'. Much has been written about Hardy's philosophy, and I do not intend to add to it. He himself was at pains, though he spoke of the poet's task as 'the application of ideas to life', to contradict those who found a philosophy of life in his work. What critics called his philosophical tenets were, he said, only 'impressions' or rationalisations of moods. He vigorously disclaimed the title of pessimist, preferring to be thought of as a meliorist, and showing in his idea of an emergent consciousness in the universe a certain affinity with the doctrine of Emergent Evolution. It is, indeed, not difficult to sympathise with critics who found the deepest-dyed pessimism in his work: at times his 'purblind Doomsters' are indistinguishable from those which Dr Johnson wrote of in satirising Soame Jenyns: 'As we drown whelps and kittens, they amuse themselves now and then with sinking a ship, and stand round the fields of Blenheim or the walls of Prague, as we encircle a cockpit.' But we must not coagulate a poet's moods into a philosophical system, any more than we must expect consistency from his ideas. Nor should we disregard the more positive and brighter aspect of Hardy's beliefs. 'Both as man and as conscious artist,' Mr J. I. M.

Stewart reminds us, Hardy was 'a product of that ethical idealism – at once urgent and substantially traditional – which so commonly cohered with the agnosticism of the period.' He himself gave us the ideal groundwork of his art when he said that human nature is 'neither ghastly, hateful, nor ugly; neither commonplace, unmeaning, nor tame, but . . . slighted and enduring; and withal singularly colossal and mysterious.' Or when he jotted down in his diary of August, 1882: 'An ample theme: the intense interests, passions, and strategy that throb through the commonest lives.' We may disagree with this generous humanism of his: but if we disregard it, we shall lose much of the value of his poetry. For it is part of the pattern as he saw it, about which he said, ' . . . in life the seer should watch that pattern among general things which his idiosyncrasy moves him to observe, and describe that alone': or again, in a note for *The Dynasts*, 'The human race to be shown as one great network or tissue which quivers in every part when one point is shaken, like a spider's web if touched.' . . .

. . . Hardy, in his shorter poems, evoked his genius most successfully through the personal and the lyrical. His lyrics are seldom pure; they are nearly always clouded by personal experience: and, even when the poem seems to be a pure distillation, it almost certainly had its sources in some real incident or flesh-and-blood person. The exquisite poem 'To Lizbie Browne' [94], for instance, is not addressed to any ideal or composite rustic charmer: Lizbie Browne was a gamekeeper's daughter whom Hardy fell in love with as a boy.[4] Again, a poem will fly off in pure lyric vein at the start, but come to earth on a moralisation before the end: examples of this are 'Shut Out that Moon' [164*] and 'Proud Songsters' [816*]. In his old age Hardy said that 'his only ambition, as far as he could remember, was to have some poem or poems in a good anthology like the *Golden Treasury*. The model he had set before him was "Drink to me only" by Ben Jonson.' This latter is a startling piece of information. But then we remember that Hardy from childhood was devoted to music, could tune a fiddle at the age of six, and learnt to refine in his verse–rhythms the lilting, pausing, lolloping measures he had first loved in country–dance tunes. So it is not after all very surprising if he took the Ben Jonson poem as his model. And something of its simplicity and musical utterance are indeed achieved in ten of Hardy's lyrics: 'To Lizbie Browne', 'I Say, "I'll Seek Her"' [172], 'When I Set Out for Lyonesse' [254*], 'Regret Not Me' [318], 'Lines to a Movement in Mozart's E-flat Symphony' [388*], 'In Time of "The Breaking of Nations"' [500*], 'Weathers' [512*], 'The Fallow Deer at the Lonely House' [551*], 'This Summer and Last' [800], and 'The Self-Unseeing' [135*]. . . .

To have written ten such poems is enough to set Hardy amongst our good lyric poets; but to have written nearly all of them in old age is a wonder. If Hardy's mind was born old, his heart remained young:

> But Time, to make me grieve,
> Part steals, lets part abide,
> And shakes this fragile frame at eve
> With throbbings of noontide.   [52*]

The idealisms of his youth were never quite extinguished. They can be heard in the wistful last stanzas of 'The Oxen' [403*] and 'The Darkling Thrush' [119*], both of which are straining after 'some blessed Hope' in a bleak world. The passion that moves behind his love poems is the passion of young manhood seen through a golden haze of restrospect. I shall speak of them in a moment. But first we must allow that this backward-looking stance is vulnerable to criticism. 'We two kept house, the Past and I, The Past and I' [249]. It is supposed to be a dangerous menage for a poet. Nostalgia, we are told, is an enervating emotion, likely to corrupt his work. I can readily believe it; indeed, any emotion is dangerous to a poem: there is only one thing more dangerous – the lack of it. The poet has somehow to distance himself from his emotions and the objects which gave rise to them, without losing touch with them altogether. Hardy distanced himself by the simple device of writing most of his poetry in old age: he kept in touch because – again I can think of no more scientific phrase for it – his heart remained young; also, he evidently had what we might call a good sensuous memory. He was a nostalgic, yes; both in the strict sense of one who feels homesickness – this is part of the emotional tone of his natural piety towards the parents, friends, and places of his youth – and in the looser sense of brooding constantly over the past. But the verse in which he embodies such brooding seldom shows the tenuousness or oversweetness which are signs of a morbid nostalgia. It is saved from them partly by deliberate roughnesses of technique and his habit of weaving homely images and colloquial phrases into the poetical texture, partly by sheer force of sincerity. There are times, indeed, when we feel that the sense of the transience of things, which is perhaps a poet's strongest motive, has become a monomania with Hardy: but at least his variations on this theme are extremely diverse, ranging from some of the best of the intimate poems to such unusual lyrics as 'The Five Students' [439] or 'During Wind and Rain' [441*]. Both of these offer us a subtle use of refrain, a technical device which Hardy employed in a masterly way to underline the pathos and inevitability of things passing. [Quotes 'The Five Students'] . . . In 'The Five Students' it is noticeable how the romantic and plangent refrain-lines in each stanza are balanced by the hard, factual, forthright imagery of the lines which precede them: this is one of many possible examples of Hardy's technical skill, and one which should be pondered by critics who airily refer to his prosiness; a more attentive study of the texts will show that he used the prosaic to set off and correct the conventionally 'poetic'.

Another technical skill I must not omit – Hardy's flair for blending the gay and the humorous with the poignant. This again has received, I think, inadequate critical attention. It is an extremely difficult thing to do, without breaking up the *legato* of the poem or ruining its texture. 'A Gentleman's Second-Hand Suit' [869] is an excellent instance of this flair. Better still, because it uses colloquial turns of phrase even more adroitly, while preserving the lyrical rhythm and tempo, is 'He Revisits His First School':

> I should not have shown in the flesh,
> I ought to have gone as a ghost;
> It was awkward, unseemly almost,
> Standing solidly there as when fresh,
>   Pink, tiny, crisp-curled,
>   My pinions yet furled
>   From the winds of the world.
>
> After waiting so many a year
> To wait longer, and go as a sprite
> From the tomb at the mid of some night
> Was the right, radiant way to appear;
>   Not as one wanzing weak
>   From life's roar and reek,
>   His rest still to seek:
>
> Yea, beglimpsed through the quaint quarried glass
> Of green moonlight, by me greener made,
> When they'd cry, perhaps, 'There sits his shade
> In his olden haunt – just as he was
>   When in Walkingame he
>   Conned the grand Rule-of-Three
>   With the bent of a bee.'
>
> But to show in the afternoon sun,
> With an aspect of hollow-eyed care,
> When none wished to see me come there,
> Was a garish thing, better undone.
>   Yes; wrong was the way;
>   But yet, let me say,
>   I may right it – some day.   [462]

That charming poem, with so much of his personality in it, brings us to the most personal of all his poems – and the best. A little must be said about the human situation behind them. Hardy's first marriage went wrong. There were faults, very possibly, on his side which made him a difficult man to live with. His wife, when the glamour of their Cornish courtship faded, was seen to be snobbish, small-minded, and incapable of living gracefully in the shadow of Hardy's genius. But a greater shadow fell upon her and darkened their relationship. Some mental derangement of hers has been hinted at, and veiled references may be found in a number of the poems: for instance 'Near Lanivet' [366*], 'The Blow' [419], 'The Interloper' [432*], 'The Man with a Past' [458], or 'The Division':

> But that thwart thing betwixt us twain,
>   Which nothing cleaves or clears,
> Is more than distance, Dear, or rain,
>   And longer than the years!   [169*]

Whatever 'that thwart thing' may have been, his wife's death when the poet was seventy-two swept away the long estrangement there had been between them, releasing a gush of reminiscence and poetry. I believe the best of these 1912–13 poems to be some of the finest love poetry in our language: indeed, one may wonder if there is in any language a parallel to this winter-flowering of a poetry of sentiment which had lain dormant in the poet's heart throughout the summer of his age. The emotional range of the poems is remarkable, from the agony of bereavement and remorse in 'The Going' [277*] to the almost ecstatic acceptance of 'After a Journey' [289*]; from the delicate pathos of 'The Haunter' [284*], in which the dead wife is speaking, to the no less delicate melancholy, strengthened by sinewy phrasing and a few clear-cut images, which makes 'At Castle Boterel' [292*] so haunting a farewell to love. The variety of emotion is equalled by that of stanza-form: it is as though the diverse moulds had been preparing through a lifetime, and now those scenes from the past ran freely into them, each recognising its own. Tricks of technique, which had at times been wasted on inferior material or had called too much attention to themselves, now came into their own – such as the triplet rhyming of 'The Voice':

> Woman much missed, how you call to me, call to me,
> Saying that now you are not as you were
> When you had changed from the one who was all to me,
> But as at first, when our day was fair.   [285*]

Looking at these poems with a poet's calculating eye, one's first response
may be, 'My word, how everything came off for him then!' But it did not
come off just because he had had fifty years' experience of using words.
Beneath their grace and appealing diversity, the 1912–13 poems have
good bone, formed by the sincerity, the refusal to overstate an emotion
or falsify a situation, which we have noticed before. There might so
forgivably have been flecks of self-pity, or sentimentality, even in the
best of these poems. That there are none is due not to the carefulness of a
poet who has feared to give too much of himself away lest it muddy the
stream of his verse but to the unselfconscious recklessness with which
Hardy did give himself: and the moral quality of that self may be
gauged, I believe, by the poetic quality of what was thus created.
Therefore, identifying these poems so closely with their maker, and
ourselves, as we read them, with the experiences they speak of, we
respond with a kind of jubilation as the moods of regret and muted
reconcilement in 'After a Journey' expand through the last two stanzas
into the faithful affirmation of 'I am just the same as when Our
days were a joy, and our paths through flowers'. [Quotes 'After a
Journey'] . . .

Such, then, is the tenderness of Thomas Hardy. I do not know any
other English poet who strikes that note of tenderness so firmly and so
resonantly. You must forgive me for using what is called 'emotive
language' about his work: but, when one is deeply touched by a poem, I
can see no adequate reason for concealing the fact. And, with Hardy at
his best, it is the poem – the whole poem, not any high spots in it, which
makes the impression. We shall be offended by his frequent use of
archaic or uncouth or stock-poetic words, if we detach them from their
contexts – words such as 'domicile', 'denizenship', 'subtrude', 'thus-
wise', 'hodiernal', 'fulgid', 'lippings', 'unbe'. But if we allow the
momentum of the poem to carry us over them, as often it can, they will
seem very small obstacles; and without them his poetry would lose
something of its characteristic flavour. The same is true of his
alliteration. Hardy's words, his epithets particularly, seem to be
frequently chosen – here a far-fetched one, there a flat one – simply for
alliteration's sake: but if, instead of dwelling upon the phrase, we seek to
comprehend the poem as a whole, we find such oddities and flatnesses
falling into place. It cannot, of course, be denied that the massive
deployment of a simple idea, though apt enough for a work on the scale
of *The Dynasts*, becomes in a short poem grandiose and cumbrous:
circumlocution is a serious danger to Hardy's lyrics. Yet he often, by a
secret formula in which craft and innocence are somehow combined,
manages to absorb his circumlocutions in the body of the poem. One
can think of few less promising lines to start a poem – or more ponderous
ways of saying 'when I am dead' – than 'When the Present has latched

its postern behind my tremulous stay': yet the poem it begins is one of Hardy's finest. The language of poetry is, after all, an artificial language, whether the poet uses a poetic diction throughout a poem, or whether he varies it with colloquial phrases. The only question is, has he achieved balance and congruence; and the final test of this is whether the poem survives as a whole or in fragments.

The poem I have just referred to, 'Afterwards' [511 *], is in form a set of variations on a theme. The first three lines of each stanza are increasingly sonorous and 'poetic', while the last line of each is a simple, colloquial statement, made more telling by the relative artificiality of the lines which precede it. Now, if I am right in judging this to be a whole poem, you may still wish to ask how far its wholeness has been achieved by artifice – by a deliberate counterpoising of the two elements I have mentioned. I believe that where personal poetry is concerned the wholeness of a poem must depend not only upon technical skill, not even upon technical skill backed by imaginative power, but also – and perhaps most – on a certain wholeness in the poet himself. Great poems have been written by immature, flawed, or unbalanced men; but not, I suggest, great personal poetry; for this, ripeness, breadth of mind, charity, honesty are required: that is why great personal poetry is so rare. It is an exacting medium – one that will not permit us to *feign* notable images of virtue. False humility, egotism, or emotional insincerity cannot be hidden in such poetry: they disintegrate the poem. Thomas Hardy's best poems do seem to me to offer us images of virtue; not because he moralises, but because they breathe out the truth and goodness that were in him, inclining our own hearts towards what is lovable in humanity. [Ends by quoting 'Afterwards'] . . .

SOURCE: 'The Lyrical Poetry of Thomas Hardy' (The Warton Lecture on English Poetry, delivered 6 June 1951), printed in *Proceedings of the British Academy* (1951), 155–63, 166, 167–8, 169–71, 172–4. See also C. Day Lewis's *The Shorter Poems of Thomas Hardy* (Dublin: 1944), and *The Poetic Image* (London, 1947), esp. pp. 150–3.

NOTES

1. Charles Morgan, as an undergraduate at Oxford, felt on meeting Hardy his 'power of drawing reverence towards affection': quoted in F. E. Hardy, *Life* . . ., vol. II.

2. J. I. M. Stewart, in *English Studies* (1948).

3. Cf. Middleton Murry: 'The unity which comes of the instinctive refusal of a great poet to deny experience . . . gives, as it alone really can give, to personal

emotion what is called the impersonality of great poetry , *Aspects of Literature*. [See Part Two of this Casebook – Eds.]

   4. [Her real name was Elizabeth Bishop; see Gittings, *The Older Hardy*, p. 89 – Eds.]

Douglas Brown 'Hardy's Elegiac Power' (1954)

. . . We reach, then, the gathering point in Hardy's poetry: where elments of balladry and folk song, of the severe, consistent acknowledgement of all that open experience reports, of the poignant nostalgic impulse, and the peculiar response to the profound moment, all fuse in elegiac poetry. That several of the most moving of these poems are inspired mainly by the death of Hardy's first wife and by his memories afterwards, should not absorb our attention. All his best writing takes its origin in immediate experiences and recollections. But the elegiac poetry of Hardy is excellent because the grief is absorbed into the texture of the occasions and memories, measured and controlled by the dramatic situations. The grief is deep; the area of sorrow, the sense of the transitoriness of human happiness, the knowledge of dereliction, loneliness, are the field of these elegies. The originating pressure is personal; but the manner of the best poems is restrained, impersonal, often ruefully simple. They take the measure of things quietly, without striking attitudes – and that is the most insidious temptation when grief is treated in poetry. Hardy's achievement is to have moved where that temptation seems not to have existed; he is most directly himself when most powerfully distressed.

   The point is best made by comparing one of Hardy's short elegiac pieces (not itself among the finest) with one of the movements of *In Memoriam*. Here is Tennyson:

> Dark house, by which once more I stand
>   Here in the long unlovely street,
>   Doors, where my heart was used to beat
> So quickly, waiting for a hand,
>
> A hand that can be clasp'd no more –
>   Behold me, for I cannot sleep,
>   And like a guilty thing I creep
> At earliest morning to the door.

> He is not here; but far away
>   The noise of life begins again,
>   And ghastly through the drizzling rain
> On the bald street breaks the blank day.

Now this is very moving: the voice's rhythm plays so subtly against the metre in the first stanza; the moment of recognition so painfully disturbs and breaks the opening of the third. There is an eloquent certainty in the speech, beyond Hardy's range. Yet one feels, for all that, there is something *presented* about the whole. The rhetorical apostrophes point to a slightly factitious quality in the occasion, as though it were staged for the purpose of concentrating our pity. The repetition,

> . . . waiting for a hand,

> A hand that can be clasp'd no more –

asks sympathy. The slant upon oneself, the picture of the 'guilty' figure, makes us feel he crept there for the sake of the poem. Serious and sincere as it is, it reads too like the poem of a grief-stricken attitude. It is not altogether 'posed', yet is it altogether pure either? The apparent restraint in the strong image of the close seems after all to be calling a good deal of attention to itself: 'ghastly', 'bald' and 'blank' are insistent.

The texture, here, is tarnished. That is not to deny the truth of Tennyson's anguish; his elegy is moving, a valid statement of human desolation in bereavement. But let us contrast it briefly with Hardy's 'Just the Same' (which may well owe something to memories of Tennyson's poem). Few poets have learnt from other poets more expertly than Hardy, with such a flair for what to take and what to leave in order to strengthen and enrich the original, personal gift.

> I sat. It was all past;
> Hope never would hail again;
> Fair days had ceased at a blast,
> The world was a darkened den.

> The beauty and dream were gone,
> And the halo in which I had hied
> So gaily gallantly on
> Had suffered blot and died!

> I went forth, heedless whither,
> In a cloud too black for name:
> – People frisked hither and thither;
> The world was just the same.   [650]

Beside Tennyson's poem, much here seems almost incompetent; this poet has not Tennyson's verbal assurance. His grief seems a smaller thing. Yet his infelicitous language sounds a deeper music. In the sparse statement of the broken opening line his grief is more simply what it claims to be; at the same time it is more acquiescent, subdued to its place in the universal scheme. The little meditation that follows seems to fumble unaffectedly; but yet 'the world was a darkened den' makes the dark house and the long unlovely street seem like stage properties by comparison. When the 'beauty and dream' appear, measuring the loss, a touch of gentle irony, even of self-parody, keeps the situation distant and accessible to different points of view. The halo was no halo at all, but a person, and mortal. The third stanza lilts for a moment to a ballad tune; the emotion in the second line is, so to speak, social. Then, abruptly, the door actually opening, the daylight world entering and the cloud dissolving, the ballad tune falls away.

> People *frisked* hither and thither,
> The world was just the same.

The eccentric word seems to guarantee and extend the occasion. The awakened perceptions are far more subdued and natural. The oblivious people moving so absurdly are more poignant than the far-away noises left undefined, and the blank day that seemed to be arranged like a backcloth for grief. Hardy is perhaps less deeply moved than Tennyson; but he never gives you the feeling that the furniture has been draped in readiness, and the blinds drawn. And it is this thorough-going simplicity that constitutes Hardy's strength in elegiac poetry, and compensates for apparent deficiencies in skill, for the failure of the consort to dance together.

Nearly all of the elegies are dramatic, rather than personal, in form. The presence of the human person – whatever may be owing to Hardy's own experiences in his own person – is a part of the dramatic technique. The 'I' is rather a function of poetic impersonality than an assertion of the poet's self. Indeed, one group of the elegiac poems offers no references to Hardy's own love, and no direct reference to his past. These are dramatic poems. 'During Wind and Rain' [441*] is such a poem, and the powerful early 'Neutral Tones' [9*] is another. 'Bereft' [157*] has something of the quality of 'During Wind and Rain', trivially vivid in its recollected actualities of clock and crock, disturbing in its evocation of gloom and place, haunting in its ballad-refrain. 'Beyond the Last Lamp' (how suggestively typical the title!) uses the refrain differently, but again with a curious weight of endorsement; sliding time and memoried place are here most telling [257*]. We cannot know, and it does not concern us to enquire, what private griefs of the

later years of his first marriage may be absorbed into 'In Tenebris 1'
[136*]; but it may come as something of a shock to anyone who has
taken Hardy's elegiac power to originate solely in his own private
knowledge of loss and bereavement, to find such a moving elegy
composed long before 1912. Some of his finest elegies have the universal
mutability of life for theme, like 'Exeunt Omnes' [335*], which
integrates subjective feeling and altering perceptions with crabbed
expressiveness. The 'spectral mannikin' of 'His Immortality' [109*]
suddenly brings the apprehension of the general human plight into
sharp focus; in several little ways one is reminded of George Herbert.
'The Clock-Winder' [471*], though with hints of the macabre, is
slightly but genuinely effective; so also is 'Where They Lived' [392].
The more personal elegies for George Meredith [243*] and for his
mother [223*], with its gripping third stanza, have a place of their own.

Of the elegies remaining, most take their origin in some moment of
recollection, or of the surging of grief. The personal suffering is absorbed
into the dramatic context, and fantasy stretches back over the years to
give metaphorical extension to the feeling of transitoriness, or of
bereavement. It is best to treat first of the shorter, as it were, lighter,
poems – poems of the brief impulse rather than of the exposed and
explored recollection. There is a passage in 'The Last Time' which
seems to bring to a point this sense of the particular, the controlling
instant, that imparts strength to the poems:

> The clock showed the hour and the minute,
> But I did not turn and look: [651]

In Hardy's poetic art, the clock always shows the hour and the minute.
Sometimes that minute is there, and gone: as in the delicate song 'The
Dream is – Which?' [611] or in 'When Oats Were Reaped' [738], with
its touching final lines, or in 'The Walk' [279*], which also moves
towards a poignant directness of feeling, or the lively 'The Prospect'
[735], or 'Without Ceremony' [282*], so gentle and natural.

Sometimes the moment is extended without being deepened, as in
'The Phantom Horsewoman' [294*] or 'An Anniversary' [407], to
produce verse of unequal power. Sometimes the ballad–tune tilts the
poetry too far and too easily away from the stress of grief, as in 'The
Division' [169*], or even 'Something Tapped' [396*]. One of the most
haunting of all these smaller poems is 'The Self-Unseeing' [135*]; it
catches all the qualities of this group of elegies: so song-like and airy in
tread, so pregnant and exact in word, so subtle – within its deliberate
limits – in music. [Quotes the poem.]

Hardy's supreme achievements lie in more extended elegy; but not
all the extensions are equally successful, although most have at least an

unequal power. 'Near Lanivet' [366*] is one such; the early, rather coarse-grained 'At Waking' [174*] is another. Sometimes the memory itself absorbs the consciousness, and the disconcerting present is only half-hinted. Sometimes the singing quality distances everything, yet endorses the grief with the weight present in balladry. Such a poem is the memorable 'Overlooking the River Stour' [424], full of delicate perceptions, and then so moving, despite the easy singing, in the last stanza, that reveals the rain on the intervening window, the blurring of vision, the regret for the lost occasion behind the shoulder. Hardy's sensuousness usually appears in decisive strokes; here it flows confidently. In 'At Rushy–Pond' [680], coloured by phantom-like sensations and slightly macabre feelings, the sensuous quality is more characteristic. The opening is self-conscious. One feels the poetry is being 'made'. But when the genuine memory comes, strength flows in.

And at this point we are left with the five great elegies that are the summit of Hardy's achievement: 'A Broken Appointment', 'After a Journey', 'The Going', 'At Castle Boterel' and 'The Voice'. In 'A Broken Appointment' [99*] Hardy manages a severity of speech and a compelling force in the rhythms that distinguish this from any other of his poems. Of the elegies, it is the most obviously fine, for it meets more than halfway our notion of what such a poem ought to sound like. The final effect of the compression – with its suggestion of self-mastery – and of the unassailable rhythm, is to endorse the situation with grave, affirmative weight. The recollection becomes deeply representative, it addresses us in its own right without regard to anyone's personal suffering. The validity speaks in those details that come back so eloquently upon the memory. Phrases like 'as the hope–hour stroked its sum' in this poem, or 'saw morning harden upon the wall' in the desolate 'The Going' [277*], make us aware of a poetic mastery that we can identify as a supremely *natural* use of the language of conversation and meditation, unassuming, pretending nothing. Yet again and again we are made to feel that the odd or simple words exist in a unique way for this very occasion. At the same time we can detect as an undercurrent that strong pressure towards defining and articulating the elusive sensation, that we feel in the uncertain prose of some memorable passages in the novels. Hardy has a rare energy and determination of spirit, and a rare genuineness, a power of undeceived fidelity to his experience; and these resolve his speech into a manner at once original, idiosyncratic, and furnished with touches of apparent clumsiness or naïveté; which gradually reveal themselves as peculiar accuracies of apprehension, or quiet, tactful indications of a personal predicament far less simple than at first it seemed.

'After a Journey' [289*] is perhaps the subtlest of these elegies. It presents more vividly and poignantly than any other the bewildering activity of memory. But the presentation is unobtrusively controlled by a steadfast, disenchanted acknowledgement of time present: of the ghostly, 'flitting', shifting quality of the past joy, the past occasion, the dead person, with which the memory conjures and beguiles. In no other poem do we feel so near to Hardy himself, a frail, diffident and bereaved man alone in the darkness – a darkness both actual, part of the situation presented, and metaphorical – and at the mercy of the shifting perspectives of reminiscence, recollection, and meditation. In no other poem does the double situation, present and past, seem so actual. The dead woman, the haunting memory of forty years gone by, come upon the consciousness with peculiar definition: the ghost –

> Facing round about me everywhere,
>   With your nut-coloured hair,
> And gray eyes, and rose-flush coming and going. . . .

Equally distinct and candid is the record of the figure in the present moment, 'lonely, lost', who tracks the lively phantom through time and place – the phantom whose very absence constitutes the present moment.

> Yes: I have re-entered your olden haunts at last. . . .
> I see what you are doing: you are leading me on. . . .

The slow, gentle, meditative manner of the verse preserves a balance trembling between the reality of the 'olden haunts', the unseen waterfall, the glowing presence of the living woman, all that memory creates; and the darkness and emptiness of the forty years between, the reverberant waterfall, the hollowness of the sound that calls from the empty cave, the 'scanning' across the dark space. It is as though memory, by flinging the bridge, made more vivid the fearful depths of the gulf of time, 'deriding Time'.

Then, as in the overwhelming final passage of 'The Voice', the present moment emerges in an act of profound realisation. Memory has not deluded; it is acknowledged with gratitude because it holds what little can be held of the most prized and valued experience. There has been no deception, no flinching from the present loneliness. That is why, even from the first line of the poem, there is a curious, disconcerting emphasis upon seeing, as if with wide-open eyes: viewing, scanning, gazing into the darkness. The watchfulness of the bereft tracker, lost in the haunted place, distinguishes with superb integrity the fact from the fiction, and the fact in the fiction, and precisely values both.

Ignorant of what there is flitting here to see,
  The waked birds preen and the seals flop lazily;
Soon you will have, Dear, to vanish from me,
  For the stars close their shutters and the dawn whitens hazily.
Trust me, I mind not, though Life lours,
  The bringing me here; nay, bring me here again!
    I am just the same as when
Our days were a joy, and our paths through flowers.   [289*]

The moment, with all its implications of irreparable loss, is known through and through, and accepted. How marvellously the preening and the flopping of bird and seal dismiss the evasive phantom! The words are secure in their accuracy, and their relevance to the occasion. The vanishing of the wraith means both a going and a coming of light. The stars close their shutters, darkening in an intimate, homely way, and seeming to shut out a greater darkness of loneliness; and the dawn whitens hazily, *whitens* with the numb, empty, colourless quality of the grief-stricken consciousness as it acknowledges the illusoriness of the visitation and the derision of time, and perceives through a haze of bewilderment and uncertainty the dawn of days still to be lived through, alone.

In the superb 'At Castle Boterel', the utterance rises out of an honourable, natural simplicity to a memorable, engraved kind of style unique in Hardy. First there are trivial, apparently accidental particulars of recollection, seen 'distinctly yet', and then the memory distends in the mind. The broken phrases move in and out of the irregular metre, constructing, reconstructing, with a sensation of shift and sway and alteration. Then, out of the moment emerges the assessment:

It filled but a minute. But was there ever
  A time of such quality, since or before,
In that hill's story? To one mind never,
  Though it has been climbed, foot-swift, foot-sore,
    By thousands more.

Primaeval rocks form the road's steep border,
  And much have they faced there, first and last,
Of the transitory in Earth's long order;
  But what they record in colour and cast
    Is – that we two passed.

The primaeval rocks make the transitoriness both poignant and yet

natural and acceptable. Gradually the poetry returns to the particular,
to a person, a moment, and the present time:

> And to me, though Time's unflinching rigour,
>   In mindless rote, has ruled from sight
> The substance now, one phantom figure
>   Remains on the slope, as when that night
>   Saw us alight.
>
> I look and see it there, shrinking, shrinking,
>   I look back at it amid the rain
> For the very last time; for my sand is sinking,
>   And I shall traverse old love's domain
>   Never again.   [292*]

It is worth repeating that the centre – what Mr Pound called the *clarity* –
in Hardy's finest verse, is the desolation in the present time, accepted
and condoned, not without pain, as the transitory quality of the human
condition. His language is a language of thorough integrity, of actual
and human relations; his matter is mutability and the place of loss in the
texture of life; his method is the candid submission of the spirit to
recollection, and its alterations of focus. But his 'solid centre' is the
desolation. That is the essence of the most powerful of all his lyrics, 'The
Voice'.

The essence of the poem may be felt in its movement. Gradually the
swinging ballad-tune of the ironically easy opening alters and breaks
down. A listless, unhappy rhythm responds to the listless breeze of the
third stanza. Then the profound and bitter acknowledgement of the
present moment impels a transformation. The cold sense of abandon-
ment, the faltering of spirit and body, the perceptible sound of the wind
bewilderingly confused with the haunting memory of the voice, all these
act out their forlorn movement through the consciousness in the final
breakdown of the rhythm. Characteristically, the temporary impulse of
recovery comes (alongside the piercing despair) in the folk-song accent
of the penultimate line; then even the impulse dies.

> Woman much missed, how you call to me, call to me,
> Saying that now you are not as you were
> When you had changed from the one who was all to me,
> But as at first, when our day was fair.
>
> Can it be you that I hear? Let me view you, then,
> Standing as when I drew near to the town
> Where you would wait for me: yes, as I knew you then,
> Even to the original air-blue gown!

Or is it only the breeze, in its listlessness
Travelling across the wet mead to me here,
You being ever dissolved to existlessness,
Heard no more again far or near?

Thus I; faltering forward,
Leaves around me falling,
Wind oozing thin through the thorn from norward,
And the woman calling.   [285*]

Such moments do not happen often in the history of a·language.

SOURCE: extract from *Thomas Hardy* (London: 1954), pp.
170–81.

Samuel Hynes   The Hardy Style (1956)

Unfavourable judgements of Hardy's poetry have generally been of two
kinds: either philosophical or stylistic. The philosophy has been
criticised either because it is wicked – the 'village atheist' school of
Chesterton – or because it gets in the way of the poetry (Hardy, says
R. P. Blackmur, was a 'sensibility violated by ideas'[1]). The style has
been criticised either because it is not poetic, or because it does not exist.
Maugham described it, writing of his transparent Edward Driffield:

He was for long thought to write very bad English, and indeed he gave you the
impression of writing with the stub of a blunt pencil; his style was laboured, an
uneasy mixture of the classical and the slangy, and his dialogue was such as
could never have issued from the mouth of a human being.[2]

Although this passage is meant to describe the novels, it applies as well
to a common view of the poems, a view which began with the first
reviewers of Hardy's verse, and which still continues. In those early
reviews, certain points were made again and again: Hardy's rhythms
were prosaic, 'arbitrarily irregular,' 'clumsy'; his language was 'needlessly inflated,' 'persistently clumsy,' 'unexciting and unpoetic'; his
range was narrow and monotonous. Even a reviewer as perceptive and
sympathetic as Lytton Strachey gave his approval in a curiously left-
handed way: 'It is full of poetry,' Strachey wrote of *Satires of
Circumstance*, 'and yet it is also full of ugly and cumbrous expressions,
clumsy metres, and flat, prosaic turns of speech.' [See review in Part
Two, above – Eds.] It was, one perhaps had to admit, poetry; but it was

certainly not poetic. 'Poetry is not his medium,' *The Spectator* concluded.
'He is not at home, he does not move easily in it. . . . Mr Hardy is a
master of fiction, but not a master of music.'³ And the *Saturday Review*
added, somewhat more generously: 'So far as it is possible to be a poet
without having a singing voice, Mr Hardy is a poet, and a profoundly
interesting one.'⁴

Any reader of Hardy's poetry must recognise that some of these
judgements, at least, are just. Hardy's poems do seem awkward,
halting, and often ungrammatical. The language ranges from the
dialectal to the technical, and is full of strange, tongue-twisting
coinages. The sentences move crab-wise across the page, or back toward
the subject of the verb: 'They know Earth-secrets that know not I,' a
characteristic poem ends [113*]. And there are awkward inversions,
which Hardy carried to greater lengths than any other poet writing in
English. For example, there is the last line of this stanza from 'At a
Bridal':

> Should I, too, wed as slave to Mode's decree,
> And each thus found apart, of false desire,
> A stolid line, whom no high aims will fire
> As had fired ours could ever have mingled we;   [6*]

These are the things we think of when we think of the typical Hardy
style; and they are all there in the poems. But in justice to Hardy we
must add two substantial qualifications to this idea of his style: that his
poems are not *all* awkwardness; and that awkwardness, like the
melodiousness which he does not have, may be functional in the poem.

The first point, because it is the easiest, we will consider first. It is a
simple fact that, quantitatively speaking, Hardy is syntactically and
grammatically orthodox more often than not. Many of the best poems
are almost conversational in style, and do little violence to prose syntax
or to the rules of grammar. 'A Broken Appointment' is a slight, but
entirely successful, example of this kind of poem:

> You did not come,
> And marching Time drew on, and wore me numb. –
> Yet less for loss of your dear presence there
> Than that I thus found lacking in your make
> That high compassion which can overbear
> Reluctance for pure lovingkindness' sake
> Grieved I, when, as the hope-hour stroked its sum,
> You did not come.

> You love not me,
> And love alone can lend you loyalty;
> – I know and knew it. But, unto the store
> Of human deeds divine in all but name,
> Was it not worth a little hour or more
> To add yet this: Once you, a woman, came
> To soothe a time-torn man; even though it be
> You love not me?   [99*]

One recognises at once that this is a Hardy poem; but 'clumsy', 'awkward' and 'prosaic' are not the right terms to describe its distinctive style. In form it is an answer to the 'blunt pencil' view of Hardy's art. The stanza is a fairly involved one: Hardy uses it with grace, adjusting long sentences to the rhyme scheme easily and employing inversion to make the rhyme only once. Its ease is not quite the ease of prose speech – Hardy always insists on the essential formality of poetry, on what Patmore described as 'the necessity of manifesting, as well as moving in, the bonds of verse' – but this is true of conventional poetry in general, and describes nothing peculiar to Hardy.

It might be easier to define Hardy's style negatively, in terms of what it is not. First of all, it is not melodious or 'lyric' in any conventional sense – only the most tedious (and least typical) of Hardy's poems can be said to sing. His characteristic pace is erratic and abrupt, the pace of thoughtful speech or of spoken thought. In 'A Broken Appointment' this pace is to a considerable extent a function of the syntax, which is slow and involved in the first stanza, and is broken by many stops in the second. The syntax is not particularly odd, and it is not, as it often is in Auden and Eliot and even Shakespeare, ambiguous – one can always establish in Hardy's verse what modifies what. Only one phrase, 'Grieved I,' stands out as a violation of normal order, because, although it is the main clause of the sentence, it is held off for four lines, and because it is inverted where the metre does not require inversion. The withholding of the admission of grief implies a relationship which is common in Hardy – the personal response is consistently subordinated to the situation, the 'I' is introduced modestly, almost apologetically, into an external scene which is the thing in the poem that really matters (in this Hardy is the antithesis of the Romantic poet, who uses the external world as a reflector of himself). As for the unnecessary inversion, one finds it often in Hardy – it is one way of reminding the reader, after a passage of easy prose syntax, that the poem is still operating within 'the bonds of verse.'

Another element in the poem which affects the pace is its sheer oral difficulty; it is hard to read, and impossible to read musically. Hardy rarely uses sound to smooth his poetic texture, but rather, as here, to roughen it (try reading aloud 'Than that I thus found lacking in your make'). The same is true of his arrangement of stresses; though the over-all pattern is generally regular, the exact location of stresses may be puzzling in spots, especially where the compound words of which Hardy was so fond leave the stress hovering over two or three syllables. This oral roughness has led some critics to conclude that he had no ear; but rather, I think, he heard a different kind of music, and a kind which should not sound strange to the modern reader's ear – it is not so different, after all, from the dissonances of Meredith and Patmore and Hopkins, or, for that matter, of Pound and Eliot.

'A Broken Appointment' offers no really outlandish examples of Hardy's peculiarities of diction. There are no neologisms (unless you count 'lovingkindness' and 'hope-hour'), no dialectal or archaic words, nothing to stumble over. Yet the poem is typical in this respect, that from it one can infer no norm of diction – all language, abstract and particular, fresh and trite, old and new, is equally available to the poet. . . .

At this point we can say, then, of Hardy's style that it is assertively unmusical and often harsh, and that this harshness is a function of the manipulation of syntax, sound, and diction so as to defeat lyric fluidity and to restrict the movement of the verse to a slow, uneven, often uncertain pace. The question of the way in which this style can be regarded as functional in the poems remains. The answer lies, I think, in the quality which Hardy praised in Barnes: 'closeness of phrase to his vision.'

The vision in Hardy's case is . . . his sense of the irreconcilable disparity between the way things ought to be and the way they are: the failure of the universe to answer man's need for order. That failure is a constant in Hardy's writing; and because of that failure the idea of poetic order is a very different thing for Hardy from what it was for his predecessors. Hardy says (in 'In Tenebris II') 'if way to the Better there be, it exacts a full look at the Worst' [137*]. The 'worst' is suffering, mortality, change, death – all meaningless in a meaningless, indifferent universe. Hardy did not try to reconcile man to his predicament, or to resolve the evident disparities and contradictions of existence – he merely recorded them: he was, as he put it, 'humbly recording diverse readings of [life's] phenomena as they are forced upon us by chance and change'.[5] The 'worst' was the actual phenomenal world, the way things are. Like other modern poets (notably Pound in the *Cantos* and William Carlos Williams), Hardy restricted himself largely to his vision of the actual, a poetic world without abstract ideals or absolutes, and strove for 'closeness of phrase' to that vision.

One result, and this is also true to some degree of the other poets mentioned, was an uncompromising fidelity to fact and detail ('Oh, but it really happened' was, for him, a valid defense of a poem). One cannot read far in Hardy's poems without noticing the precision of observation, the command of minute detail. Sometimes there is nothing more and the poem seems merely trivial, a description, or more often, since Hardy's method was primarily dramatic, an anecdote; but often detail and vision fuse and support each other, and the poem succeeds. 'A January Night' succeeds in this way, because detail precedes vision and prepares us for it:

> The rain smites more and more,
> The east wind snarls and sneezes;
> Through the joints of the quivering door
>   The water wheezes.

> The tip of each ivy-shoot
> Writhes on its neighbour's face:
> There is some hid dread afoot
>   That we cannot trace.

> Is it the spirit astray
> Of the man at the house below
> Whose coffin they took in to-day?
>   We do not know.   [400]

This is a very characteristic poem, in that all we are allowed to *know* is the substantive situation – the wind, the rain, and the writhing ivy. The dread is in what we do not and cannot know, the forces or the emptiness behind the actual. The poem does not explain anything, nor does it set this particular experience in the context of any system of belief; rather it dramatises man's *inability* to explain, his ignorance and his horror.

Man's ignorance, and his inability to reduce the universe to significant order, are the principal factors in Hardy's vision, and in his poetry. One result, as we might expect, is a style built upon tensions and disparities. These tensions and disparities function in many ways: form against idea, prose syntax against metrical necessity, one level of diction against another, image against image, or image against abstraction. The poetic materials are likely to be heterogeneous, and their combinations apparently whimsical – one rarely feels in Hardy's verse the force of poetic decorum at work. This is odd if one considers the Victorian decorousness of the man, but not strange in the light of his thought. For Hardy's thought, while it had not achieved a system of belief, had freed him from traditional belief, and with this philosophical freedom went a poetical freedom as great, and as empty. Chance rules Hardy's universe, and often it seems to determine his style as well. And why, after all, in a lawless universe should there be laws governing poetry? Why *not* make poems out of clashing incongruities, since this is the way the world is?

This argument seems to lead us to the conclusion that Hardy's poems are good or bad by accident, that he did not really have control of his medium. This critical conclusion did persist throughout Hardy's poetic career, and he was understandably annoyed by it: 'The reviewer,' he complained, 'so often supposes that where Art is not visible it is unknown to the poet under criticism. Why does he not think of the art of concealing art?'[6]

The notion that the machinery and the effort of creation should not be visible in the final work is not an uncommon one – Yeats says much the same thing in 'Adam's Curse.' But Hardy seems to mean something more here. In his aesthetic (in so far as he had one), 'art' usually means the technical finish, the conventions operating within a work; in the remark quoted above he seems to be saying that *his* intention is to eliminate convention from the surface of his work. The acceptance of conventions implies the acceptance of the idea of order which produced them; like other late Victorians Hardy was driven by his rejection of inherited· beliefs to a rejection of inherited poetic methods and to a search for new ones. 'There is no new poetry,' he wrote in his notebook, 'but the new poet – if he carry the flame on further (and if not he is no new poet) – comes with a new note. And that new note it is that troubles the critical waters.'[7] The 'new note,' he makes clear, is the voice of his thought: style is a metaphor for belief.

Like Donne, Hardy was profoundly disturbed by a 'new philosophy,' and like Donne he found in a harsh and jagged style a way of transforming his disturbance into poetry. His gifts were less than Donne's, his intellect less tough, and so the results are less often successful poems. But the relation of style to thought is much the same, and is based on the same perception – that a breakdown of beliefs invalidates the conventional styles in which those beliefs were expressed, and that at such a time the artist, if he is to be true to his vision of reality, must find a personal style for his personal vision.

Hardy defined *style* in his essay, 'The Profitable Reading of Fiction':

Style, as far as the word is meant to express something more than literary finish, can only be treatment, and treatment depends upon the mental attitude of the novelist; thus entering into the very substance of a narrative, as into that of any other kind of literature. A writer who is not a mere imitator looks upon the world with his personal eyes, and in his peculiar moods; thence grows up his style, in the full sense of the term . . . Those who would profit from the study of style should formulate an opinion of what it consists in by the aid of their own educated understanding, their perception of natural fitness, true and high feeling, sincerity, unhampered by considerations of nice collocation and balance of sentences, still less by conventionally accepted examples.[8]

This is, in its essentials, a standard romantic treatment of literary values. The attitudes of the artist – his 'sincerity,' his 'true and high feeling' – are what matter; the literary tradition is hampering convention, and the verbal surface of the poem is mere 'literary finish.' The trouble, of course, is that if you take away the tradition and the literary finish there is nothing left; the most exquisite feeling depends upon words and conventional forms for objective existence. But Hardy never seemed to see this; in his aesthetic, technique was rigorously separated from and subordinated to thought, and thought in turn was a private, almost solipsistic, act. One finds, scattered through his notes, remarks like this: 'My weakness has always been to prefer the large intention of an unskillful artist to the trivial intention of an accomplished one: in other words, I am more interested in the high ideas of a feeble executant than in the high execution of a feeble thinker.'[9] Surely few modern critics would consider this separation of the artist into thinker and executant a realistic one, but apparently for Hardy it was a necessary distinction.

It was necessary, I think, because it could be made into a kind of declaration of independence – independence both from traditional systems of belief which he could not accept, and from the stylistic conventions which he associated with those beliefs. Hardy's poet is a man alone with his 'mental attitudes' and those attitudes are his only guide, the only fit object of his fidelity. Consequently, when he defines *style*, he does so in terms which most critics would probably think more properly defined *tone*, a considerably narrower critical concept. By making style identical with tone, Hardy points up two important and related qualities of his verse – the distinctive personal voice, and the consistently personal point of view. Belief, and the lonely believer, are the coordinates of his poetic reality. Thus a conventional poetic act, a striving after a 'nice collocation and balance of sentences' is an act of infidelity, and a harsh and personal tone the mark of a true heart.

Hardy tried . . . to write monistic poetry – poetry, that is, in which the actual is the only reality, and in which there is no other, invisible world above and beyond the actual, to which the things in a poem refer and from which they derive significance and value. Such a position, consistently held, would seem to have certain necessary effects on a poet's style: he would not use symbols to make reality visible, since only the visible *is* real; he would avoid metaphor for the same reason – metaphor implies that two obviously different objects or events partake in a common reality; he would rather favor direct description, in which a hawk is a hawk and not a handsaw, or similes, which assert the discreteness of the elements involved.

This, in fact, does describe Hardy's practice pretty well. He is neither a symbolic nor a metaphorical writer; in his poems things remain intransigently things. (In the two poems quoted in this chapter, for example, only the second line of 'A Broken Appointment' – 'And marching Time drew on, and wore me numb' – could be called metaphorical, and the metaphor there is mixed and vague.)

But Hardy apparently found the style proper to his belief, like the belief itself, inadequate. If the unseen reality could not come in the front door as philosophy, it could come in the back door as superstition; if it could not clothe itself in symbol and metaphor, it could appear as omen and abstraction – 'our old friend Dualism,' says Hardy, is 'a tough old chap.' Hence the phantoms, ghosts, and dreads in the poems; hence also the presence among the meticulous particulars of abstract words – Crass Casualty, Time, Change – and personifications of the sort that populate the Overworld of *The Dynasts*. These terms have one quality in common: they all refer to the dark, inexplicable side of existence. The superstitions in the poems are all frightening superstitions ('Signs and Tokens' [479] catalogues some of these); the Overworld includes spirits of Pity, Irony and Rumour, but not of Happiness or Joy or Peace.

The tension between particular and abstraction may be spelled out (as in 'Hap' [4*]) or simply implied (as in 'A January Night' [400]); in either case, one area of language qualifies and casts doubt upon the other – they are, in other words, antinomial. This relationship does not, as metaphor does, imply a necessary relationship between the terms – it assumes no order. It simply points to an incompatibility in the nature of things. It is a fundamental stylistic manifestation of Hardy's vision.

We may see a further effect of this vision in the general flatness of Hardy's descriptive language. While description is often sharp and detailed, one rarely feels the shock of recognition that comes from seeing experience in a new light; the light is always the same – Hardy's twilight. He seems to select his modifiers carelessly, as though any syllable would do, and they are consequently often obvious or simply trite (adjectives like *dear, sweet,* and *fine* are among his favorites). Perhaps because things in Hardy's verse are always and only things, he depends for his poetic force more upon action than upon description, upon what things do rather than on what they are. This is just another way of saying what I have said before, that Hardy is essentially a dramatic poet.

Action in poetry may operate in two ways: through dramatic scenes and through the use of verbs and verbals. Hardy's poems are almost always scenic in this sense – figures in a landscape, meeting, speaking, parting, returning. Often the point of view is located outside the action, and the speaking voice is the ironic observer, who records what *he* said and what *she* said, and comments ironically on how wrong they were;

this is essentially the relation of audience to actors. Other poems are dramatic in that they are set as dialogues, often with one voice that of God, Nature, or some other personification of the nature of things. Such situations enabled Hardy to identify the terms of his antinomies with individual characters, and thus to make dramatic the conflict between them.

A dependence on verbal action seems to follow logically from this emphasis on the dramatic; conflict is active, and it can best be established through language denoting action. It is not surprising that Hardy's most striking and original words and phrases tend to be verbs or words derived from verbs; of the 200-odd coined words in the *Collected Poems* half are verbals – words like *aftergrinds, downstairward, outskeleton, self-widowered, unadieu'd*.[10] Many of the barbarisms which have troubled Hardy's critics are simply verbs used as adjectives or nouns: *bleed, float, scan, shines*, for example, all do the work of nouns in the poems. Such coinages, like the superstitions, generally refer to the dark side of existence.

To demonstrate how Hardy's stylistic oddities *may* function to express his vision of the world is not to say that they always *do* function effectively. The ways in which they succeed, and the ways in which they fail, can best be seen by examining in some detail two typical poems – one relatively weak and one very good.

IF IT'S EVER SPRING AGAIN
(*Song*)

If it's ever spring again,
    Spring again,
I shall go where went I when
Down the moor-cock splashed, and hen,
Seeing me not, amid their flounder,
Standing with my arm around her;
If it's ever spring again,
    Spring again,
I shall go where went I then.

If it's ever summer-time,
    Summer-time,
With the hay crop at the prime,
And the cuckoos—two—in rhyme,
As they used to be, or seemed to,
We shall do as long we've dreamed to,
If it's ever summer-time,
    Summer-time,
With the hay, and bees achime.   [548]

One can immediately point to a number of technical flaws in this poem: the multiple and awkward inversions and the comic *flounder-around her* rhyme in the first stanza, the padding in the second (there is no point to the parenthetical *two* in the thirteenth line or in the last three words of the fourteenth, and the final line is entirely filler). Cuckoos rhyme and bees chime to make the rhyme scheme, not because rhyming and chiming are natural to them. The device of repetition is overworked and ineffective; the last lines of the stanzas in particular are feeble as refrains. One may legitimately conclude that the general slackness and ineptness of the poem is simply the result of Hardy's taking on a musical form to which his talents were not equal. Such a form makes metrical demands which simply silence Hardy's characteristic tone of voice – it is striking here that the metrical norm is dominant throughout the poem, and that diction and syntax are wrenched and padded to fit it, whereas in his best poems the opposite is more likely to be the case.

But such a conclusion does not get to the heart of the poem's weakness. The fundamental failure is a failure of tension; the poem is not antinomial, and in the absence of his principal formal element, Hardy goes slack. Dramatically, the poem is all *then*; the *now* is implicit in the title, but it has no existence in the poem itself. We do not see the rustic beatitude of spring and summer in contrast to anything; as observers we have nothing to stand on. Nor do the words themselves work upon each other to produce tensions; the language is entirely the language of conventional bucolic bliss, unqualified by the irony that the actual imposes. The nostalgia which suffuses the poem has no clear origin, and so remains gratuitous and sentimental.

As a contrast to this failure, we may consider one of Hardy's finest poems, 'Bereft':

> In the black winter morning
> No light will be struck near my eyes
> While the clock in the stairway is warning
> For five, when he used to rise.
> Leave the door unbarred,
> The clock unwound.
> Make my lone bed hard –
> Would 'twere underground!
>
>
> When the summer dawns clearly,
> And the appletree-tops seem alight,
> Who will undraw the curtains and cheerly
> Call out that the morning is bright?

When I tarry at market
No form will cross Durnover Lea
In the gathering darkness, to hark at
Grey's Bridge for the pit-pat o' me.

When the supper crock's steaming,
And the time is the time of his tread,
I shall sit by the fire and wait dreaming
In a silence as of the dead.
    Leave the door unbarred,
    The clock unwound,
    Make my lone bed hard –
    Would 'twere underground!   [157*]

Like 'If It's Ever Spring Again,' this is a memory poem, but there the
similarity ends. 'Bereft,' though it employs a fairly involved stanza
form, is not 'musical' – the voice speaks in the accents of despair, not of
melodious nostalgia. As in so many of Hardy's poems, the principal
tension lies in the relation of past and present, but in this case we know
exactly what each term implies. The past means *order*, especially the
orderly relating of time and action; the speaker is the kind of woman
who says, 'There's a right time for everything.' We find this assumption
in each stanza of the poem (excepting the refrain, which images the
present); when 'he' was alive, life was a series of pleasing and
appropriate actions – rising in the morning, supper at night, and a bed
that was not lone and hard. Even the rhythms of these passages 'keep
time.' The present, in contrast, is existence without order, time without
its appropriate action – the clock has run down. The rhythms are
uneven, out of time.

The images in the poem are individually flat and undecorated, the
modifiers ordinary, the verbs exact and literal. As in many of Hardy's
poems, there is little metaphorical use of imagery. The poem depends
rather on the manipulation of carefully selected details – dark and light,
the furnishings of a cottage, a few homely references to the world
outside – which can be taken quite literally. Through these details a
physical setting is created which is detailed and actual; the grieving
widow has a context, and from the context we infer her character – neat,
orderly, diligent, methodical. Because this context exists so precisely,
the refrain can work powerfully against it without metaphor or other
emotive heightening. The unbarred door, the unwound clock are, in
the speaker's world, highly charged symbols of her loss, which is the loss
of the ordering force in her life. But without the carefully composed
literal world of the poem, the symbols would have little power to move
us.

The world of the poem is not, of course, a product of the imagery alone. Rhythm also has its role, as I have suggested, and so does diction. The language is plain and unadorned, almost colloquial (but with a touch of the dialectal, perhaps, in *cheerly* and *tarry*); it is suitable both to the speaker and to the occasion.

We respond to the poem, or we accept what it says about grief, then, because it has, through the integrity of its imagery, its rhythms, and its language, 'proved' to us that that grief is real. By giving us the world of the speaker's past in its bare actuality, Hardy has justified the burden of his refrain and has made a poem which is moving and beautiful.

These examples suggest that while Hardy's style was often an effective medium for the expression of his personal vision, it was severely limited in range. This limitation is essentially the limitation of his vision, for in Hardy style and belief were one. He could not write poems of song or celebration – in his experience he found nothing to sing about and nothing to celebrate. He could neither reason nor argue in verse, and the occasions on which he tried – his 'philosophical' poems – were disastrous. Certain themes and certain aspects of experience were closed to him: religion was something other people believed in, love was only available to him as a theme when it was either betrayed or past, sex was cruelty but never ecstasy, and human happiness was a delusion or a memory made bitter by the unhappy present. Art, politics, urban life – all common themes among his successors – he ignored; his world was the dark side of Wessex, and it was there that he succeeded as a poet.

But Wessex is a private country, and its accent is private, too; if he achieved 'closeness of phrase to his vision' there, it was *his* vision, and no one else's. So, though it is striking, it is perhaps inevitable that so fine a poet as Hardy has had virtually no influence on twentieth-century poetic style. Like Hopkins, he can be imitated, but his style is too personal, too eccentric to be used. Later poets, notably Auden and Dylan Thomas, have expressed their admiration for Hardy's poetry, but the mark of it is discernible in Auden only in his early schoolboy verse, and in Thomas not at all. Hardy died as a poet, as he died as a man, without heirs.

SOURCE: chapter 4 of *The Pattern of Hardy's Poetry* (Chapel Hill, N. Car.: 1956), pp. 56–73).

NOTES

1. R. P. Blackmur, 'The Shorter Poems of Hardy', *The Southern Review*, VI (Summer 1940).
2. W. Somerset Maugham, *Cakes and Ale* (1930), pp. 134–5.

3. T. H. Warren, *Spectator* (5 April 1902).

4. *Saturday Review* (11 Jan. 1902).

5. Preface to *Poems of the Past and the Present*.

6. *The Life* . . . , p. 384.

7. Ibid., p. 300.

8. Harold Orel (ed.), *TH's Personal Writings* (London: 1967), pp. 122–3.

9. *The Life* . . . , p. 310.

10. These are catalogued in an appendix to E. C. Hickson's *The Versification of TH* (Philadelphia: 1931), pp. 120–7.

C. B. Cox and *A. E. Dyson* on 'After a Journey' (1963)

Hardy's first wife, Emma, died in November 1912. After her death, he discovered that she had written three very personal manuscripts about her life. The first two were so distressing to him that he destroyed them. The third, *Some Recollections*,[1] includes reminiscences about Emma's early life. An account of her happy childhood is followed by an enthusiastic description of her first meetings with Hardy. On reading the manuscript Hardy was stricken with remorse, for their later married life had been extremely unhappy. In the early months of 1913, he revisited the places in Cornwall, where their young love had flourished, and 'After a Journey' describes this search into the past. Some of his best poems were written at this time. He composed at least fifty poems concerning Emma during the year after her death, and many of these recall phrases or incidents from *Some Recollections*. She tells how she showed Hardy 'the solemn small shores where the seals lived, coming out of great caverns very occasionally', and this detail Hardy uses in his poem.

> HERETO I come to view a voiceless ghost;
>   Whither, O whither· will its whim now draw me?
> Up the cliff, down, till I'm lonely, lost,
>   And the unseen waters' ejaculations awe me.
> Where you will next be there's no knowing,
>   Facing round about me everywhere,
>   With your nut-coloured hair,
> And gray eyes, and rose-flush coming and going.
>
> Yes: I have re-entered your olden haunts at last;
>   Through the years, through the dead scenes I have tracked you;
> What have you now found to say of our past –

Scanned across the dark space wherein I have lacked you?
Summer gave us sweets, but autumn wrought division?
   Things were not lastly as firstly well
      With us twain, you tell?
But all's closed now, despite Time's derision.

I see what you are doing: you are leading me on
   To the spots we knew when we haunted here together,
The waterfall, above which the mist-bow shone
   At the then fair hour in the then fair weather,
And the cave just under, with a voice still so hollow
   That it seems to call out to me from forty years ago,
     When you were all aglow,
And not the thin ghost that I now fraily follow!

Ignorant of what there is flitting here to see,
   The waked birds preen and the seals flop lazily;
Soon you will have, Dear, to vanish from me,
   For the stars close their shutters and the dawn whitens hazily.
Trust me, I mind not, though Life lours,
   The bringing me here; nay, bring me here again!
     I am just the same as when
Our days were a joy, and our paths through flowers.   [289*]

'After a Journey' is a most suitable poem with which to introduce a study of twentieth-century verse. Both its mood of uncertainty and its personal rhythms point forward to characteristically modern developments. Hardy published his last novel, *Jude the Obscure*, in 1895, and from this time until his death in 1928 devoted himself to poetry. Jude has much in common with the heroes of many twentieth-century novels. He does not have deep roots in his community, but becomes homeless, moving from place to place in search of a fulfilment he cannot find. There is a strong element of autobiography in Hardy's depiction of Jude, and the perplexities dramatised in this novel become the theme of his later verse. On a first reading a poem such as 'After a Journey' might seem a conventional piece of nostalgic writing, but its surface simplicity covers a profound, almost tragic awareness of the enigma of human life. As in Walter de la Mare's 'The Listeners' and Edward Thomas's 'The Sign-Post' . . . the apparent conventionality of theme and treatment hides highly original attitudes of mind. These poets do not employ the experimental techniques of Ezra Pound and T. S. Eliot, but they are similarly oppressed by the loneliness of modern man. They are still using typical romantic language and imagery, but these are transformed by the pressure of personal experience.

Hardy was a young man when in 1859 Darwin's *Origin of Species* was published. The theory of evolution persuaded some writers, such as G. B. Shaw, to believe that civilisation was developing new and better forms, and that we were moving towards a society of supermen. In contrast, Hardy was disturbed by the breakdown of traditional Christian beliefs, and became increasingly pessimistic. He tried to find some rational explanation for the mystery of the universe, but his doubts grew like a cloud over his sensibility. 'After a Journey', like so many of the later poems, considers death with a most disturbing honesty, and offers few consolations. T. S. Eliot and W. B. Yeats succeeded in some degree in reconciling religion with rationalism. Eliot became a Christian and Yeats developed his own individual brand of mysticism. Their verse is not without doubts and equivocations, but in many great poems they escape from pessimism. Hardy, de la Mare and Edward Thomas are typically modern in their acceptance of uncertainty, and this is one reason why they have had so much influence on post-1950 verse.

Recent poets have been influenced not only by Hardy's personal self-questionings, but also by his technique as a poet. Just as the traditional, countryside way of life, celebrated in early novels such as *Under the Greenwood Tree*, breaks down, and characters such as Clym Yeobright, Tess and Jude become isolated, so Hardy's poetic language moves from simple, musical ballads to the individual tone of voice in 'After a Journey'. The importance of Hardy in the development of modern verse has often been underestimated. When the *Collected Poems* were published, Ezra Pound wrote: 'Now *there* is a clarity. There *is* the harvest of having written 20 novels first.' W. H. Auden, Dylan Thomas and Philip Larkin have all testified to their debt to Hardy. Like Browning, whom he studied with admiration, Hardy escapes from the conventional rhythms of Swinburne towards a more conversational, dramatic manner. The voice that speaks in 'After a Journey' is quiet, gentle, melancholy and completely honest. There are no false postures, or bardic pretence, only an uncompromising reflection of deeply moving personal experience. It is this honesty which has particularly influenced Larkin, and poems of his such as 'No Road' and 'Church Going' owe much to Hardy.

The construction of 'After a Journey' provides a good example of Hardy's mature technique. The rhyme scheme – ab ab cd dc – is regular in each stanza, and contributes much to the lyrical quality of the poem. The short, penultimate line, rhyming with the previous one, assists this singing quality of the verse. We are reminded of Hardy's love of music, and that he spent much time in studying metrical forms and in trying to achieve novel sound effects. Lines such as 'Summer gave us sweets, but autumn wrought division' and 'For the stars close their shutters and the dawn whitens hazily' have a rich and poignant music. But this lyrical quality is repeatedly disturbed and broken in the poem, and this innovation points forward to the later development of free verse. The first line of the poem – 'Hereto I come to view a voiceless ghost' – has five clear stresses, and is a normal iambic line; but the second line, personal and questioning, immediately breaks down this regular pattern. The alliteration in 'whither' and 'whim' continues the lyrical effect, but the rhythm is close now to the speaking voice. The words 'will', 'whim', 'now', 'draw', and 'me' are all stressed in some degree. 'Whim' is heavily stressed, and then the last three words have a slow movement, as if Hardy is pondering over this question. In the third line, the movement reflects the experience precisely, and there is no attempt to impose an iambic pattern. The long pauses after 'cliff', 'down', 'lonely' and 'lost' suggest both the uncertain moments of the narrator, following this spirit of his wife, and his emotional condition, not knowing any longer how to move purposefully in this world. The fourth line is typical in its mixture of a lyrical tone with the personal speaking voice. Like nearly all the rhymes in the poem, 'awe me' is a full rhyme, adding to the sense of pattern and musical effect. A break in the movement of the line is made by the two unstressed syllables that lie together at the end of 'waters' and 'ejaculations'. This break in the lyrical flow suggests Hardy's own voice; but the music of this line, one of the most evocative in the poem, is almost beyond analysis. This mixture of lyricism and conversational tone continues throughout the poem. There are many feminine endings to lines – 'draw me', 'awe me', 'knowing', 'going', 'tracked you', 'lacked you', etc. – and these, making the lines drop away at the end, create the prevailing melancholy cadences of the poem. Although the rhyme scheme is constant from stanza to stanza, and the penultimate line is always short, the number of syllables in each line conforms to no fixed pattern. The fifth line, for example, has nine syllables in the first stanza, twelve in the second, thirteen in the third, and eight in the fourth. The arrangement of stresses and syllables accords with the demands of Hardy's experience, and works in opposition to any conventional metrics.

In all his poems Hardy continues to introduce 'poeticism'. There are many words and phrases taken straight from romantic jargon – 'Whither, O whither', 'olden haunts', 'wrought', 'twain' and 'Life lours' – in 'After a Journey'. These archaic words might suggest at a first quick glance that the poem is simple and traditional, recording a universal experience of loss. But the accuracy of the observations, both of the scene itself and of personal emotions, makes this use of language by no means conventional. We see how 'the waked birds preen and the seals flop lazily', and we are given a most poignant description of Hardy's own feelings. As in the poetry of de la Mare and Edward

Thomas; old poeticisms are given a new flavour.

Lyricism and the speaking voice, poeticisms and precise descriptions, combine to present Hardy's dramatic sense of the influence of the past on the present. The poem shifts between the pictures of young love and the situation of the old man, wandering just before dawn through these old familiar scenes. As always in Hardy, the contrast is between a simple, happy past and an uncertain present. Although the poem describes a moment in time, when the poet's memories of his wife are so acute that he feels her presence like a ghost, the moment achieves its rich significance because of its relation to the past. The poem shifts backwards and forwards between past and present, until we hardly know in what period of time we are living. The feeling of transience is overwhelming. As Hardy revisits the cliff, the waterfall and the cave, his experience is almost like a dream, an illusion of the senses. We feel the contrast between his present wanderings and the warm-blooded reality of the past, between the wraith-like spirit who leads him on and the young girl, with her nut-coloured hair, grey eyes and rose-flushed cheeks.

From the beginning the poem is full of uncertainty. The ghost is voiceless, unable to ascribe any meaning to death, drawing Hardy back into the past. The 'unseen waters' evoke a sense of great beauty, but also suggests danger. It is night, and the noise of the sea is like some voice from the other side of life, speaking to him through the darkness of the mind. In the second stanza Hardy recalls the failure of his marriage. Through 'the dead scenes', 'the dark space', he tries to find again the young girl he once loved. With an unequivocal sincerity he writes: 'Things were not lastly as firstly well With us twain . . . ' The archaic language makes this simple acknowledgement of failure profoundly moving. The third stanza begins with Hardy speaking intimately to his dead wife. Their melancholy tone, followed by pictures from the past, remind us of the pathos of the fading of love. The fact that Emma Hardy is dead obtrudes through all the fancies of the poem. The intimate tone is directed to a person who exists in the past, and who can never be recalled. This indicates the correct interpretation of the last stanza. Dawn approaches, and the birds and seals move about with no thought for the past. As in traditional stories, the ghost must disappear at cock-crow. The tender word 'Dear', followed by 'vanish', reminds us that these memories, so powerful at this moment, must also fade. These lines not only reflect Hardy's own loss, but link his grief with the dying faiths of his time. The old romantic certainties, with their glorification of man, have no meaning in the twentieth century. The image of the stars closing their shutters reminds us of much other modern literature, picturing the dying of the light and the birth of despair. Hardy is particularly successful in his poetry in evoking a sense of twilight or gloom. The 'unseen waters', the stars closing 'their shutters', the dawn whitening 'hazily', beautifully suggest the half-light through which he moves.

After these uncertainties and the overwhelming nostalgia for the past, the last three lines become a pitiful cry. He is not the same as forty years ago. The time when 'our days were a joy, and our paths through flowers' is gone for ever. Yet 'despair' is not quite the right word with which to end this study of 'After a Journey'. Hardy concludes the poem by asking to be brought again to such moments when his mind is invaded by the wonder of the past; and there is a quality of stoic acceptance in the honest recognition of the facts of his experience. His journey brings him to the half-light of an incomprehensible world. He rejects all comfortable belief in progress, and shoulders the burden of the twentieth-century consciousness.

SOURCE: chapter 1 of *Modern Poetry* (London: 1963), pp. 34–40.

NOTE

1. Emma Hardy, *Some Recollections*, edited by Evelyn Hardy and Robert Gittings (Oxford: 1961).

L. E. W. Smith on 'The Impercipient (At a Cathedral Service)' (1964)

> That with this bright believing band
>   I have no claim to be,
> That faiths by which my comrades stand
>   Seem fantasies to me,
> And mirage-mists their Shining Land,
>   Is a strange destiny.
>
> Why thus my soul should be consigned
>   To infelicity,
> Why always I must feel as blind
>   To sights my brethren see,
> Why joys they've found I cannot find,
>   Abides a mystery.

Since heart of mine knows not that ease
  Which they know; since it be
That He who breathes All's Well to these
  Breathes no All's Well to me,
My lack might move their sympathies
  And Christian charity!

I am like a gazer who should mark
  An inland company
Standing upfingered, with, 'Hark! Hark!
  The glorious distant sea!'
And feel, 'Alas, 'tis but yon dark
  And wind-swept pine to me!'

Yet I would bear my shortcomings
  With meet tranquillity,
But for the charge that blessed things
  I'd liefer not have be.
O, doth a bird deprived of wings
  Go earth-bound wilfully!

    * * *

Enough. As yet disquiet clings
  About us. Rest shall we.   [44]

A certain ungainliness in the sentence construction of this poem is at first somewhat off-putting; but, on closer inspection, it is just this apparent infelicitousness that gives the poem its complex, tentative, humble tone. Each of the first three stanzas is a complex sentence in which the main verb is witheld. The first two stanzas are almost identical in pattern; two or three noun clauses as subjects of a main verb which comes as the first word of the last line. This noun-clause-subject construction is nearly always awkward in English; it is associated with classical translations, with prayer, incantation, and some parts of the Bible. These two stanzas are private meditations, Hardy bitterly alone among the praying congregation 'at a cathedral service'. Their tone is determined by their construction: their awkwardness is, in part, Hardy's awkwardness. In these first two stanzas his thoughts follow the patterns of the Christian worship, although his sympathies are apart. He is in the congregation, but not with it.

  In the third stanza there is a slight change of focus, which is reflected in the grammatical construction. The main verb, 'might move', is still with-held in the complex sentence, but here it is adverbial clauses that make up the first part of the stanza. The effect is to throw the emphasis on the word 'might', and the meaning behind this word, with the doubt cast by the clauses introduced by 'since', serves to isolate Hardy even further, because we know that 'their sympathies and Christian charity' were *not* moved by his 'lack'.

So in the fourth stanza he is only conscious of himself: 'I am like . . . .' There is still only one complex sentence, but the main verb, 'I am', comes right at the beginning. He is concerned here with his own position and feelings.

The word 'Yet' that introduces stanza five is a grammatical QED after the four complex sentences of the first four stanzas. We are working towards simplicity of statement. Here the sentence is still 'complex', but its form is much more direct, and the balance between the two parts of the sentence throws the emphasis on the word 'But'. The tone here is less tentative: it is direct and clear, with a cutting edge of bitterness. He is, in a way, answering back. But having reached this direct confrontation, he then quietly retreats: the last two lines of this stanza, introduced by the poignant 'O', are a genuine *crie-de-coeur*.

And then follows the utter simplicity and humility of the last stanza. Only two lines are necessary, but there are three simple, reduced sentences. It is this simple grammar that conveys to us Hardy's own simplicity, humility and 'Christian charity'.

The rhyme scheme also contributes to the tone of the poem. There are only two rhymes in each stanza; and one of these, the awkward weak rhyme of *be, me, destiny, infelicity*, etc., runs on through all the stanzas. This helps to unify the whole poem (like the service in the cathedral), but it is significant that it is the weaker rhyme that is repeated: Hardy's position throughout the poem is not a strong one; but his own strength of character comes out in the second, stronger rhyme of each stanza; *band, stand, Land; consigned, blind, find;* etc. The rhymes of the last two lines of the poem follow on from the previous stanza, adding to the simplicity of this quiet close.

The rhythm of the poem is closely related to the development of feeling. In the first three stanzas the basic iambic metre is rarely disturbed; it repeats like the chanting in the cathedral. The rhythm in these stanzas is over longer units, controlled by the form. The run-on lines, divided at the commas, give a wave-like motion: but we feel, possibly because the line-break comes at the stronger rhymes, that we are being led into more restless movement.

There is a small but significant change in the third stanza: the semi-colon in the second line breaks the rhythm abruptly. We begin to feel Hardy's unease. The repeated All's Well, with its capitals, breaks the flow too, preparing us for the slight tone of sad cynicism in the last two lines.

Stanza four, where Hardy feels himself most isolated, is the most eccentric in rhythm. Many of the iambic feet are reversed to trochees giving that uneasy feeling that Tennyson used in the 'Willows whiten, aspens quiver' stanza of 'The Lady of Shalott'.

The fifth stanza begins with the strongest rhythm in the poem: this is, in a way, Hardy's testimony. All the syllables of 'Yet I would bear my short . . . .' have just about the same value, all of them strong. An extra weight is also put on 'But' and 'charge' of line three, and on 'not have be'. This is where the poet's bitterness is most evident. But after this outburst, he settles back to a quiet iambic metre.

The row of asterisks is an unusual device to use in a poem. Here it serves as a barrier between the heat and bitterness of feeling of the first five stanzas, and the humble passion of the last two lines. It is better these two things were kept apart, and with the asterisks Hardy removes himself from the argument. But he still feels deeply, and this comes out in the rhythm of these last two lines, broken into three sentences, with the run-on from 'clings' to 'about us', in which we still feel some of the mud that has been thrown clinging to us. But the quiet 'Rest shall we', with its open, questioning tone, provides a perfect close.

Something of what Hardy thought of Christianity, and his own attitude towards his lack of faith, is indicated by the imagery of the poem. The final 'bird deprived of wings' image seems to show that Hardy was no willing agnostic. Earlier he has said his soul was 'consigned to infelicity', and that he felt 'blind'. The 'faiths' of 'this bright believing band' seem 'fantasies', and their 'Shining Land' seems 'mirage-mists'; but this is only how they appear *to him*; he is no atheist saying they *are* so: the important word is 'seem'. There is no doubt that for Hardy to have accepted Christianity would have been self-deception: the phrase 'heart of mine' meant much to Hardy: by it he means that place in us where we *know*, intellectually, emotionally and instinctively; and here, no Christ 'breathes "All's Well"' to him. (The word 'breathes' makes his approach to religion personal and intimate.)

The difficult thing to assess in this poem, I find, is how far Hardy feels and implies that the 'faith' of 'this bright believing band' is self-deception. The alliteration of 'bright believing band' has, I feel, a slight edge of satire: it is a bit too pat and complacent. 'Shining Land', 'joys', 'All's Well' – it is all too good to be true. The important stanza here is the fourth. The company is 'inland', and yet it can hear 'the glorious distant sea', whereas, to the realist Hardy, the sound is the wind through the dark pine. Here the 'company' is surely deceiving itself. The images, too, are relevant. The 'dark and windswept pine' is a lonely and battered object with which Hardy can identify himself – it is a true Hardy symbol; and although the company says 'the glorious sea', Hardy knows they can use that adjective only because they are 'distant';

if they were near, or if they could imagine it more truthfully, they would know the sea is cruel, stormy and bitter.

But what distressed Hardy even more, and this perhaps implies a failure of faith in the 'believers', is their lack of 'sympathies and Christian charity'. He had been charged with atheism: but it was not true that he wanted to do away with 'blessed things'. It was just that he had looked into his heart, and found, if he was to be honest with himself, he could not believe. The faith was not there. If they were true Christians they would sympathise with his 'lack' and 'shortcomings': they could act out of strength, optimism and faith, but yet they accused him. And then, in the last two lines, in spite of his weakness, pessimism and deprivation, Hardy shows that he is the one who can act with sympathy, compassion and 'Christian charity'.

> Enough. As yet disquiet clings
> About us. Rest shall we.

These two lines could well be a motto for the world today.

We have arrived at the 'meaning' of this poem without attempting anything like a paraphrase. I doubt that a paraphrase could, without going into great lengths, say what this poem is about. It is concerned with investigating that complex no-man's-land between 'belief' and 'lack of belief', and the inter-action of those who believe and those who cannot, especially when it appears that those who do not believe seem to practise the beliefs more faithfully than the 'believers'. This complexity of 'meaning', what the poem is really about, comes through the inter-action of form, tone, rhythm, rhyme and imagery: it is because all these are so closely inter-related that I find this such a satisfying poem. The closer I look, the more moving I find it to be: it engages so much of the reader's attention and sympathies.

SOURCE: essay in *The Critical Survey* (1964), pp. 223–5.

Philip Larkin   'A Poet's Teaching for Poets' (1968)

I had always known Hardy as a novelist when I was young but I hadn't read his poems particularly. I'd always rather assumed with Lytton Strachey that 'the gloom was not relieved even by a little elegance of diction'. But when I was about 25, I suppose, I was in some digs which faced east and the sun used to wake me very early in the morning – you know, about six. It seemed too early to get up, so I used to read, and it happened that I had Hardy's own selection of his poems, and I began to read them and was immediately struck by their tunefulness and their feeling, and the sense that here was somebody writing about things I was beginning to feel myself. I don't think Hardy, as a poet, is a poet for young people. I know it sounds ridiculous to say I wasn't young at 25 or 26, but at least I was beginning to find out what life was about, and that's precisely what I found in Hardy. In other words, I'm saying that what I like about him primarily is his temperament and the way he sees life. He's not a transcendental writer, he's not a Yeats, he's not an Eliot; his subjects are men, the life of men, time and the passing of time, love and the fading of love.

I think most poets who are well-known today have loved Hardy's poems at one time or another. I think Auden has; I think Dylan Thomas did. Vernon Watkins told me that although Dylan Thomas thought Yeats was the greatest modern poet, Hardy was the one he loved. Betjeman clearly loves him; . . . Cecil Day Lewis clearly does; and yet these are all very dissimilar poets. I rather think that they may have found what I found: that Hardy gave them confidence to feel in their own way. When I came to Hardy it was with the sense of relief that I didn't have to try and jack myself up to a concept of poetry that lay outside my own life – this is perhaps what I felt Yeats was trying to make me do. One could simply relapse back into one's own life and write from it. Hardy taught me to feel rather than to write – of course one has to use one's own language and one's own jargon and one's own situations – and he taught one as well to have confidence in what one felt. I have come, I think, to admire him even more than I did then. Curiously enough, what I like about Hardy is what most people dislike. I like him because he wrote so much. I love the great Collected Hardy which runs for something like 800 pages. One can read him for years and years and still be surprised, and I think that's a marvellous thing to find in any poet.

I can't imagine why people say Hardy had no ear. In almost every Hardy poem in the 800 pages, barring one or two about the death of Edward VII and that sort of thing, there is a little spinal cord of thought and each has a little tune of its own, and this is something you can say of very few poets. Immediately you begin a Hardy poem your own inner response begins to rock in time with the poem's rhythm and I think that this is quite inimitable. There are no successful imitators of Hardy. I think Hardy's diction is often quaint – one has to concede that. I don't think it's any quainter than a good many other poets', but often in Hardy I feel that the quaintness, if it is quaintness, is a kind of striving to be accurate. He might say, 'I lipped her', when he means 'I kissed her', but after all, that brings in the question of lips and that is how kissing's done. When Hardy says that a bower is 'roof-wrecked', I don't know whether 'roof-wrecked' is thought to be quaint but it means precisely that the roof is wrecked. It's a kind of telescoping of a couple of images. I think people are a little unfair to Hardy on that. He can often be extremely direct. 'I should go with them in the gloom hoping it might be so.' 'Not a line of her writing have I, not a thread of her hair.' Donne couldn't be more direct than that. . . .

SOURCE: extract from 'A Man Who Noticed Things', in *The Listener*, 25 July 1968; this was an edited version of a conversation with Victor Scannell on Radio 4.

Kenneth Marsden   Hardy's Vocabulary (1969)

. . . Discussions of rare words and peculiar usages, contorted syntax and linguistic mixtures, always occupy a large part of any discussion of Hardy's language. This is natural enough, but probably unfortunate in the long run. In the first place, there is a natural tendency to exaggerate their frequency and their strangeness. (Less than 1 per cent of Browning's 34,746 rhymes are either imperfect or forced, but these have been enough to give him a reputation for eccentric rhyming.)[1] In the second (if one must look for Hardy's weaknesses), it distracts attention from the area of true weakness. The really unsatisfactory work is not the odd, strained, gnarled, 'mixed' poems, but those whose technical accomplishment covers hollowness. Such poems as 'A Bygone Occasion' [557], 'The Rift' [579*], 'I Look in Her Face' [590], 'Could I but Will' [595] and 'I Knew a Lady' [601] are quite vacuous, unless one considers that it is interesting to know that Hardy was influenced by the Victorian drawing-room ballad. Poems such as 'The Two Wives' [600] and 'The Singing Woman' [605] are in their different ways products of the desire to write poems which . . . is part of Hardy's poetical physiology. All these are linguistically smooth and all are ultimately worthless.

The badness of 'My Cicely' [31*], pointed out by several critics, is a special kind of badness – Hardy's. The poem, therefore, has its own attractions, since Hardy's good work as well as his bad depends on – or is an extension of – his personality. (MacDowall, perceptive as usual, calls it 'a curious and shadow-haunted poem'.)[2] Critics never seem to object to 'Any Little Old Song' [665*]; it has appeared in several anthologies and selections (including the Penguin *Hardy* in 1960), but it seems to me to be completely negligible, from its ominous title onwards. The linguistic deadness of this poem is clear enough. It is, however, easy to jump to unwarranted conclusions about Hardy's use of similar language. Mrs Nowottny gives a general account of this problem: 'the difficulty for the critic, especially when there is no conspicuous innovation at the level of vocabulary, is to arrive at an understanding of those processes in the poem which enable familiar words to convey unique quality'.[3]

It is fairly easy to find places where this difficulty has been too much for the critic, or has never been faced at all; for instance, E. Blunden comments:

They [Hardy's poems] have their share of stuffed-owl simplicities, such as the observation in the railway waiting room,

> The table bore a Testament
> For travellers' reading, if suchwise bent.[4]

We can only agree – if this gobbet is accepted as the solitary piece of evidence for the charge; but this is a stultifying procedure. If one reads 'In a Waiting-Room' instead, one finds that it begins in this way:

> On a morning sick as the day of doom
>> With the drizzling gray
>> Of an English May,
> There were few in the railway waiting-room.
> About its walls were framed and varnished
> Pictures of liners, fly-blown, tarnished.
> The table bore a Testament
> For travellers' reading, if suchwise bent.   [470*]

Surely the drabness of the last phrase is in key with everything else? Is not the scene, the situation and the feeling well rendered? Furthermore, is the phrase so drab really? Is there not a subdued irony to it – an implication that nobody will be so bent? This is heightened when we find that the plainest evidence of its having been used is that some commercial traveller ('bagman' is Hardy's word) has been doing his calculations on the Gospel of St John!

Another example, from G. M. Young:

Much might be said of these few stanzas only ['In Tenebris 1']. I will only note: the simplicity of their metrical structure, the perfect carrying-through of the stated theme: contrasted with this, the awkwardness in places of the diction, the obstinate choice – as it seems, for careless it is not – of the lifeless word

> No more that severing scene
> Can *harrow* me . . . [5]   [136*]

This is plainly a more subtle misunderstanding. Young has specifically excluded carelessness and seems to be considering the word in context; but is 'harrow' lifeless and, if not, why does he fall foul of it?

The first thing to notice is that 'In Tenebris I' is not only about despair and 'unhope' but the pain connected with them; 'pain', 'smart', 'scath', 'faint'; next to remember what a harrow does to the ground; then to observe 'severing' in the previous line. 'Harrow' is part of a powerful image cluster, not a lifeless word. We ought to notice, too, the heavy stress on the word; it is not intended to be passed over lightly in any sense.

The short answer to the second question is that Young, typical here of many critics, thought it lifeless because his preconceived ideas about Hardy caused him to expect lifeless diction:

> He was imperfectly educated, cramped by a book-language which he could not shake himself free of, and writing it with a stilted and self-conscious clumsiness. . . .
> His errors are not those of an untrained taste feeling towards a style which will not come. They are errors of practice in following unfortunate models – prose translations of the classics, for example – without perceiving their imperfection.[6]

The danger inherent in this attitude is that when an author gets a reputation for clumsiness the quality of his words may no longer be noticed at all.

. . . most of Hardy's triumphs are poems which subdue difficulties *and* show signs of the struggle; smoothness and ease are frequently danger signals. It would be strange if this were always so; he does have his less idiosyncratic successes, as 'I Look into My Glass':

> I look into my glass,
> And view my wasting skin,
> And say, 'Would God it came to pass
> My heart had shrunk as thin!'
>
> For then, I, undistrest
> By hearts grown cold to me,
> Could lonely wait my endless rest
> With equanimity.

> But Time, to make me grieve,
> Part steals, lets part abide;
> And shakes this fragile frame at eve
> With throbbings of noontide.   [52*]

The linguistic variation here is no greater than is to be expected among
good poems; it is, in fact, one of the few successful Hardy poems which
could be by someone else. (There is a resemblance to Yeats, whose
Song, 'I thought no more was needed', might almost be an answer to it,
since it takes the opposite side in the Body/Soul conflict.)

On the other hand, 'The Pedigree' would be spotted instantly as
Hardy; situation, structure, theme, are all typical. The surprising thing
is that the vocabulary is much less so; a 'Hardy' effect has been obtained
with a standard, consistent, vocabulary. Only when this has been
achieved do the usual peculiarities appear.

> I bent in the deep of the night
> Over a pedigree the chronicler gave
> As mine; and as I bent there, half-unrobed,
> The uncurtained panes of my window-square let in the watery light
> Of the moon in its old age:
> And green-rheumed clouds were hurrying past where mute and
> cold it globed
> Like a drifting dolphin's eye seen through a lapping wave.   [390]

In 'At Castle Boterel' we see something different again; this is a poem
mainly in a very plain style, but at one point it modulates into 'Hardy'
language and out again without incongruity. First come five stanzas of
what might be described as impressive ordinariness; then

> And to me, though Time's unflinching rigour,
> In mindless rote, has ruled from sight
> The substance now, one phantom figure
> Remains on the slope, as when that night
> Saw us alight.
>
> I look and see it there, shrinking, shrinking,
> I look back at it amid the rain
> For the very last time; for my sand is sinking,
> And I shall traverse old love's domain
> Never again.   [292*]

'Time's unflinching rigour' and 'mindless rote' are typical examples of
his philosophical language; 'phantom' is a favourite word; 'ruled' shows

a boldness of metaphor not in evidence elsewhere in the poem. But they arise naturally out of the precise situation and provide a slight generalisation in a very individual poem; which then returns to its concrete situation and language. The two changes of linguistic level are achieved smoothly and the sixth stanza is not at odds with the others.

To show how Hardy's use of language enables his poems to live 'on the dangerous edge of things', as so many of them do, it is necessary to consider a complete poem, 'The Five Students':

> The sparrow dips in his wheel-rut bath,
> The sun grows passionate-eyed,
> And boils the dew to smoke by the paddock-path;
> As strenuously we stride,–
> Five of us; dark He, fair He, dark She, fair She, I,
> All beating by.

> The air is shaken, the high-road hot,
> Shadowless swoons the day,
> The greens are sobered and cattle at rest; but not
> We on our urgent way,–
> Four of us; fair She, dark She, fair He, I, are there,
> But one – elsewhere.

> Autumn moulds the hard fruit mellow,
> And forward still we press
> Through moors, briar-meshed plantations, clay-pits yellow,
> As in the spring hours – yes,
> Three of us; fair He, fair She, I, as heretofore,
> But – fallen one more.

> The leaf drops: earthworms draw it in
> At night-time noiselessly,
> The fingers of birch and beech are skeleton-thin
> And yet on the beat are we, –
> Two of us; fair She, I. But no more left to go
> The track we know.

> Icicles tag the church-aisle leads,
> The flag-roped gibbers hoarse,
> The home-bound foot-folk wrap their snow-flaked heads,
> Yet I still stalk the course –
> One of us . . . Dark and fair He, dark and fair She, gone:
> The rest – anon.   [439]

The first task, undertaken mainly through language, is the neutralising of possibly ludicrous associations, since memories of 'Ten Little Nigger Boys' can be aroused by the poem. This is done mainly by the almost complete cutting out of details regarding the fates of the students; there is only the laconic 'elsewhere' or 'fallen one more'. This avoids the mistake Wordsworth made in 'We are Seven':

> The first that died was sister Jane:
> In bed she moaning lay,
> Till God released her of her pain;
> And then she went away.

The next trouble is that of Stock Responses; there are two possible, based on the Seasons/Life parallel and the 'I am left alone by death of friends' motif. It must be admitted that the poem does depend, to some extent, upon these responses, but they are controlled by a precise use of words; the effect is worked for, and there is no encouragement to the reader to construct his own poem. This is achieved (in contrast to the deaths) by a delicate use of detail. The 'mechanical' nature of the poem's progression is lessened by slight variations; for instance, the changes in the order of the students in line 5.

The key to the first stanza is violence: 'dips', 'wheel-rut', 'passionate-eyed', 'boils', 'strenuously', 'beating'. Thus, one of the stock associations of Spring is used, but the other, delicacy (young tender leaves and so forth), is contradicted. The sparrow, it should be noted, is not a 'romantic' bird. The second, Summer, stanza has for its key, still heat ('hot', 'shadowless', 'swoons', 'sobered', 'rest'). 'Sobered' was originally 'darkened' and it is one of Hardy's good revisions; it is not only exact but provides a link by contrast to the first stanza; 'shaken' sounds violent, but probably refers to heat-haze, not thunder. In the third, Autumn, stanza, the 'hurrying' word is 'press', which is milder than the 'strenuously' of the first stanza and the 'urgent' of the second; the implication of 'briar-meshed' points the same way. The semantic connection between 'mould' and 'press' probably plays its part too.

The fourth stanza, early Winter, is full of quietness, stillness and menace ('drop', 'earthworms', 'noiselessly', 'skeleton-thin', 'fingers'). The earthworm image could have been imitated from Tennyson's *Geraint and Enid*,

> While some, whose souls the old serpent long had drawn
> Down, as the worm draws in the wither'd leaf
> And makes it earth . . .

since both are rather menacing. But the idea is hardly out of the way.

The last stanza, dead of Winter, depends of course upon cold. The visual accuracy of the first line and the aural of the second are both important. There is, I think, a ghostly effect created from 'gibber', via the 'squeak and gibber' of the Roman ghosts mentioned in *Hamlet*. (This may be far-fetched, but the connection was made by me and another reader independently).

Words which have to be considered are 'beating', 'beat' and 'stalk' (which was objected to in 'In Time of "The Breaking of Nations"'[500*]. The primary meaning is 'to march proudly' which is accurate here. The OED adds that it is frequently used of ghosts, plagues, etc., which tends to support the possible implications of 'gibber'. The meaning is different from that of 'stalk' in 'In Time of "The Breaking of Nations"' so Hardy is evidently in full control of this word. With regard to 'beat', 'a course habitually traversed by anyone', the chief points are to note the word 'habitually', and to be unaffected by the modern limitation of the word to policemen. 'Beating' is presumably 'beating a path', though intransitive uses in this sense are rare.

There are a number of compounds in the poem; 'wheel-rut', 'paddock-path', 'briar-meshed', etc. One line has three: 'The home-bound foot-folk wrap their snow-flaked heads'. Frequent use of compounds is one of the marks of Hardy's style, as mentioned earlier. Often they are alliterative, e.g. 'paddock-path', 'foot-folk', and Dr Hickson has a long list of these.[7] (The use of such linked nouns as 'ball and blade', 'sun and shower' is common also, especially in Hardy's poorer poems; for instance, 'And kings invoked for rape and raid/His fearsome aid in rune and rhyme', 'The Sick Battle-God' [64].) Groom points out that some of the examples of compounds he gives (e.g. 'copse-cloth'd', 'coppice-crowned') 'have a certain piquancy and in their context are suggestive of pathos; but of the delicate touch which changes the ordinary into the poetic, they show not a trace'.[8] This is perhaps overstated, but it is hard to disagree with his opinion that Hardy uses them mainly for compression or as 'a useful metrical expedient'.

Here, as often, one must distinguish between use and origin. Dorset dialect – much closer to Anglo-Saxon – undoubtedly could provide a sense of familiarity with compounds: 'if you ask one of the workfolk (they always used to be called "workfolk" hereabout – "labourers" is an imported word)'.[9] 'Foot-folk' is obviously normal enough to anyone with such a background. The frequent use of compounds is, perhaps, one reason for the high proportion of monosyllables in the poem (noted by Evelyn Hardy).[10] Finally, on page 201 of Purdy's *Thomas Hardy: A Bibliographical Study* the reader can see two unpublished stanzas of this poem. They prove that if Hardy often wrote inferior verse he did not always publish it.

Accusations of a monotonous obsession with Death lose much of their sting – and truth – when we see how different in tone Hardy's handlings of the subject are. His elegy on his mother, 'After the Last Breath', is a striking variation on the theme:

> There's no more to be done, or feared, or hoped;
> None now need watch, speak low, and list, and tire;
> No irksome crease outsmoothed, no pillow sloped
>   Does she require.
>
> Blankly we gaze. We are free to go or stay;
> Our morrow's anxious plans have missed their aim;
> Whether we leave tonight or wait till day
>   Counts as the same.
>
> The lettered vessels of medicaments
> Seem asking wherefore we have set them here;
> Each palliative its silly face presents
>   As useless gear.
>
> And yet we feel that something savours well;
> We note a numb relief withheld before;
> Our well-beloved is prisoner in the cell
>   Of Time no more.
>
> We see by littles now the deft achievement
> Whereby she has escaped the Wrongers all,
> In view of which our momentary bereavement
>   Outshapes but small.   [223*]

This elegy is not one of Hardy's pondering poems. The tone, firm but not dogmatic, is that of a man quietly confident that he knows what he thinks and what he is going to say. The form, perhaps based on the Sapphic stanza of Hardy's favourite Latin poet, Horace, is well adapted to this form of speech; the three long lines, slow-moving but free from contortion, are succeeded by the 'clinching' short line which rounds off each stanza, marking firmly each stage in the argument. Hardy frequently ends a poem with a slight variation in the structure and here the final double rhyme provides one.

When considered linguistically, the poem shows a similar care and tone. The first stanza has at the beginning an unbroken run of monosyllables; the change comes with 'no irksome crease outsmoothed', itself an effective mixture since the harshness of 'irksome' is followed logically by the softness of 'outsmoothed', paralleling the action itself. The quiet felicity of 'sloped' is notable, but easy to miss.

Stanza 2 is again largely monosyllabic. The key word both in sound and meaning is 'anxious', emphasising the uncertainty of the mourners as to whether they would be able to carry out their provisional intentions. The heavily polysyllabic opening of stanza 3 contrasts with most of the poem so far, and the contrast is heightened in the third line where the Latinate 'palliative' stands against the flat colloquialism of 'silly face'.

Stanza 4 is, by comparison, a little romantic; for instance, 'savours', 'well-beloved', 'prisoner in the cell of Time'. The fine paradox is striking, however. The final stanza begins with the bold telescoping of 'little by little' to 'littles', followed by the syllabic contrast of 'deft achievement' and two typical Hardyan usages, the personification of 'Wrongers' and the affix-construction 'outshapes'. Finally, 'momentary bereavement' turns this elegy for one person into a *memento mori* for himself and us; the bereavement is but momentary since everyone's time is short.

Despite the serious objections which have been made against Hardy's verbal amalgam, much of his strength is derived from it. If some of his words are rare, they are often fitting as well; if they are dialect, they remind us of what standard English has lost; if archaic, they frequently justify their revival; and if invented, they are sometimes worth the trouble. Hardy's own needs take precedence over the rules of others. This mélange, which does not seem a possible language for any human being, has been made into a personal, living, language. Hardy has created it to enable him to say certain things. He is at the farthest extreme from '. . . the perfect type of English secondary writer, condemned recently but for all time by Henri Davray with his: "Ils cherchent des sentiments pour les accommoder à leur vocabulaire".'[11] Rémy de Gourmont has provided an even more apposite summary: 'Le style est une spécialisation de la sensibilité.'

The places where this personal idiom emerges most clearly are such poems as 'To an Unborn Pauper Child' [91*], 'Nature's Questioning' [43*] and 'A Commonplace Day' [78]. It is significant that these poems have . . . been quoted as examples of excellence in some other category; significant not necessarily of a small number of good poems, but of the way in which the poems are integrated; achievement in one mode accompanies achievement in another. Another poem which shows how an apparently disparate vocabulary has been forced into a personal style is 'In Front of the Landscape'.

Plunging and labouring on in a tide of visions,
    Dolorous and dear,
Forward I pushed my way as amid waste waters
    Stretching around,
Through whose eddies there glimmered the customed landscape
    Yonder and near

Blotted to feeble mist. And the coomb and the upland
    Coppice-crowned,
Ancient chalk-pit, milestone, rills in the grass-flat
    Stroked by the light,
Seemed but a ghost-like gauze, and no substantial
    Meadow or mound.   [246*]

There is obviously much to comment upon here besides the vocabulary. The stresses are strong and yet the rhythm seems fluid and supple enough. There is a rhyming-link, sustained through the poem, by which the fourth line in the first stanza of a pair supplies the rhyme for the second and sixth lines of the second stanza. To attack the vocabulary is only too easy; 'Dolorous and dear' seems too vague to mean anything. . . . There is the peculiar 'customed' and the 'dead' compound 'ghost-like'. But the description, despite its occasional verbal precision, e.g. 'rills in the grass-flat/Stroked by the light' and conciseness, e.g. 'coppice-crowned', is intended to be ominous and generally vague; the idea of moving through a 'tide of visions' would be ludicrous if allowed to become too vivid; 'customed' landmarks are indistinct and unsubstantial. This welding of manner and matter continues throughout: for example, the last two stanzas:

Thus do they now show hourly before the intenser
    Stare of the mind
As they were ghosts avenging their slights by my bypast
    Body-borne eyes,
Show, too, with fuller translation than rested upon them
    As living kind.

Hence wag the tongues of the passing people, saying
    In their surmise,
'Ah – whose is this dull form that perambulates, seeing nought
    Round him that looms
Whithersoever his footsteps turn in his farings,
    Save a few tombs?'   [246*]

Among other things, there should be noted the precise successful use of 'bypast'; the appropriateness of 'body-borne' (Hardy's alliterative compounds often justify themselves); the ambiguity of 'translation'; the colloquial 'wag'; the abstract 'surmise'; the learned 'perambulates'; the semi-archaic 'farings'; and the rightness here of another early vogue word 'looms' (four uses in *Wessex Poems* alone). All these should be noted; and also the way in which these recalcitrant words are yoked together, slaves to Hardy's meaning and intentions.

Mr Southworth observes rather grudgingly: 'Too persistent reading of his poetry dulls one's sense of incongruous or unfelicitous associations of strange bedfellows.'[12] Perhaps Hardy himself should be allowed to answer:

He subjoined [TH in his notebook after a note about *Moments of Vision* – Eds] the Dedication of *Sordello* where the author remarks: 'My own faults of expression are many; but with care for a man or book such would be surmounted, and without it what avails the faultlessness of either?'[13]

SOURCE: extracts from *The Poems of Thomas Hardy* (London: 1969), pp. 160–72, 177–8.

NOTES

1. H. H. Hatcher, *The Versification of Robert Browning* (Columbus, Ohio: 1928), p. 108.
2. Arthur S. MacDowall, *TH: A Critical Study* (London: 1931), p. 245.
3. Winifred M. T. Nowottny, *The Language Poets Use* (London: 1962), p. 105.
4. Edmund Blunden, *TH* (London: 1940), p. 264.
5. G. M. Young, Introduction to *Selected Poems of TH* (London: 1940), p. xxvi.
6. Ibid., p. xiv.
7. E. C. Hickson, *The Versification of TH* (Philadelphia: 1931).
8. Bernard Groom, *The Formation and Use of Compound Epithets in English Poetry from 1579*, SPE Tract No. 49 (Oxford: 1937), pp. 317–18.
9. F. E. Hardy, *The Life . . .* , p. 313.
10. Evelyn Hardy, *TH: A Critical Biography* (London: 1954), p. 134.
11. Ezra Pound, *ABC of Reading* (London: 1934), p. 88.
12. J. G. Southworth, *The Poetry of TH* (New York: 1947), p. 126.
13. F. E. Hardy, *The Life . . .* , pp. 378–9.

Jean Brooks The Homeliest of Heart–Stirrings: Shorter Lyrics (1971)

. . . Whereas the best of Hardy's philosophical poetry is shaped by passionate personal feeling, the cry of unadulterated joy or sorrow which certain theories of poetry regard as indispensable to lyric form seems to be missing, or to exist at low tension, in many of his successful lyrics. Nor can one find the subtleties and ambiguities on which the modern reader of Eliot or Empson has been trained to exercise his talent for the elucidation of mysteries. It is perhaps difficult not to feel a sense of disappointment on first reading, for example, 'Life and Death at Sunrise':

> The hills uncap their tops
> Of woodland, pasture, copse,
> And look on the layers of mist
> At their foot that still persist:
> They are like awakened sleepers on one elbow lifted,
> Who gaze around to learn if things during night have shifted.
>
> A waggon creaks up from the fog
> With a laboured leisurely jog;
> Then a horseman from off the hill-tip
> Comes clapping down into the dip;
> While woodlarks, finches, sparrows, try to entune at one time,
> And cocks and hens and cows and bulls take up the chime.
>
> With a shouldered basket and flagon
> A man meets the one with the waggon,
> And both the men halt of long use.
> 'Well,' the waggoner says, 'What's the news?'
> '–'Tis a boy this time. You've just met the doctor trotting back.
> She's doing very well. And we think we shall call him "Jack."
>
> 'And what have you got covered there?'
> He nods to the waggon and mare.
> 'Oh, a coffin for old John Thinn:
> We are just going to put him in.'
> '–So he's gone at last. He always had a good constitution.'
> '–He was ninety-odd. He could call up the French Revolution.'

[698*]

There are no tricks to discover here. It is difficult for the most ardent student of ambiguity to make the poem carry a meaning other than the one intended by the poet. Hardy has ventured so near the prosaic in matter and manner that one is tempted to think that he set out to prove to himself how much 'poetry' he could do without. Yet, like Wordsworth's deceptively simple 'A Slumber Did My Spirit Seal', the poem grows in depth and richness until one realises that its centrality of theme has subtly changed one's awareness of life.

The observation of a chance encounter between two countrymen, and their fragment of completely natural conversation, seems at first sight too trivial to carry much significance. Yet the prosaic conjunction of two men is made poetic by the conjunction of life and death embodied in their meeting. Quiet acceptance of the eternal rhythms of human life is reflected in their brief unemotional exchange of news. The baby, taking the name of the dead man whose memory reaches so far back into the past, promises for the future the only kind of continuity the human race can hope to attain. Hardy's hawk-like vision, which so often in his poetry and novels sets tiny individual figures in a landscape, gradually extends to link his two speakers, through the old man and baby and the distant figure of the doctor, mediator of life and death, not only to their local social context but also to the whole of human history. Finally these ephemeral human lives are set firmly in the larger rhythms of nature. Their conjunction takes place to the dawn chorus of wild birds and farm livestock. Hardy's affectionate and slow-moving enumeration by species suggests the eternal recurrence of natural things, and with them, of leisurely funeral waggons eternally meeting and passing the hurry of new life. These things go onward the same though Dynasties pass. And the whole of sentient life – birds, farm animals, human beings – is set in the vast timeless context of the insentient universe in which they live and die – the landscape of hill, wood, pasture, copse, and morning mist.

Like so many of Hardy's lyrics, 'Life and Death at Sunrise' (subtitled 'Near Dogbury Gate, 1867') begins with a precise evocation of time and place. The details of the moment when 'the hills uncap their tops' to reveal their reality while human figures emerge from and disappear into the fogs that 'still persist' at the foot, show a naturalist's exact observation of phenomena, yet they are emotionally charged with the imponderable mystery of life and death. Natural features of the landscape, night, and mist arouse deep traditional responses which turn the hills into watchers from an Overworld of unobscured reality, and the foggy lowland into the darkling plain of blinkered human action. Apart from the one simile of the hills as 'awakened sleepers', which brings overtones of resurrection into this poem of life and death, and the personalising metaphors of 'uncap' and 'look', the details of the poem are not of the kind to satisfy the image-hunter. Hardy seems to depend more on factual statement than suggestion; yet the steady piling up of

observed detail of this moment of sunrise manages to suggest more than
the content of the statements. When the scene has been set, human
action appears in the second stanza. The movement of sentient life
counterpoints the stability of the insentient landscape with another kind
of stability – the perpetual recurrence of the life cycle. Things have not
shifted during night; only the individual actors in the drama are likely
to be different. The last two stanzas focus on the two individual figures –
the most important features of Hardy's landscape – to bring the
dramatic immediacy of homely colloquial speech into the descriptive
but as yet non-dramatic scene. At this pivotal point of time and space
evoked by the details of the first two stanzas, no extraneous comment
from the poet is needed to realise the conjunction of light and dark
inherent in the exchange of words.

The effect of the poem springs from the reality of a normal everyday
experience honestly recorded and felt; the moment of insight into our
relationship to the rhythms of the universe from the unflinching
response of Hardy's senses to all facets of the objective world. Lyric
ecstasy gives way to loving fidelity to what he sees and hears; yet this
very devotion to fact produces lyric emotion.

The only way of expressing emotion in the form of art is by finding an 'objective
correlative'; in other words, a set of objects, a situation, a chain of events which
shall be the formula of that *particular* emotion; such that when the external facts,
which must terminate in sensory experience, are given, the emotion is
immediately evoked.   (T. S. Eliot: *Selected Essays*)

In this homely Wessex scene Hardy has found an objective correlative
for his intuitions about life and death. In the simple but precise diction,
the natural speech rhythms straining against metrical rigidity, in the
verse form itself, he has found the means to infect his readers with those
intuitions. While all four stanzas keep roughly to the metrical pattern of
three stresses in the first four lines and six in the last two, the wide
variations in speech stress and number of syllables to the stress make the
movement of each stanza very different. Syllabic and speech stress do
not pull too far apart in the first stanza. As the stability of the landscape
gives way, however, to the eccentricities of human and animal life, the
tension between regular metre and irregular speech stress becomes
more elastic: a crisp six-syllable line of alternating stress and unstress,
such as 'The hills uncap their tops', has grown to nine syllables of
completely natural speech rhythm in

'Well,' the waggoner says, 'What's the news?'

as human speech and movement gradually dominate the insentient natural scene. The 'closeness of phrase to his vision' which Hardy admired in his fellow Dorset poet William Barnes has been achieved here.

The unpretentious nature of both phrase and vision may call for a redefinition of lyrical quality. Hardy himself, in his Preface to *Select Poems of William Barnes*, objected to too severe a classification that would exclude much of the finest English poetry as well as his own characteristic mixture of lyrical, dramatic, narrative, and contemplative elements in the same poem.

> . . . many fine poems that have lyric moments are not entirely lyrical; many largely narrative poems are not entirely narrative; many personal reflections or meditations in verse hover across the frontiers of lyricism . . . the same lines may be lyrical to one temperament and meditative to another; nay, lyrical and not lyrical to the same reader at different times, according to his mood and circumstance . . .
>
> One might, to be sure, as a smart impromptu, narrow down the definition of lyric to the safe boundary of poetry that has all its nouns in the vocative case, and so settle the question by the simple touchstone of the grammar-book, adducing the *Benedicite* as a shining example. But this qualification would be disconcerting in its stringency, and cause a fluttering of the leaves of many an accepted anthology.

Other 'impromptu' definitions are just as wide of the mark. The gnarled and knotted nature of much of Hardy's thought and diction does not accord with the singing quality once thought to be essential to a lyric, though the technical challenge they present to musicians has produced several successful settings, notably Benjamin Britten's 'Winter Words'. There are some exceptions: few people would disagree with Hardy's estimate that 'When I Set Out for Lyonnesse' [254*] has 'the song-ecstasy that a lyric should have', but in general he found 'So little cause for carolings/Of such ecstatic sound' that his poetic impulse took other directions. And though much of that impulse is personal, it is difficult to make 'Life and Death at Sunrise', 'An Unkindly May' [825*], or 'The Sheep-Boy' [764] fit exactly the definition of Ruskin: 'Lyrical poetry is the expression by the poet of his own feelings'. There is too much fact within the feeling for most of his poetry to exist as simple cries of joy or sorrow; too much contemplation for the complete merging of poet and subject that takes place in 'pure' lyric, though 'Weathers' appproaches this rare purity. But the isolated details of experience that he selects to relate in the significant pattern of a poem imply his subjective response where it is not explicit, and the complex of objective reality and subjective response add up to a poetic unity (not invalidated by the contrasts of mood and experience which may be contained within a

single poem) that can be called lyrical, however mixed the genres
within the poem may be.

Hardy's best lyrics are moments of vision that have found their
objective correlative in something close to common experience which
yet evokes the underlying deeper reality that he admired in Turner's
late paintings. All the unremarkable and usually unremarked aspects of
routine life are brought into consciousness by Hardy's penetrating
vision in a search for the attainable significance that does not aspire
beyond the world of here and now. He finds it in the burning of an old
photograph, a car 'whanging' down a country road, a thrush singing in
the gloom of a death-marked landscape at the turn of the century, an
old woman raking up leaves, a girl who 'passed foot-faint with averted
head' the scene of her former love, a boy at midnight on the Great
Western,

> Bewrapt past knowing to what he was going,
>   Or whence he came,   [465*]

a mysterious couple promenading beyond the last lamp on Tooting
Common, whose human quality of sadness immortalises the scene in the
poet's memory, 'the mould of a musical bird long passed from light' in a
museum, the loss of a drinking glass, a broken appointment, a moment
of indecision whether to meet or not, the memory of imperfections in a
face or in social graces, the scene of youthful pleasures, old furniture, a
dream of the loved one in old age, a map on the wall, a family pedigree
which mocks illusions of individual free will and significance, a glance
in the mirror, a visit to his first school, the death of a cat, a superstition
that 'this candlewax is shaping to a shroud', a flash of sunlight reflected
from the coffin of a fellow-poet and friend. Poems like 'After the Last
Breath' [223*] and 'The Announcement' catch the imperceptible
moment when the death of a person makes an undefinable difference to
routine rhythms:

> They came, the brothers, and took two chairs
>   In their usual quiet way;
> And for a time we did not think
>   They had much to say.
>
> And they began and talked awhile
>   Of ordinary things,
> Till spread that silence in the room
>   A pent thought brings.

> And then they said: 'The end has come.
>   Yes: it has come at last.'
> And we looked down, and knew that day
>   A spirit had passed.   [402]

Our awareness of the moment when things have changed their look and quality is enlarged by the quiet prosaic observation of habitual actions that sustain life, the suggestion of regular recurrence in the repetition of the word 'And', the sudden tightening of natural speech rhythms to end the second stanza on three stressed monosyllables which bring expectation of change; the dramatisation of that change, as in 'Life and Death at Sunrise', in colloquial speech; the respectful embarrassed gesture, 'And we looked down' in the presence of the reluctantly-voiced mystery which has brought the larger rhythms of the cosmos into intersection with the ordinariness of the daily round.

Often in Hardy's world, as in Samuel Beckett's, 'nothing happens, nobody comes, nobody goes', as a glance at some of his titles may indicate – 'A Commonplace Day' [78], 'A Broken Appointment' [99*], 'Nobody Comes' [715*], 'She Did Not Turn' [582], 'You Were the Sort that Men Forget' [364]. Yet, like Beckett, Hardy extracts significance from the insignificant. The moment of awareness can be projected as strongly from what does not happen as from a dramatic conjuncture of persons, time and place, as in 'A Commonplace Day':

> Wanly upon the panes
> The rain slides, as have slid since morn my colourless thoughts; and yet
>   Here, while Day's presence wanes,
> And over him the sepulchre-lid is slowly lowered and set,
>   He wakens my regret.   [78]

The poet's attempt to define the quality of an uneventful day begins, characteristically, at the twilight hour, which in many poems – 'Nobody Comes', 'At Day-Close in November' [274*], 'Birds at Winter Nightfall' [115], 'The Darkling Thrush' [119*], and others – carries a traditional emotional charge of loneliness, sadness, loss and regret. The striking metaphor 'turning ghost' gives the lead to 'the pale corpse-like birth . . . bearing blanks in all its rays', and the images of colourlessness which define the insubstantiality of the day. The colloquial 'scuttle' suggests the undignified character of its insignificance in a precise concrete verb which, in true Hardy fashion, is immediately swallowed up like the day itself in the abstract Latinate grandeur of 'the anonymous host/Of those that throng oblivion' and the formal 'ceding his place, maybe,/To one of like degree'. But the cautious colloquial 'maybe' which punctuates the formal phrase and the personification of the day cast doubt on the poet's complete assent to its insignificance.

When the time of day has been precisely set, stanza 2 brings place and person into conjunction with it. The fireside seems to be a favourite spot for contemplation, as poems like 'The Photograph' [405*], 'Logs on the Hearth' [433*] and 'Surview' [662] bear additional witness. The poet's physical presence in the poem by a physical fireside gives authenticity to an experience that can only be made significant by the human capacity to feel and think. His precise, orderly actions reinforce the 'end-of-the-day' atmosphere, which closes in again with the dragging extent of the fourth line, unpunctuated by the pauses that characterise the human action of the previous lines, and the overwhelming alliterative weight of 'beamless black'. In stanza 3 his meditating mind brings human values into fruitful tension with the uneventfulness of the day through pondering on what he has *not* done to make it significant – a characteristic Hardeian affirmation through negation. His relationship as a human being to 'this diurnal unit' is suggested by the compound of cancelling opposites in 'corpse-like birth' and the 'blanks' in its 'rays', for only conscious human action can realise the dormant potentialities that each day is born with. The preponderance of cloddish 'u's and heavy alliterating 'b's and 'd's end the stanza with the brutish thump of the cosmic insignificance which the conscious human mind has to face and transform.

Stanza 4 develops the link between the poem's human consciousness and the dull world he inhabits by the simile of colourless thoughts; outer and inner environments slide, with the long vowels and repetitions of 'n', to one dead level of insignificance, until the positive turn 'and yet'. The humanised image of Day as a dead person returns, in a context which stresses the actualities of place – 'Here' – and time – 'while Day's presence wanes' – and these antidotes to insubstantiality are joined by the most powerful positive of all – human emotion. Stanza 5 moves in closer to the poet's meditating mind to turn over the irrational feeling of regret.

The idiosyncratic rhythm of the overheard voice is now in full swing, with all the stops and starts, slow hesitations, and eccentricities of thought in process, so the stanza can carry such Hardeian medievalisms as 'that I wot of' and 'toward' – which gives a better sense of forward motion than a commoner word. Hardy's unflinching look at the worst in this stanza – the commonplaceness of the day, unmarked by any significant human action that he knows of – is immediately and characteristically balanced in stanza 6 by his tendency to hope for the best and believe that there was some extra-sensory reason for his emotion. The scrupulous hesitancy of 'Yet, maybe' – for he will not pretend to absolute conviction – serves to emphasise the outward swing from the personal to 'the wide world' which began in stanza 5 and is carried on in 'some soul,/In some spot undiscerned on sea or land', and the unpunctuated rush of the 'enkindling ardency' which brings the imagined positive impulse to a soaring conclusion in the last three lines. The fire of matter and manner in this penultimate stanza balances the dying embers of the second; the prefix of the unusual compound 'upstole' gives a lift to the 'waning' imagery that predominated in the first half of the poem. The final stanza does not lose the impetus of the upward lift, though Hardy's respect for truth qualifies the hope of the noble intent by making it potential rather than actual; 'benumbed at birth/By momentary chance or wile' – a misfire. Yet the human emotion of regret for the 'thwarted purposing' of the day which created his moment of vision remains valid, as the most important thing in the poem, and ends it with an affirmation of waking awareness that balances all its corpses. The feeling cannot be explained by reason, but the irrational and supernatural which Hardy's respect for scientific truth rejected intellectually persists in powerful emotional tension with that scrupulously presented truth in the 'undervoicings' of the poem. . . .

Hardy himself was no life-denier. Poems such as 'Let Me Enjoy' [193] and 'Great Things' [414*] bear direct witness to his pleasure in the simple sensuous joys of the world as it is. Even 'For Life I Had Never Cared Greatly' [492] denies the initial denial by admitting the ebb and flow of life's appeal, 'till evasions gave in to its song'. Only a man who loved life in every fibre of his being could feel so keenly the betrayal of its potentialities in the sight of a starving thrush, a blinded bird, or an unwanted pauper child. His inability to put misery out of view is a direct corollary of the intense wish to justify life and joy, and the interaction of these two emotions a major source of his resonant power. Only a man who upheld the value of life and the individual human being is capable of the compassion that begins 'To an Unborn Pauper Child' with 'Breathe not, hid Heart: cease silently,' and consistently negates the negating injunction by the living personal rhythms of his own voice affirming painfully, honestly, against the rigid metrical pattern, the value of human emotion – 'unreasoning, sanguine, visionary' – which

> can hope
> Health, love, friends, scope
> In full for thee; can dream thou'lt find
> Joys seldom yet attained by humankind! [91*]

The affirmation is all the more impressive for refusing to deny the life-denying realities of travails, teens, and Time-wraiths their power and place in human experience. The manuscript shows Hardy's indecision

between 'seldom' and 'never' in the last line. His final choice of 'seldom'
is more accurate; but the hope of joys remains a hope rather than a
conviction. However, its truth is accepted without question because it
has been hardly won through a struggle with life's denials. Where the
tension between what is and what ought to be is missing in thought and
structure, the result is a lesser poem. 'To C.F.H. on Her Christening
Day' and 'The Unborn' make the same indictment of birth, but without
the sense of painful personal involvement that springs from Hardy's
conflicting allegiances to scientific truth and human aspiration. The
beginning of 'To C.F.H.':

> Fair Caroline, I wonder what
> You think of earth as a dwelling-spot,
> And if you'd rather have come, or not?   [793]

pales before the immediate dramatic power of an injunction to stop
breathing. The equivalent question to the pauper child, 'Wilt thou take
Life so?' comes, not as a desultory speculation to start a poem, but as a
fitting climax to the failure of life's illusions set out in the previous
stanza, and it gains resonance from the poet's knowledge, which he
never allows us to forget as he voices his desires for the child, that it is *not*
free 'To cease, or be', but 'Must come and bide'. The prayer for 'good
things with glad' in the last stanza of 'To C.F.H.' is less effective than
the scrupulously cautious hope that ends 'To an Unborn Pauper Child'
because it does not rise out of the travails and teens that invariably
balance good things and glad. The sense of painful personal struggle
towards affirmation of life is less effective in 'The Unborn' [235*],
where it is left distanced and undramatic. The tension in 'the news that
pity would not break/Nor truth leave unaverred' does not come to life in
the verse form, the clichés, the abstractions, the generalised vagueness of
'crowding shapes'. But it can be felt in the anguished hesitations and
broken personal rhythms of a man experienced in life's travails and
teens addressing a potential human being who comes to stand for the
human predicament.

In 'To An Unborn Pauper Child' the Hardeian idiosyncrasies of
rhythm and diction enact what it means to be human, with illusions of
freedom, against the predestination of the verse pattern. It means
dignity and tenderness: Hardy has managed to suggest both by using
the second person singular throughout, hallowed by Biblical and
traditional associations and the intimacy of its continuing usage in
dialect. It means sublimity and simplicity: the rolling Latinate
grandeur of 'unreasoning, sanguine, visionary' and 'Ere their terrestrial
chart unrolls' is followed immediately by short monosyllabic statements. The Revelations image of cosmic power in Stanza IV leads to a

stanza on man's weakness in which only one of the Anglo-Saxon words is not a monosyllable. It means losing the concrete joys of life – 'songsingings' – to ghostly abstractions in the march of Time, and human aspirations to the process of physical decay:

> Hark, how the peoples surge and sigh,
> And laughters fail, and greetings die:
> Hopes dwindle; yea,
> Faiths waste away,
> Affections and enthusiasms numb;
> Thou canst not mend these things if thou dost come. [91*]

It means being part of the cosmic rhythm of suffering as an individual, and as a member of the human race; and it means companionship in suffering, helplessness, and loss of illusion. It means accepting fully the human being's inability to change the nature of things: the dream of doing so as a 'vain vow' – but nevertheless a positive contribution to the value of life, as the hammer-blows on 'Health, love, friends, scope' indicate. It means, finally, feeling the complex emotion that inspired the poem: the love-hate relationship with life; the compassion and reverence for the human individual subjected to its ills; the irrepressible desire to hope for the best while believing that it cannot be, which affirms the significance of life denied to it by the cosmic scheme. . . .

Hardy was no mean poet of great occasions as well as small, as 'The Convergence of the Twain' [248*] can demonstrate, and war stirred him as the most obvious expression of cosmic futility and missed opportunities for lovingkindness. Other poets have written better songs for the men who march away and the girls they leave behind them, and his heart was not in a call to National Service. But few have integrated more successfully an Overworld philosophy of war as an image of tragic cosmic absurdity with the microscopic details of its physical impact on human beings and lesser creatures; as in the impressive 'And There Was a Great Calm', written to celebrate the Armistice of 1918.

> . . .
> Aye; all was hushed. The about-to-fire fired not,
> The aimed-at moved away in trance-lipped song.
> One checkless regiment slung a clinching shot
> And turned. The Spirit of Irony smirked out, "What?
> Spoil peradventures woven of Rage and Wrong?"
>
> Thenceforth no flying fires inflamed the gray,
> No hurtlings shook the dewdrop from the thorn,

No moan perplexed the mute bird on the spray;
Worn horses mused: "We are not whipped today";
No weft-winged engines blurred the moon's thin horn.   [545*]
. . .

He is nearer to Owen in 'The Man He Killed' [236*], where he
emphasises by the very limitations of the speaker's viewpoint the sinister
distortion of communication that abstracts humanity from the ordinary
kindly individual. But the internal rhyming and repetition, the
hesitations of speech that recapture the perplexity of the common
soldier as he tries to rationalise the absurdity of war which turns friend
into 'foe' when they are 'ranged as infantry' on opposite sides, are pure
Hardy. In this poem and 'And there was a Great Calm', Hardy
comments on the significance simple words may be made to carry. They
can be destructive of communication, but he also finds in 'many an
ancient word/Of local lineage like "Thu bist", "Er war"', a more
constructive significance in their similarity to the language that

    they speak who in this month's moon gird
At England's very loins . . .   [498]

Hardy's view of patriotism was unfashionably catholic.

    Then said I, 'What is there to bound
My denizenship? It seems I have found
    Its scope to be world-wide.'   [494]

But it makes a poem like 'Drummer Hodge' more representative of the
universal Unknown Soldier than Rupert Brooke's 'The Soldier'.
Brooke's soldier is narrowly centripetal: his death means only 'that
there's some corner of a foreign field/That is for ever England'.
Drummer Hodge dies for a cause and in a country he does not
understand, beneath foreign stars he cannot name,

        Yet portion of that unknown plain
            Will Hodge for ever be;
        His homely Northern breast and brain
            Grow to some Southern tree,
        And strange-eyed constellations reign
            His stars eternally.   [60*]

Hardy's characteristic unsentimental response to a dead man's physical
relationship to environment, creative and centrifugal, which is reported
with a dignified simplicity and restraint that is indicative of deep

feeling, gives the local lad from Wessex the importance of a citizen of the world and the cosmos that Brooke's 'richer dust' and 'pulse in the eternal mind' cannot compass.

The significance of death in war lies less in the 'glory and war-mightiness' than in 'the long-ago commonplace facts/Of our lives' ('The Souls of the Slain') enshrined in the memory of the living by death's very power to deny. This is the long-awaited revelation whose Pentecostal imagery and elemental setting at Portland Bill, where 'contrary tides meet', as Hardy's note tells us, provide 'undervoicings' of the intersection of the timeless with time that make 'The Souls of the Slain' [62*] a memorable war poem, in spite of the 'senior soul-flame' in incongruous military command of impalpable 'sprites without mould'. In time of the breaking of nations, significance resides in the individual human being asserting the eternal rhythms of life against the abstract negation of death – the transformed body of Drummer Hodge contributing to the true meaning of patriotism; the common soldier puzzling out in his own slow, country way why he killed another common soldier called 'the foe'; 'a maid and her wight' indulging in a passion older than the Anglo-Saxon words, and a man and an old horse engaged in the eternal occupation of taming the earth from which they grew.

Hardy's intensely personal yet universal affirmations of life against the negations of old age and death can perhaps be justly assessed by comparing them with the equally valid but very different affirmations of another poet who wrote some of his finest poetry in and about old age, W. B. Yeats. The insistent question of mortality is raised both in Yeats's 'Among School Children' and Hardy's 'He Revisits His First School' by the discrepancy between the youth of the children and their elderly visitor. In contrast to the detailed realism of the children in their schoolroom that begins Yeats's poem, Hardy's poem gives more prominence to the unwished-for physical presence of the poet, 'standing solidly there as when fresh', than to the children, who exist only as an undefined 'they' of the future in the third stanza. The whole poem develops from the half-humorous, half-apologetic deprecation of his intrusive physical body, unbecoming in its old age, to a fanciful superstition of his return as a ghost.

> Yes; wrong was the way;
> But yet, let me say,
> I may right it – some day. [462]

The ghostly image, 'beglimpsed through the quaint quarried glass/Of green moonlight, by me greener made', is more acceptable and more in harmony with place and children than the reality, but in spite of its whimsical treatment, Hardy can admit no transformation of the reality except through death.

To Yeats too the harsh reality of 'a sixty-year-old smiling public man' in the midst of children is one that cannot be denied. Yet 'Both nuns and mothers worship images'; the changeless conceptions of love-blinded eyes defeat the physical negation of 'Old clothes upon old sticks to scare a bird'. The poem, more complex than Hardy's single lyrical mood, develops from the realism of the encounter with children and nuns through a reverie on the poet's beloved Maud Gonne as a child and as an elderly woman, to an extended statement of his personal philosophy that ends in a symbolic image of tree and dancer which reconciles the mortality of the individual with the recurring cycle of life to whose changeless image the individual contributes her changing body.

> O chestnut-tree, great-rooted blossomer,
> Are you the leaf, the blossom or the bole?
> O body swayed to music, O brightening glance,
> How can we know the dancer from the dance?

Hardy makes the point more simply, and more physically, in 'Heredity':

> I am the family face;
> Flesh perishes, I live on,   [363*]

and many of his lyrics (for example, 'At Waking' [174*], 'Thoughts of Phena' [38*], 'He Abjures Love' [192*]), realising the bleakness of life without illusions, clearly recognise the value of images to worship.

There can be sad acceptance, but no reconciliation to perishing of the flesh in Hardy. Grief is the one note that suffuses 'I Look Into My Glass' [52*], which presents the dissonance between passions still strong and the ageing physical body. There is none of the rage that batters the language and rhythm of Yeats's 'The Tower':

> What shall I do with this absurdity –
> O heart, O troubled heart – this caricature,
> Decrepit age that has been tied to me
> As to a dog's tail?
>   Never had I more
> Excited, passionate, fantastical
> Imagination, nor an ear and eye
> That more expected the impossible –

The passion of imagination that is so strong in Yeats is able to call up 'images and memories' of those who had peopled his environment, and of his own literary creations; and to leave to 'young upstanding men' those qualities which had affirmed him as a man – his full acceptance of both body and soul, his pride, and faith that 'Death and life were not/ Till man made up the whole'

> And further add to that
> That, being dead, we rise,
> Dream and so create
> Translunar Paradise.

The strongest passion in Hardy is of human affection, as the second stanza of 'I Look Into My Glass' bears witness. No triumph of imagination or compulsion on his soul to 'study/In a learned school' (Yeats) could make the distress of 'hearts grown cold to me' (Hardy) 'seem but the clouds of the sky' (Yeats). Yet the value of his passion is affirmed just as strongly through his sadness at its loss as Yeats's through his more complex assertion.

Hardy had no faith in a translunar Paradise to leave to anyone. Like Camus, he can leave no more than the experience of having known plague (by which Camus here means death) and remembering it,

. . . of having known friendship and remembering it, of knowing affection and being destined one day to remember it. So all a man could win in the conflict between plague and life was knowledge and memories . . . how hard it must be to live only with what one knows and what one remembers, cut off from what one hopes for! (Camus: *The Plague*)

Hardy has achieved this miracle of integrity by accepting Camus's definition of the double face of knowledge: 'Knowing meant that: a living warmth, and a picture of death'. His ability to touch the two chords simultaneously puts him in the front rank of elegiac poets. His first wife's death in 1912 released his full poetic power in the elegiac vein; but the death of a lesser creature suffices to bring out Hardy's idiosyncratic affirmation of living warmth through a vivid picture of its negation by death. 'Dead "Wessex" the Dog to the Household' [907] misses fire, like some of his philosophical poems, because the mouthpiece – Wessex himself – is beyond the suffering his death causes, the verse form is rather too jaunty for its subject, and there are few concrete details about the dog or his relationship to Max Gate to give the quality of the loss. But in 'Last Words to a Dumb Friend', the tenderness of immediate memory recreates through tightly-controlled couplets and directly-felt observations the dead cat's relationship to his human family and environment. The natural first reaction of any pet-

lover, never to have another, followed by factual details of the
impossibility of blotting out his memory by blotting out 'each mark he
made', rises to a deeply personal, creative meditation on the relationship of any living creature to the negation of death:

> Strange it is this speechless thing,
> . . .
>
> Should – by crossing at a breath
> Into safe and shielded death,
> By the merely taking hence
> Of his insignificance –
> Loom as largened to the sense,
> Shape as part, above man's will,
> Of the Imperturbable.

The negation inevitably calls up the affirmation of the value of life; the
empty scene speaks of the importance of the missing figure.

> And this home, which scarcely took
> Impress from his little look,
> By his faring to the Dim,
> Grows all eloquent of him.

We are left with the harsh reality of knowledge, and the inextricably-
linked pain and triumph of human memory and emotion that enshrine
the significance of life in its relation to the physical fact of death:

> Housemate, I can think you still
> Bounding to the window-sill,
> Over which I vaguely see
> Your small mound beneath the tree,
> Showing in the autumn shade
> That you moulder where you played.   [619*]

But Hardy, perhaps, like Camus's Tarrou, would have called that
winning the match.

SOURCE: extracts from *Thomas Hardy: The Poetical Structure* (London: 1971), pp. 49–57, 59–62, 75–80.

Thom Gunn 'The Influence of Ballad-Forms' (1972)

John Crowe Ransom has called Hardy a Victorian Poet, and it is certainly true that Hardy wrote quite a lot of his poetry during the Victorian era. Even though his first book of it was not published until 1898, many of his poems in later volumes are followed by nineteenth-century dates. And the characteristics of his poetic style, for better or worse, are fully defined in all he wrote before 1900. It improves, but it does not become different in kind. On the other hand we often find Hardy treated like Hopkins as one of the first of the moderns; he and Hopkins, in fact, are the poets we usually find at the start of an anthology of twentieth-century English poetry. And, unlike Hopkins, he lived well into the twentieth century, for if he was born eight years after the death of Sir Walter Scott, we may notice that toward the end of his life he was reading Proust, whom he both influenced and outlived. So we can find good reason for thinking of Hardy as either a nineteenth-century poet or a twentieth-century poet.

Yet most of the time his poetry is of either century only in rather superficial ways. It is true that there is a lot of Victorian subject matter and that he produces a lot of Victorian ideas: the social scene is often one that we recognise from novels of the time, and there is much made of evolution, loss of faith, and the death of God. But in his most successful poems (and it is by these that we must define him) the social background is not usually very important, and the ideas are present only in such a general way that they do not belong to specifically Victorian thought. Rather, what we may find in his best poetry is an emotional reaction to ideas, which can be a very different matter.

It is also true that when we come to a poem like 'The Convergence of the Twain', we can find writing like this, in which he describes the shipwrecked *Titanic* at the bottom of the sea:

> Over the mirrors meant
> To glass the opulent
> The sea-worm crawls – grotesque, slimed, dumb, indifferent.
>
> [248*]

The image may remind us, a touch, of Tennyson or Beddoes. But they would have used it in connection with psychological breakdown, whereas Hardy uses it to show how those most powerful in society are in the end completely powerless before the processes of nature and time. It is a theme as characteristic of other centuries as of the nineteenth – we may think of the fall of magistrates, or of the sea's defeat of Sir Patrick

Spens. The statement and the feeling (to put it in another way) do not really belong to any specific time because they are commonplaces of every time. But – we may point out – there is an abruptness, almost a brokenness to the tone, a savagery to the language, that we like to think of as typical of much twentieth-century poetry. Again, though, if we look at the passage closely and in context, we see that it is acting in concert with explicit general statements, in a completely traditional and unfragmentary way, very far from the ways of that generation of modernists with which Hardy's life span overlapped.

Perhaps my thought might be clearer if I were to take a complete poem. Around the middle of Hardy's collected poetry comes a poem called 'In Time of "The Breaking of Nations" ', and it is about the start of the First World War. It has been often anthologised, but it is easy to underrate because of the simplicity of its expression, and of what may strike the reader as an obviousness to the sentiment.

> Only a man harrowing clods
>   In a slow silent walk
> With an old horse that stumbles and nods
>   Half asleep as they stalk.
>
> Only thin smoke without flame
>   From the heaps of couch grass;
> Yet this will go onward the same
>   Though Dynasties pass.
>
> Yonder a maid and her wight
>   Come whispering by:
> War's annals will cloud into night
>   Ere their story die.   [500*]

I wouldn't find the style of this poem very easy to date if I were to come across it printed anonymously. It is direct and economical, without drawing attention to itself, though the eye hesitates on what seem at first a couple of weaknesses in the diction. But, as often in Hardy, what at first may seem weak turns out in the end to be a strength. One of the words is 'stalk' – surely, we think, it entered the poem only for the rhyme, but then we realise, with our attention fully upon it, that the word does properly indicate the stiff, ungraceful movement of the man and the old horse over the bare earth and, by implication, over the centuries. The phrase 'a maid and her wight' may jar us too, though only slightly: why these archaisms, we ask, when a phrase like 'a girl and a boy' would do as well? But of course the slight archaisms take us out of the specific year when the poem was written, and help to suggest those patterns of human and vegetable behaviour that the poem is about.

For between these two images – the one of resigned human labour to keep the land fruitful and the other of human love which will end by making the body fruitful, there is the even more powerful and much more ambiguous one, of couch grass, the perennial weed, that invades the fields humans have cultivated, and will always continue to do so, and that has been gathered in heaps to burn by the humans, who continue their temporary defeats of it. Humans survive, and *it* survives, in spite of the burning, survives through its very neutrality, like the 'slimed sea-worm'. It burns in 'thin smoke without flame' – that is, not violently but continuously. The image is brief, but sharp, and the struggle between man and the simplest forms of life is like a parody of all wars. Or, better, we could say that all wars are like a parody of it, it being the more elementary struggle.

All flesh is grass: we war against the couch grass as we war against each other: yet the wars will never completely succeed, and various human activities will always continue. Put like this, the poem would amount to no more than truism, but it is saved from such by the succinct clarity of the images of the harrower and the burning weed. The general assertions belong equally to the nineteenth and the early twentieth century, but in essentials the poem belongs specifically to neither. And the same can be said of pretty well all of Hardy's best poetry. John Crowe Ransom has said:

Either he was not influenced by the current styles of poetry that were admired in his lifetime, or else he was not adaptive and could not change from the style which he came into at the outset, as into a style that suited him. For the one reason or the other, he continued in it, though he widened its range.[1]

He continued in it. That is, he didn't go through the dramatic developments of style that we find in many of the writers who have been of most weight for modern readers. James and Yeats have their early, middle, and late styles, but Hardy found quite early a way of writing large and open enough to last him for a long life-time, and in which he could realise most of his greatest poems.

The reason he is of neither century is the obvious one. The single important influence on him is that of the Ballads, and the majority of his poems derive either directly or indirectly from them. Donald Davidson, writing of the novels, said that 'the characteristic Hardy novel is conceived as a *told* (or *sung*) story, or at least not as a literary story; . . . it is an extension, in the form of a modern prose fiction, of a traditional ballad or an oral tale.'[2] If this is so of his prose, how much more obviously it is of his poetry. From beginning to end of his collected poems we find ballads of all varieties, from the laborious 'The Dance at the Phoenix' [28], through the fine melodrama of 'A Trampwoman's Tragedy' [153*] to the grotesque dialogue of 'Her Second Husband Hears Her Story' [840*] in his last book, where a woman in bed with her second husband tells him how she prevented her drunken first husband from making love to her, by sewing him into the sheets of the bed and thus inadvertently smothering him to death. (As the second husband remarks in the last line, 'Well, it's a cool queer tale!')

The ballad so dominates his poetry that when we come to such poems as 'I Need Not Go' [102] or 'I Say, "I'll Seek Her" ' [172], we know at once, before we perceive the more direct hints at identity, that the girl in each of the poems is a *dead* sweetheart, because the writing is such that we are given ballad expectations, and we sense that – as in 'The Unquiet Grave – the living man is still in love with the dead girl. We have a similar kind of expectation when we start reading 'Who's in the Next Room?'

> 'Who's in the next room? – who?
>   I seemed to see
> Somebody in the dawning passing through,
>   Unknown to me.'
> 'Nay: you saw nought. He passed invisibly.'
>
> 'Who's in the next room? – who?
>   I seem to hear
> Somebody muttering firm in a language new
>   That chills the ear.'
> 'No: you catch not his tongue who has entered there.'
>
> 'Who's in the next room? – who?
>   I seem to feel
> His breath like a clammy draught, as if it drew
>   From the Polar Wheel.'
> 'No: none who breathes at all does the door conceal.'
>
> 'Who's in the next room? – who?
>   A figure wan
> With a message to one in there of something due?
>   Shall I know him anon?'
> 'Yea he; and he brought such; and you'll know him anon.'
>   [450*]

I don't remember my first reading of this poem. But I am pretty certain that I recognised its pattern by the time I reached the end of the first

stanza. Who 'passed invisibly' but Death? This is what I mean by
ballad expectations. I am not even sure, explicitly, where these
expectations come from, being unable to find a precise parallel in any
ballad I can remember. The unnamed visitor could of course be a god
or an angel, but there are reasons already to be found in that first stanza
for our thinking it something less exalted, something fearful yet
commonplace, more suited to the tone of the ballad. For we have to
remember that gods and angels make virtually no appearance in the
Ballads.

Why then, if we were to come to the poem fresh, without even
knowing it was by Hardy, do we think of ballads, given the facts that it is
not a narrative and that it is not in any kind of ballad metre? First, I
would say, because there is a suggestion of the homely riddle – the riddle
being, in the first stanza, 'what is a presence but invisible?', and in the
last, 'who collects dues yet is not a tangible person?' Such riddles belong
to all folk lore, but particularly occur in ballads. Secondly, the poem
consists of a dialogue – the first four lines of each stanza spoken by one
person, the last lines being the ambiguous answers of the other. The
speakers are distinct – the first voice is close to panic, its tone is urgent
and suspicious, the second is more measured, and on the whole rather
laconic. They are distinct, but we do not know the sex, age, or situation
of the first speaker, and of the second we cannot even be sure that it is a
mortal: still less is there any suggestion of personality in either. (In the
ballad of 'Edward', similarly, there is no suggestion of personality in the
voice of either mother or son.) Lastly we think of ballads because of the
complete simplicity of language – a simplicity both cause and effect of
the author's impersonality: for though he is in fact artful and
sophisticated, all the artfulness and sophistication are concealed within
the form of the ballad dialogue.

If we can get all this from the first stanza, what does the rest of the
poem add? The whole point of the form is that the speaker should ask
three questions and get the answer No and that in the final stanza the
question should be answered Yes. The poem depends on the pattern of
the build, the increasing horror of understanding, all the more because
we are familiar with the pattern from ballads and fairy tales. I have
suggested that the poem seems more simple than it really is. The
plainness of the language is so tense and controlled that a word that is
only slightly unusual can have a disproportionately chilling effect, –
e.g. the word 'firm' in the phrase 'Somebody muttering firm' already
'chills the ear', even before we are told that it does. There is the brilliant
impetuous clumsiness to the first line of each stanza, and by contrast the
measured tone of each last line, the poem ending with an almost
contemptuous (and almost epigrammatic) dismissal of the questioner:
'Yea he; and he brought such; and you'll see him anon.' There is

nothing you can do about it, human being, with all your panic and
nerves and longing for explanations.

The poem suggests, without melodrama, all the terrors and strangeness implied by the folk personification of death. Homely and familiar
materials, expressed in simple language, are used to produce primitive
and rather complex emotions. The poem could not have been written
without the old Ballads on which it is consciously modelled. . . .

I would now like to discuss a poem, 'During Wind and Rain', in
which, while it is wholly Hardy's own, the strengths and potentials of
the ballad are more completely and energetically used than in perhaps
anything else he wrote. What is more, as I hope to show, the genuine
ballad mystery is its lifeblood.

> They sing their dearest songs –
> He, she, all of them – yea,
> Treble and tenor and bass,
>   And one to play;
> With the candles mooning each face. . . .
>   Ah, no; the years O!
> How the sick leaves reel down in throngs!
>
> They clear the creeping moss –
> Elders and juniors – aye,
> Making the pathways neat
>   And the garden gay;
> And they build a shady seat. . . .
>   Ah, no; the years, the years;
> See, the white storm-birds wing across!
>
> They are blithely breakfasting all –
> Men and maidens – yea,
> Under the summer tree,
>   With a glimpse of the bay,
> While pet fowl come to the knee. . . .
>   Ah, no; the years O!
> And the rotten rose is ript from the wall.
>
> They change to a high new house,
> He, she, all of them – aye,
> Clocks and carpets and chairs
>   On the lawn all day,
> And brightest things that are theirs. . . .
>   Ah, no; the years, the years;
> Down their carved names the rain-drop ploughs.   [441*]

The first stanza firmly establishes the pattern, and it is a very detailed one. Most of each stanza consists of a picture showing the activity of what seems to be a growing family. We never know at any point how many there are in the family, and that is not important, but the activities show them in harmony – in the first stanza literally in musical harmony. The vagueness about their number is clearly deliberate, and contrasts with the precision of observation that shows elsewhere. 'Treble and tenor and bass,/And *one* to play' or 'The candles mooning each face' – that is, the light does not completely illumine, like the sun or an electric lamp; it illumines only what is directly in its path, and leaves other surfaces in a clear-cut shadow. The second stanza shows them all in a different kind of activity – clearing moss from the pathways, an occupation similar to that of burning couch grass, a quiet clearing of space in nature so as to make room for human assertions. In the third stanza the activity is of breakfasting out of doors – again there is specificity where it is needed to make the picture clear ('With a glimpse of the bay'), and a lack of it where it is not needed – we still do not know how many there are in the family now, though it sounds as if it is still growing. And we do not know exactly what the pet fowl are. But the generalness of the family and the generalness of the pet fowl are part of the same point – for the family's harmony is based on certain general rhythms of life which are also those of birds and animals. This takes me three-quarters of the way through the poem, but I have still not described it all. Each picture of activity is cut short by 'Ah, no' and an exclamation about 'the years,' for the scenes are pictures from the past, and they are being recalled 'during wind and rain,' and each final line consists of an image from the present, an image of the natural destructiveness of the storm. 'How the sick leaves reel down in throngs.' – 'See, the white storm-birds wing across.' – 'The rotten rose is ript from the wall.' The language is suggestive, pictorial, and ominous. As contrasted to the ordered and harmonious health and ease of the family at their music, the leaves 'throng', they are sick, they go through a drunken dance of death. The movement is slow, the final lines being packed with difficult consonants, so that we cannot read them very quickly, and in one of them there is also a heavy alliteration. What is more, these final lines rhyme with the first lines of the stanzas, separated rather than joined by the five intervening lines. Separation is also the point of 'Ah, no', the words immediately preceding: for this set of images is a complete denial to the other set describing the family.

We have the pattern then: a contrast between past and present through two sets of images, and we have a loose narrative progression in the first set (those to do with the family). Comment is *implied*, only, by a certain complexity in the juxtapositions between the two sets. For the disturbing fact is that if we find the rhythms of the busy and burgeoning family to be 'natural' ones, we have to admit that the rhythms of the storm denying them are equally natural.

And so we come to the last stanza, which superficially seems to follow exactly the same pattern. The first image, of the family is once again of lighted, airy, spacious activity, but the tone is here deceptive. They are moving house:

> Clocks and carpets and chairs
> On the lawn all day,
> And brightest things that are theirs.

It is an extraordinary picture, suggesting highlights on polished wood and clockface in the open sunlight. But wait – the first line was 'they change to a *high* new house', and the high new house might be the outdoors itself. All the circumstances are omitted, we are not told how or why their furniture should be left *all day* out of doors (though it seems to me possible that they are being evicted). Whatever is happening, it is odd enough to constitute a strong hint that the pattern is broken, the harmony is only apparent, and the family is in some way ended: and the mystery is all the greater in that the scene is as bright and airy as the other scenes that came before it, yet it may be the start of tragedy. As usual, it is followed by the denial, because even this scene is lost in the past, but it is in this stanza that the two sets of images (those to do with the family and those to do with the storm) come closest together in their import. The image from the past is bright, and the image from the present is dark, but the first implies calamity, and the second is of annihilation. And, in this final line, for the first time the image from the present refers directly to the remembered family:

> Down their carved names the rain–drop ploughs.

'Ploughs' suggests not only the movement of a raindrop in a furrow, but also its obliterating action. Time and the elements are actually beginning to wipe out even their names and memories: the storm of the present is merely a most destructive embodiment of time and its inevitable process of ruin and denial.

I would like to suggest that the strength of this poem is directly related to the presence of . . . three kinds of ballad-omission. . . . First in the narrative: there is even less linking of narrative than in 'Sir Patrick Spens'; instead there is a loose progression, for what we are given is a series of scenes which we must link for ourselves. Secondly there are the omissions of motive and character: we are never told the circumstances of the family, even the approximate number of people in it, nor is there any differentiation made between its members, and we are not given any reason for their 'change' in the last stanza. The third kind of omission . . . is far the most difficult for a modern writer to manage, and it succeeds largely because of the way Hardy has managed the two other kinds – there is an almost complete omission of social and historical context, and what remains is there in primitive simplicity but without any false naivety. The family amounts to an emblem of human fruitfulness, of the whole of human life as it should be – but, amazingly, it is done without portentousness. On the contrary, Hardy presents it with clarity and modesty: we believe in the family first and only later realise how inclusive is its presentation. The emerged mystery is the subject of the poem: life in memory co-existent with death in the present. And though the poem is far from being a direct imitation of a ballad, the Ballads have been indispensable to its writing, and it is almost inconceivable without them.

The ballad is the chief native source of our literature, and it remains a body of poems that has been constantly drawn upon as a means of renewal. For the Elizabethans the original Ballads were still a live form, and we have extracts from current ballads in Elizabethan and Jacobean plays, and sophisticated, clearly 'authored' ballads like the patriotic ballads of Drayton or the anonymous 'Tom o' Bedlam'. By the eighteenth century the ballad seemed an escape into the exotic from a literature that appeared to have become over-polite and over-urbane. In the nineteenth century it influenced in some sense almost every poet of importance. And in the twentieth the form has been at least tried out by many poets from Pound onward. At present it is probably more healthy as a living and popular form than at any time in the last two hundred years: most obviously in the ballads of Bob Dylan; but the Beatles's 'Eleanor Rigby' is a perfect urban equivalent of the traditional ballad, and Robert Hunter's words for the Grateful Dead or Robbie Robertson's for the Band are good ballads and good poems by any standard.

The traditional ballad, in fact, being a source, contains material enough for endless draughts, and is not only the indirect source for most of the short poems in English literature, but the direct and conscious source for poems as different as a song by Shakespeare, a song by Blake, the Lucy poems, 'The Ancient Mariner', 'The Lady of Shalott', 'Who's in the Next Room?', 'Miss Gee', and 'The Ballad of Hattie Carrol'. The writers of different times may be searching for different things, but they can find them, or think they find them, in the ballad.

Josephine Miles has examined very brilliantly how the ballad has been used as a means of renewal. In the eighteenth century she finds it 'blurred' with Spenser to become part of the eighteenth century 'sublimity'. On the other hand, she says,

in the nineteenth and twentieth centuries there was a strong urge away from epic and epic scope and upholstery, toward depth, delicacy, and implication. And here again, other forces in the ballad seemed to serve: not its lords and ladies of high degree this time, but rather its quick and implicative narrative style, which got rid of adjectives in favour of verbs, let objects do the work of persons, and saw persons in basic family relation and in basic simple confrontation.[3]

I need scarcely point out how aptly all that Miss Miles says here applies to Hardy. She is not, in this passage, speaking of him, but it reads like a description of 'During Wind and Rain'. (Though I would still insist that if the urges away from and toward are common to Hardy and other nineteenth-century poets, he goes about them in a different way from any of his contemporaries.)

The characteristic of Hardy's poetry that seems to place it most firmly among that of his contemporaries is that it is narrative poetry. One of the major concerns of Victorian poets was to find a modern substitute for the epic, whether in longer attempts like the *Idylls of the King* or *The Ring and the Book*, or in shorter narratives – and certainly one way in which they tried to find it was through ballads. There is, too, a temptation to think of Hardy as a novelistic poet, but I would suggest that, though some poems are, as we shall see, novelistic in presentation, we think of him so because we are remembering that he did not start publishing books of poetry until he had published almost the last of his many novels. Though in truth, as Donald Davidson showed, the novels themselves derived from ballads. Such poems as 'Who's in the Next Room?' or 'During Wind and Rain' go back to the same sources as *Far from the Madding Crowd* or *Tess*. There is a single-mindedness in Hardy's attachment to the ballads – even though he may have made nineteenth- and twentieth-century emphasis in them – that is greater than that of any of his contemporaries. Without their ballads and ballad-influenced poems there would still remain a major part of Browning's or Tennyson's work, let alone Swinburne's, Arnold's or Hopkins's. But without such poems there would be practically nothing of Hardy's poetry left, and I hope to show how the influence of the Ballads continues even into his most personal poems.

I am convinced that all good writing (as well as some bad) is the product of obsession. Hardy's mastering obsession, in his prose as well as in his poetry, was a regret for the past. I would call it nostalgia if the word didn't imply something enervating. On the contrary it was the source of his strength – that is, the strength of his best poetry, and of the ideas most powerfully realised in it. Not the didactically presented ideas, the Pessimism, but the ideas implicit in and inseparable from such a poem as 'During Wind and Rain'. In any case it is incontestable that a large majority of his poems deal with a calling up of the past, usually combined with a regret for its passing, whether it is a public past (as in the ballads to do with the Napoleonic wars), or private (as in the poems of 1912–13 about his first wife), or a kind of combination of the two (as in 'During Wind and Rain').

There is a poem of his called 'Old Furniture', two stanzas of which sum up his feeling about the past in much of its complexity:

> I see the hands of the generations
>   That owned each shiny familiar thing
> In play on its knobs and indentations,
>   And with its ancient fashioning
>   Still dallying:
>
> Hands behind hands, growing paler and paler,
>   As in a mirror a candle-flame
> Shows images of itself, each frailer
>   As it recedes, though the eye may frame
>   Its shape the same.   [428*]

He was prepared to follow those frail images, those hands behind hands, for their own sake, but also as means of defining the present. Surely there has been no poet, even in medieval or Elizabethan times, who was more obsessed with the fact that the important and vivid Now slides immediately into the past, 'first memory, then oblivion's swallowing sea.' ('The To-Be-Forgotten' [110*]). We live in the present, but we are conscious creatures, and we are weighed down by memories, which are all partial losses, and which will one day become total losses. He records not as 'a momentary stay against confusion' but as a momentary stay against loss. And there is a poignancy running right through his most robust poetry from the knowledge that it *is* only momentary.

For the poetry is almost always robust, never fretful or neurotic. He particularly records his own losses as only important because they are a part of other people's losses. It is never the poetry of personality: nothing could be further from him than the Confessional poetry that was all the rage in the U.S. and England a few years back. He must have been a genuinely modest man. His first person speaks as a sample human being, with little personality displayed and with no claims for uniqueness – with as little distinguishing him beyond his subject matter, in fact, as distinguishes the personages of the ballads beyond their actions.

So he was obsessed by the past, and he finds the ballads (and forms derived from them) the perfect repository for his laments about passing time. To sum up Hardy's poetry as 'laments for the past' may seem to be rather limiting it, but after all a lot of the poetry most firmly enduring from the last three thousand years consists of exactly that. And as I have tried to show, the feeling of his poems is often one of a *general* regret: the family in 'During Wind and Rain' may have been a family he knew, it may not, but in any case the poem works for us as an evocation of possibilities which are now no longer possibilities.

But of course he was not confined to such general laments. I say 'of course' because nowadays Hardy's best-known poems are probably those to do with *personal* loss, the poems of 1912–13 about his first wife. I would like to take now a poem that is not one of this group, but which certainly seems to deal with an incident from Hardy's own past and is immediately less generalised in theme than those discussed so far.

NEAR LANIVET, 1872

There was a stunted handpost just on the crest,
    Only a few feet high:
She was tired, and we stopped in the twilight-time for her rest,
    At the crossways close thereby.

She leant back, being so weary, against its stem,
    And laid her arms on its own,
Each open palm stretched out to each end of them,
    Her sad face sideways thrown.

Her white-clothed form at this dim-lit cease of day
    Made her look as one crucified
In my gaze at her from the midst of the dusty way,
    And hurriedly 'Don't,' I cried.

I do not think she heard. Loosing thence she said,
    As she stepped forth ready to go,
'I am rested now. – Something strange came into my head;
    I wish I had not leant so!'

And wordless we moved onward down from the hill
    In the west cloud's murked obscure,
And looking back we could see the handpost still
    In the solitude of the moor.

'It struck her too,' I thought, for as if afraid
    She heavily breathed as we trailed;

Till she said. 'I did not think how 'twould look in the shade,
  When I leant there like one nailed.'

I, lightly: 'There's nothing in it. For *you*, anyhow!'
    – 'O I know there is not,' said she . . .
'Yet I wonder . . . If no one is bodily crucified now,
  In spirit one may be!'

And we dragged on and on, while we seemed to see
  In the running of Time's far glass
Her crucified, as she had wondered if she might be
  Some day. – Alas, alas! ·   [366*]

This is an anecdote, and is aiming at something very different from the other poems we have looked at so far – a circumstantiality, a uniqueness of the remembered incident. The dated title suggests that we are to treat it as a bit of autobiography, but we would do so anyway – the oddness of the incident and the prosaicness of most of the style, in combination with the depth of feeling, would be enough.

For all the verse form, which with its alternating short and long lines slightly resembles ballad-metre, it is less like a ballad than the other poems discussed. It is something like an incident from a novel, but nevertheless the ballad hovers over it, and certainly Hardy is still making use of some of the ballad's great lessons.

The first is in the narrator's sense of himself. He is almost completely impersonal. The girl's emotion emerges quite explicitly, in her speech, but the man's is largely implied: first, by the fact that he should remember something so apparently trivial, and secondly by the poem's movement – until the last line. He is participant as well as narrator, certainly, but he is essentially the first-person participant of the ballads, the general man, not different or special like the Romantic narrator nor obliquely boasting about the extremity of his emotions like the confessional narrator, but experiencing the feeling any sensitive man would feel in his place.

Until the last two words of the poem. – And here we have the omission, the great implicative lacuna, which carries the full force of emotion hitherto held in, and which it seems to me is related to the omissions of the ballads. We have the presaging of the metaphorical crucifixion, then simply 'Alas, alas!' A lot has been left out, but we do not need to know any more. It is like Sir Patrick Spens's misgivings followed by the image of the cork-heeled shoes. The worst fears have been justified, why go on?

There is another characteristic to the poem, however, and it is far from the ballads – in fact it is close to the late nineteenth century novel,

Henry James's as well as Hardy's. There is what seems like a literal transcription of the fragmentary and incomplete speech and emotion. The speech is hesitant and interrupted, like real speech. I have mentioned that the style is at times prosaic – such an effect is deliberate, and part of the poem's effect. We labour into the poem, indeed. The first line is:

> There was a stunted handpost just on the crest.

Hardly mellifluous writing. What is more, in spite of the naturalistic rendering of the speech, in spite of the prosaic patches, there are also certain phrases (all ending lines and thus needed for rhymes) which I can only call Hardyisms: 'dim-lit cease of day', 'the west cloud's murked obscure', and 'the running of Time's far glass'. Peculiar and un-euphonious, and close to poetic cliché. There is an awkwardness to such phrases that F. R. Leavis has remarked reminds us in their amateurish-ness of the Poet's Corner in some provincial newspaper.

This brings up the whole question of awkwardness in Hardy's poetry. It is of two kinds: the deliberate and the inadvertent. Poems like 'Who's in the Next Room?' and 'During Wind and Rain' contain little awkwardness of style, but they are (like the best poems of many poets) not quite typical of Hardy's work as a whole, which is marked by peculiarities of diction, metre, and structure.

There is a famous passage in his notebooks, dated 1875. He is speaking of prose-writing, but it is clear how it applies to (and comes from) his thinking about poetry:

> The whole secret of a living style and the difference between it and a dead style, lies in not having too much style – being, in fact, a little careless, or rather seeming to be, here and there. It brings wonderful life into the writing . . . . Otherwise your style is like worn half-pence – all the fresh images rounded off by rubbing, and no crispness or movement at all.
> It is, of course [he is speaking of prose-writing], simply a carrying into prose the knowledge I have acquired in poetry – that inexact rhymes and rhythms now and then are far more pleasing than correct ones.[4]

There is a certain naivety to these remarks, and indeed they could be rather dangerous advice if taken literally. You can imagine someone writing his poem and then deliberately roughing it up a bit. And you recall Kenneth Rexroth's remark: 'There is always something a little synthetic about Hardy's rugged verse. The smooth (poems) seem more natural somehow.'

I have said that Hardy doesn't strike me as a very Victorian poet, but of course no one can be completely outside his time, and we have to realise that though so much of his poetry is different from that of his

contemporaries, he is with them in reacting against Tennysonian
mellifluity – in fact he is with Hopkins and Bridges rather than with
Swinburne. They are reacting against such writing as:

> And on a sudden, lo, the level lake
> And the long glories of the winter moon.

These are beautiful lines – on the whole too beautiful. We think more
about the liquid 'l's than of water or moonlight. At the same time it's
worth noting that the first line of 'Near Lanivet' is a barbarous kind of
reaction: in 'there was a stunted handpost just on the crest,' we think
more of the 'st' sounds than of the lovers labouring up the hill.

The word to stress in Hardy's prose note is 'life' ('it brings wonderful
life into the writing'). Hardy, for all his mournfulness, is mournful
because he delights in the particulars of the present as much as a
William Carlos Williams, but unlike Williams he can see their loss
impending even as he delights in them. The particulars may be slight
and ephemeral, but he records them with precision and vividness:

> The rain imprinted the step's wet shine
> With target-circles that quivered and crossed,   [478]

or, elsewhere:

> The twigs of the birch imprint the December sky
> Like branching veins upon a thin old hand.   [735]

If these two images are not positively uneuphonious, they are not that
elegant-sounding either. But why should we care? They present things
with immediate authority. Hardy's poetry is crammed with such
images. It is one of the great pleasures of reading it that we are likely to
come across them at the most unexpected moments.

Hardy's awkwardness, whether completely deliberate or inadvertent
or even a funny mixture, comes from a concern for authenticity. It
usually succeeds when his stylistic concern is subordinated to his
concern for exact depiction of his subject. (Not surprisingly, you could
say the same of Tennyson). Rexroth's criticism is on the whole just,
though there are exceptions to it. And I think 'Near Lanivet' as a
complete poem is such an exception. The poem is full of oddities, but
those that do not succeed are small ones, and those that do are part of
what is after all a pretty odd incident. A better statement of Hardy's
conscious aesthetic would be his own sentence when speaking of Tess
Durbeyfield's face: 'It was the touch of the imperfect upon the intended
perfect that gave the sweetness, because it was that which gave the

humanity.' His poetry is never as smooth as Tennyson's or Campion's but the small imperfections have their own sweetness when they are a genuine part of his subject matter, because they indicate a faithfulness to its humanity. . . .

SOURCE: extracts from 'Hardy and the Ballads', *Agenda* (London: 1972), pp. 19–24, 28–39.

NOTES

1. John Crowe Ranson, 'Honey and Gall', *The Southern Review*, VI (Summer 1940), 12.
2. Donald Davidson, 'The Traditional Basis of TH: Fiction', in A. J. Guerard (ed.), *H: A Collection of Critical Essays* (Englewood Cliffs, N.J.: 1963), p. 15.
3. Josephine Miles, *Eras and Modes in English Poetry* (Berkeley, Calif.: 2nd edn), p. 108.
4. F. E. Hardy, *The Life . . .* (London: 1962), p. 105

David Cecil The Hardy Mood (1974)

My title may be found misleading. [My] subject . . . is Thomas Hardy's personality, its pervading mood and flavour, as revealed in his art. Such a survey should include his novels and poems: his genius appears in both. It is characterised by two strains. On the one hand he was a story-teller incurably interested in the human drama; on the other he was a poet whose temperament and views of life were of the heightened imaginative kind which more commonly utters itself in verse. His work exhibits both strains. The poems are often stories too, and the novels are notable for scenes of a 'poetic' beauty and intensity. I wish I could discuss both. But . . . I must choose . . . I will confine myself to the poems.

Lately it has been the fashion to rate these higher than the novels. I do not agree: for me Hardy needs the length of a novel like *The Mayor of Casterbridge* to display his majestic genius to the full. But the poems reveal it with an equal intensity. Sir John Betjeman thinks him the greatest poet England has produced for a century. Myself I shrink from ranking poets in this way. Poets are not tennis-players competing with one another at the same game, so that one can be judged to have won and the other to have lost. But certainly Hardy's double achievement is stupendous. He is one of the very great English writers.

A great 'Romantic' writer; he was a child of the Romantic Movement with a romantic attitude to his art. This means that his work is openly personal. The great poets of the pre-Romantic Ages, though in fact diverse and individual, were not consciously so: consciously they simply aimed at cultivating what were generally recognised as the accepted qualities of all good poetry. It was not till the Romantic Period that the poet began to feel it a duty to be 'true to himself', writing only of what meant much to him, and in his own way. Hardy's work shows that he took this for granted. All his life he wrote poems – he enjoyed writing poetry better than novels – and he wrote them for his own satisfaction, and without making any great effort to get them published. Moreover his characteristic unit was the short personal poem, the immediate impression of some passing inspiration taking shape as a song or anecdote or meditation.

This might seem to imply that he was an egotistic writer. Mistakenly; for though it is true that he wrote only about what especially happened to interest him, these things did not include Thomas Hardy: he was not self-absorbed or introspective. In fact, his works do reveal his personality more fully and truthfully than do those of a professional egotist like Byron. The professional egotist, acutely conscious of the impression he is likely to make, edits himself in order to make an intended impression. The result is that he seldom produces an accurate likeness. Not so Hardy, who simply and truthfully gives voice to his unedited feelings. These are sometimes autobiographical feelings, as in the memorable poems he wrote expressing the emotion that swept over him after his first wife's death. But even these poems contain no self-analysis, let alone any touch of exhibitionism. They are spontaneous unselfconscious cries of the heart.

For the rest his subject-matter is directly connected with his own experience. He writes about the places he knew, about Dorchester and Weymouth and the Wessex countryside, and about incidents that had taken place there in the past or present. These places and incidents are described realistically and circumstantially; they are never filtered through a poetic convention. Sitting idle at home, or out on a casual stroll, Hardy would suddenly find the creative spirit stirring within him: something made him feel sad or amused or reminiscent in such a way as to impel him to embody his feeling in verses which he wrote down for his own pleasure and for others to read if they felt so inclined. He did not certainly expect this to happen; indeed, to the end of his life he was surprised at other people's interest in his poetry. Max Beerbohm told me of a talk he had had with the octogenarian Hardy about a new literary magazine that had been just started by some young men. 'I sent them a poem', said Hardy; 'and', he added with naïve pleasure, 'they have taken it!' Since he was by this time by far the most famous and respected of living English authors, their acceptance was not to be wondered at. But it did genuinely astonish Hardy, not only because he was modest but because to him his poems were so private and personal a matter that he could not get used to the idea that they might interest other people.

The poems divide themselves into various categories representing different phases of his thought and feeling. There are the pure lyrics: Hardy was a born singer like Burns or Blake, in whom a feeling sometimes soared up irresistibly in a flight of song. He was also, as I have said, a story-teller inspired like an ancient ballad-writer to tell a tale in the heightened tone and recurrent rhythm of verse. His verse stories like those in the ballads are strange and dramatic. Hardy thought they ought to be. He once said, 'A story must be exceptional enough to justify its telling. We tale-tellers are all Ancient Mariners, and none of us is warranted in stopping Wedding Guests (in other words, the hurrying public) unless he has something more unusual to relate than the ordinary experience of every average man and woman.' Here he is speaking of his stories in prose. He meant it even more emphatically of his stories in verse. To write in metre is to sing rather than to speak. No one is inspired to sing of the flat and commonplace.

Finally, lyric and dramatic inspirations are very often deployed by Hardy in such a way as to illustrate a third strain in him, the reflective speculative strain. He generalises from small incidents to draw conclusions about the universal plan. These conclusions, apparent also in his novels, are grand and melancholy. They are grand because man's relation to the universe is the grandest possible subject. They are melancholy because Hardy took a melancholy view of such a relation. He was born sad, tender-hearted, and unhopeful. 'When I was a little boy', he once said, 'I even hated seeing boughs lopped off trees, I thought it must hurt them. I will never forget the horror I felt when I first saw a dead bird – and when I was fifteen I remember lying out in the sun one day and wishing that I might never grow older. I wanted always to stay just as I was in the same place with the same friends.' Temperamental sadness was increased by circumstances. He was brought up in nineteenth-century agricultural Dorset when the conditions of life there were peculiarly hard. Children were soon made aware of the harshness of nature, of cold and fog, and rain and wind and snow. They learned about man's harshness too. Wages were very low; man-traps were set for poachers; a man could be hanged for stealing a sheep. Hardy saw two hangings before he was sixteen. Further, he grew up in a transitional period when England was changing from an agricultural to an industrial economy. This induced in his apprehensive spirit a feeling of insecurity. His insecurity was also spiritual; for the nineteenth century saw the fading of that unquestioned religious faith which had given men spiritual solace and confidence even if their lives were hard. Hardy lost his faith, and deeply regretted the loss: for it left him with a sense that man was the helpless victim of inhuman forces which drove him forward towards no certain end, and were indifferent to his sufferings. Man's instinctive feelings of love and pity, which Hardy valued above all things, had, it seemed, no significance in the universal scheme. Hardy's view of the human predicament was tragic and ironic; tragic because it involved so much misfortune, ironic in the contrast he noted between what man hoped and wished for and what generally befell him. His irony appears in some of the names he gave to his collections of poems, *Satires of Circumstance* and of stories, *Lifes Little Ironies*.

For a typical example of his irony let me recall to you the poem 'Ah, Are You Digging on My Grave?' In this a woman lying in her grave hears someone digging in the earth above, and wonders whether it is a relation or the man she loved planting flowers of remembrance. The poet replies that it is neither; for everyone, even her enemies, have become indifferent to her memory: it is only her little dog who is digging. For a moment this news raises her spirits, only to lead to disappointment:

> 'Ah, yes! *You* dig upon my grave. . . .
> Why flashed it not on me
> That one true heart was left behind!
> What feeling do we ever find
> To equal among human kind
> A dog's fidelity!'

> 'Mistress, I dug upon your grave
> To bury a bone, in case
> I should be hungry near this spot
> When passing on my daily trot.
> I am sorry, but I quite forgot
> It was your resting-place!' [269]

Summarised in cold print, Hardy's view of life would suggest that his poems are depressing reading. Perhaps they ought to be; but they are not. Books that depress are written by those who do not respond to life, who are unable to enjoy or appreciate or love. Hardy on the contrary was unusually able to enjoy and appreciate and love. Indeed his tragic sense comes from the tension he feels between his sense of man's capacity for joy and his realisation that this is all too often disastrously thwarted. Nobody can describe pleasure better than he can. The parties in his novels, in *Far from the Madding Crowd* and *The Woodlanders*, are the most festive in our literature, and he can express their spirit equally well in poems. Listen to him singing the delights of drinking and dancing and light-hearted love in 'Great Things' [414*], the best poem about pleasure I have ever read.

Hardy's appreciation of beauty is as acute as his sense of pleasure. It is most apparent in his descriptions of the Dorset landscape, vivid, circumstantial, and made romantic by his imaginative sense of the past. He sees village and town, peopled by the picturesque ghosts of their inhabitants stretching back through Napoleonic days and Elizabethan days and medieval days, to those of the ancient Romans and still further back to prehistoric man. He is even more poignantly aware of recent ghosts – the ghosts of people he himself has known. He is pre-eminently a poet of memory, of personal memories evoked by a tune, a picture, a page from an old book, even a fleeting effect of light. These are often happy memories, so that the emotion expressed in the poems is characteristically mixed, blending pleasure in what is remembered with sadness that it is past. This mixed emotion shows at its most acute in his love poems. Once or twice he wrote a love poem expressing pure rapture ('When I Set Out for Lyonnesse' [254*]). But unqualified joy is rare in his love poems. More typical and even more beautiful is 'The Voice' [285*], where past joy is recalled with poignant bitter-sweet regret.

The poems I have referred to illustrate Hardy's manner as well as his matter. This manner is remarkable for the way it blends the realistic and the imaginative. There is a great deal of the realistic in it. Hardy never employs a deliberately poetic diction. He uses the same words as he would use in prose, and to describe the same prosaic scenes. Yet the effect is far from prosaic. For his use of these words and his vision of these scenes is soaked in the dye of his strange imagination. The stories he tells are odd, the incidents that fire his fancy are freakish. How like Hardy to have written a poem about himself sitting by the fire on a snowy night, all unaware that some fallow deer behind him are gazing in at the lighted window ('The Fallow Deer at the Lonely House' [551*]). It is at the same time a true incident, and a strange one. He loved Gothic architecture, and his taste in everything is 'gothic', delighting in grotesques and gargoyles. For him, as for so many romantics, strangeness is an essential quality of beauty.

This taste for strangeness contributes to make his manner as well as his matter very individual. Certain writers did influence him; Browning, who provided him with examples of the dramatic lyric expressed with a gothic grotesqueness, and William Barnes, with his lyrics about rustic life in Dorset. Metrically Hardy seems to have been influenced less by poems than by music. His metres, lilting and varied, recall the country dance tunes of his day. As a boy along with his father he played

the fiddle at local dances, and he loved the tunes all his life. Their
rhythms echo through his verses:

> Who now remembers gay Cremorne,
>   And all its jaunty jills,
> And those wild whirling figures born
>   Of Jullien's grand quadrilles?
> With hats on head and morning coats
> There footed to his prancing notes
>   Our partner-girls and we;
> And the gas-jets winked, and the lustres clinked,
> And the platform throbbed as with arms enlinked
>   We moved to the minstrelsy.   [165*]

His diction is equally characteristic. As I have said, it is prosaic but it
also manages to be odd. Hardy seems to take pleasure in introducing
into his poems words at once queer and unpoetic such as 'domicile' or
'stillicide'. The effect of these unusual locutions is not always happy.
Hardy's oddness leads to odd failures. Indeed, as much as Wordsworth
himself, he was an unequal poet. Like Wordsworth he seemed unaware
that a very prosaic sentence sounds comic when set to the recurrent
rhythms of verse. . . .

Sometimes too Hardy fails to fuse the divers elements of his
inspiration. Song, story and reflection clumsily jostle each other to the
disadvantage of all three. His reflections are especially troublesome in
this way. On to a lyric or a story he will tag a moral which is implicit in
what has preceded it, and is only weakened by being openly stated.
More creator than critic, he often fails to understand both the laws
governing the art of his choice and the nature of his own talent. The
result is that he is at his best only in a minority of his poems. But in these
imagination and realism reinforce each other to achieve something
uniquely memorable. As an example in his lighter vein, take 'Weathers'
[512*]. No Elizabethan song is more irresistibly lyrical than this, but
where among Elizabethan songs would we find so detailed and accurate
an evocation of the English country scene, with its sharp-eyed
observation of the drops on the gate bars, the rooks that 'in families
homeward go'.

These are picturesque features that go easily into a poem. But Hardy
is not afraid to include details that are not obviously picturesque. Boldly
he introduces the 'unpoetic' into his verses. It needed boldness. The
coming of technology had produced a problem for the poets of his time.
If they were to be true to their own experience they should speak of
modern mechanical inventions like cars and telegraph wires as readily
as poets of the past spoke of haywains and ploughs. But cars and

telegraph wires had not yet acquired imaginative associations, so that the writers tended to introduce them self-consciously. Unselfconscious Hardy was one of the first successfully to face this difficulty. Cars and telegraph wires in his verses seem as natural and as poetical as any plough or haywain (see 'Nobody Comes' [715*]).

It is his particular blend of reality and imagination that makes his love poems so memorable. 'The Voice' [285*] is as beautiful and as musical as any other love poem in English; but it has a peculiar authenticity because in it he is recalling truthfully the experiences of an individual, not a nameless figure of a lover but a specific man called Thomas Hardy. His poems bear the recognisable stamp of his personality, simple, sublime, lovable. Here we come to the central secret of the spell he casts. It compels us because it brings us into immediate contact with a spirit that commands our hearts as well as our admiration. It combines a special charm, a special nobility. The charm unites unexpectedly the naïve and the sensitive. Hardy addresses us directly, unreservedly, unselfconsciously; yet he is not unsubtle or imperceptive. On the contrary he shows himself exquisitely appreciative of delicate shades of feeling and of fleeting nuances of beauty. Similarly his nobility of nature fuses tenderness and integrity. His integrity is absolute. He faces life at its darkest, he is vigilant, never to soften or to sentimentalise; yet he never strikes a note of hardness or brutality. His courage in facing hard facts is equalled by his capacity to pity and sympathise.

SOURCE: essay in F. Pinion (ed.), *Thomas Hardy and the Modern World* (Dorchester: 1974), pp. 106–11, 111–12. (First presented as a lecture to the Hardy Summer School at Weymouth, 1973.)

T. R. M. Creighton 'Versification, Mind and Feeling' (1974)

Hardy possessed the prime requisites of a great poet: an unfailing control over the resources of language in verse, and a wide range of profound response to life. He adapts the traditional disciplines of versification to his new and independent purpose as Yeats did (though their sources, methods and purposes are enormously different) rather than evolving new modes of expression from them, as Pound and Eliot did. The following qualities especially may be indicated to the new reader, not as unique to Hardy but as acquiring a unique voice in his poetry.

1. *Rhythms* of inexhaustible variety and tunefulness form delicate patterns in themselves. Hardy's understanding of the relation of speech rhythm and underlying metre extends from the classic regularity of 'The Darkling Thrush' [119*] to the stress-scansion of 'Afterwards' [511*]. Rhythms are always organically part of the meaning. The metrical calm of 'The Darkling Thrush' matches its mood; the dactylic movement of 'The Voice' [285*] is in ironic contrast – a favourite device: cf. 'Wessex Heights' [261*] or 'In Tenebris II' and 'III' [137*, 138*] – like Bach's use of dance rhythms for some of the most intense arias in the *Passions*, and emphasises its own collapse in the last stanza.

2. The *sounds* of words expound Hardy's subjects, whether onomatopoeically ('Wind oozing thin through the thorn from norward') or by their own music ('when frost was spectre-gray'; 'the wind his death lament'). Try repeating these lines aloud and hear the vowel-sounds at work producing effects more subtle than consonantal alliteration and dissonance.

3. *Stanza forms* endlessly varied and inventive are always part of the meaning they convey, not superimposed on it, and declare why they are so and not otherwise. The number of lines in a stanza modifies its expressiveness. Relations between lines of similar or different lengths always say something. The sharp contrasts in 'A Wasted Illness' [122*] create tension; the metrical distinction between lines of nearly similar lengths produces the elegiac feeling of 'Afterwards'. The final words of lines form patterns, not only of masculine and feminine endings, but of their own syllabic length. In 'The Year's Awakening' [275*] five masculine polysyllabic endings interrupt the monosyllabic ones and the mainly monosyllabic texture of the poem dramatically. In 'Afterwards' two polysyllabic endings place a nimbus round 'mysteries' and 'outrollings'. Every aspect of *rhyme* is used suggestively. The simple rhyme of 'The Darkling Thrush' reinforces the effect of its regular metre. The complex rhymes of 'Proud Songsters' [816*] mirror the mobility of the birds and their repetition over two stanzas the confused unity of nature in which they live. The triple rhymes of 'The Voice' ('call to me, all to me', etc.), in contrast to the heavy single rhymes ('were', 'fair', etc.), continue the opposition between subject and rhythm. Internal rhymes, unrhymed lines and changes of stanza within a poem always say something.

4. *Imagery* in Hardy is sparing and restrained,[1] eschewing extended simile, metaphor or symbolism. Overt imagery is simple, illustrative but often daring: 'like the wind on the stair' in 'I Sometimes Think' [520*] or 'like the lid of a pot that will not close tight' in 'Suspense' [879*]. But imagery is inherent in Hardy's language as it is in most poets'. In 'The Darkling Thrush' not only the 'strings of broken lyres' (epitomising the nineteenth century) is imagery but also 'spectre-gray', 'winter's dregs',

'eye of day' and the funereal complex around the landscape and the century in the second stanza. Similarly, 'the primrose pants' in 'A Backward Spring' [445*], 'the wind is blurting' in 'An Unkindly May' [825*], 'much tune have I set free' in 'Haunting Fingers' [546*], and the rain 'bent the spring of the spirit' in 'She Charged Me' [303*]. A technical term, 'beheaped', affords a marvellous image at the end of 'Places' [293*]. Imagery is embedded in Hardy's words and the way he uses them, not as a decoration but a function of language. Sometimes the objects in a poem form a field of imagery. In 'The Place On The Map' [263*] the (undrinkable) sea, the drought, the woman's unweeping eyes combine to portray a dry situation. The solid natural creatures – leaves, moth, hedgehog, stars – in 'Afterwards' function as images of the speaker's sensibility in connection with the verbal imagery, 'postern' and 'quittance', and are all extinguished by the bell signifying his end.

5. *Syntax.* Hardy's verse sentences vary flexibly between brief simplicity and complex length, moving closely with the verse or opposing it in free enjambment over lines and stanzas as the poem requires, but never restricted by it. The easy prose syntax of 'The Darkling Thrush', or the strict formal structure of 'Afterwards' (every stanza but the last, where the order is inverted, beginning with a subordinate clause leading to a delayed verb), serve artistic purposes; as do the baffling sixth stanza of 'A Sign-Seeker' [30*] or lines 2–4 of 'The Voice' ('Saying that now you are not as you were/When you were changed from the one who was all to me,/But as at first, when our day was fair.'). Syntactical complexities generally reflect confusion or distress, a kind of grammar of grief; see also 'After a Journey' [289*], stanza 2. Hardy does not shun poetic inversions and other traditional usages – his practice in this respect is 'mixed', like his vocabulary – neither does he depend on them. No poet can better employ straightforward modern English in verse when he wants to.

6. *Vocabulary.* Although it is closely related to questions of grammar and syntax, I have isolated this aspect of Hardy's diction because it has often been criticised as uncouth and affected. There is little in the poems to support the view that his diction in either sense is cumbersome or out of control, or that he was unaware of its effect. He uses a 'mixed' vocabulary in two ways. First, in a number of poems – though by no means all – he mixes 'poetic', archaic, obscure or dialect words, a good many compounds ('spectre-gray', 'blast-beruffled') and a few coinages ('outleant', 'wistlessness') of his own invention, into simple modern English. The test of this vocabulary must be whether it works to produce the result – often of surprise, evocation or allusion – it seeks to achieve, to create the unique texture of his verse, not whether it is conventional or has precedents. Second, he mixes poems that have an unusually pure,

consistent and restrained diction and vocabulary among others that have features just the reverse. 'Lying Awake' [844*] and 'Four In The Morning' [681*] are examples. When he is odd, it is to achieve compression or precision, or to say, as he often does, things other poets have not wanted to say. 'Cerule' is an odd word but when you have read 'Earth is a cerule mystery . . . At four o'clock', no other seems possible. (Try substituting 'azure'.) If you want to say in verse 'I wanted to be out at 4 a.m. but didn't like getting up so early', could it be better done than: 'Though pleasure spurred, I rose with irk'? It is inconceivable that the poet capable of controlling the first poem is unaware of the strangeness of the second or out of control of either. The argument may be extended to larger structures – 'The Souls Of The Slain' [62*], 'In Front Of The Landscape' [246*], 'To Shakespeare' [370*] ['some townsman (met maybe/And thereon queried by some squire's good dame/Driving in shopward'), and the strange amalgam of cliché and fantasy in the last stanza] – to the comedy of 'Genoa' [65*], where a carefully inflated and absurd diction clashes with the 'chrome kerchiefs, scarlet hose, darned underfrocks'. If what such poems say could not have been said, these effects and contrasts not produced, by other means, then Hardy's diction and vocabulary justify themselves and we may be sure he knew what he was doing. The same is true of his frequent use of clichés. His mother's death was 'a deft achievement' in 'After The Last Breath' [223*]; in 'The Voice' she 'was all to me' and 'our day was fair'. It is not that, at a loss for a striking phrase, he reached unconsciously for a cliché but that in the context of the poem he gives the cliché, because we are so familiar with it, a light of feeling that no more studied expression could have enjoyed.

HARDY'S MIND AND FEELING

The *Complete Poems* present the composite picture of a poet's mind: a mind concerned not to explain but to declare itself, able to sustain logical discrepancies within an intuitive frame work. It is not an intellectually conceived picture, though Hardy possessed a powerfully incisive intellect, and can reconcile such rationally incompatible statements as that life is an unmitigated evil and it is greatly to be enjoyed, within the context of feeling. 'The mission of poetry', Hardy wrote (*Life*, p. 377), 'is to record impressions, not convictions'; and, as he repeatedly says in the *Life*, he had no convictions in the normal sense. He reasons from deep emotional predispositions: an intense love and reverence for life in all its forms, a profound tenderness for all living things, a hatred of violence and cruelty, and an innate need for a religious explanation of the universe. These predispositions, though reduced by his experience of reality to a sense of tragedy, colour all his work. What give unity to the inconsistent, conflicting and often mutually contradictory impressions he records in his poems are the sensibility, the cast of mind, which received them and the art which sets them down. To see the poems as a whole is quite a different experience from admiring some of the best-known anthology pieces and being surprised at the slightness, oddness or apparent triviality of some of their neighbours. All the poems illuminate each other, casting reciprocal light backwards and forwards, so that quite small pieces attain a glow which might otherwise be imperceptible – e.g. 'Sacred To The Memory' [633*], with its wonderfully resonant central line 'In bare conventionality', refracts rays from all the poems of family piety, of belief and unbelief, of memory and reflection, and of human life and values – and the whole work achieves a greatness beyond the sum of its parts, great as some of them are. . . .

We cannot avoid forming a personal relation with its owner, just as in fact we cannot in the novels. Readers and critics who share T. S. Eliot's austere views about the impersonality of poetry and the creative process are unlikely to get further with Hardy than he did. (See 'Tradition and the Individual Talent' and 'Thomas Hardy' in Eliot's *Selected Prose*.) I suppose Hardy's sadness, his dark cast of mind, will strike new readers most. Eliot, discussing Hardy as a personality, not specifically as a poet, finds him neither 'wholesome' nor 'edifying' but self-absorbed, and says that he is 'interested not at all in men's minds but only in their emotions'. It is truer to say that Hardy, though always interested in mind in himself and his fictive characters, sees emotion – or some even deeper, more mysterious force of being, the awareness of which he shares with D. H. Lawrence – as what ultimately controls men's lives; and that his sadness is both wholesome and edifying, neither negative nor enervating, because it is a product of the positive predispositions mentioned above. Hardy's enormous strength, which Eliot denies him, is to enunciate his sense of the value of life, his concern for the happiness of all living things in a universe which he sees as destructive of the first and indifferent to the second. Even when he ostensibly deplores the fact of consciousness, as in 'Before Life And After' [230*], it is sorrow at the suffering and transience of things, not at their existence, that emanates from the poem. He cannot explain why the universe is as it is; and in not attempting to do so he may show as much strength as others who have explained. He mourns, though he never fears, death and the passage of time because they consume the vitality and possibilities of the present which he loves. He leaves us, as Day Lewis writes ('Birthday Poem', *Collected Poems*), 'warmer-hearted and brisker-eyed'. He enhances life and dwells 'in tenebris' because it seems marred by a 'thwarted purposing', 'an unfulfilled intention'. It may be a metaphysically naïve attitude but Hardy is not the only poet to have made poetry out of mutability. It is hard to see why his 'pessimism', which is in other cases called a tragic sense of life, has attracted opprobrium. Perhaps it is because he faces and discharges the task of making poetry out of what Hynes calls 'experience which has no invested meaning' without investing it with a private mythological or religious significance. I do not think it true, as Hynes goes on to say, that Hardy tries 'to make poetry of monistic materialism' or of scientific humanism or of determinism. His belief in these was provisional, based on emotion and often qualified . . . His poetry is sometimes conformable to his ideas, sometimes not; and paradoxically he invests experience with a wide range of meaning by recording, as he said, 'impressions, not convictions'.

It is customary to praise the 'fidelity to life' with which Hardy does this. Certainly his delicate, acute and accurate observation of nature, of people, of emotional and psychological situations is conveyed with minute precision and extraordinary boldness – e.g. 'A Countenance' [847*], written astonishingly in 1884 – and his humour, whether darkly ironic or straightforwardly comic, plays a larger part in the deeply serious body of his work than in much poetry. But his penetration of all he touches seems to me to transcend these qualities. In exploring the waste and the fertile spaces of human experience he enlarges our knowledge and understanding of them, whether we agree with his outlook or not. He is, to use his own description of a poet who puzzled him [Browning], 'a great seer and feeler' and, as fully as any poet has ever been, a man speaking to men. Occasionally his sorrow at a creation of such blighted promise leads him to expressions of gloom that seem perverse and gratuitous, that make one smile in a way not intended; sometimes his relish for life takes him to the scandalous or sensational; and momentarily he loses touch with reality. But this occurs (only in a minority of poems, not, as Blackmur suggests, as a dominant character-istic) because he did not choose to censor his impressions or falsify his consciousness for public view. (He wrote his poems 'because he liked doing them, without any ulterior thought; because he wanted to say the things they contained and would contain': see *Life*, p. 302.) In the context of our personal relation it is seen as a complementary aspect, a kind of necessary by-product of a creative sensibility whose prevailing qualities are profundity and sensitiveness, generosity and majesty of imagination – 'his hawk's vision, his way of looking at life from a very great height', as Auden puts it.

Most academic critics from Leavis to the present express doubts about the 'greatness' of Hardy's poetry. (Hynes, the most searching, compro-

mises by calling it 'a high poetic achievement'.) One can see why.
Hardy conforms to no academically recognisable type. His art, though
rooted in tradition, defies analysis in terms of historical influence. His
independence of contemporary trends and fashions fits into none of the
pigeon-holes reserved for his age. His own casual and unselfconscious
attitude to his verse, reflected in the quotation just above, shocks
expositors of other twentieth-century poets. His poetic imagination does
not seek to transmute reality but to present it as he saw it and to
penetrate deeply into his experience of it. His meanings offer no
ambiguities for ingenious explication. But 'greatness' is a quality much
easier to withhold than to define. It is hard to see how poetry which
communicates intense and varied emotion with supreme articulacy can
be anything but very great. . . .

> SOURCE: extract from the Introduction to *Poems of Thomas Hardy:*
> *A New Selection* (London: 1974; revised edn 1977), pp. x–xvi.

NOTE

1. 'He seems often bent on showing how much poetry can do without and yet
be poetry', writes A. S. MacDowall (*TH*, 1931), p. 205: an interesting
anticipation of a remark of Eliot's in quite a different context, that some great
poets show us 'what poetry can do without—how *bare* it can be' (Henrietta
Hertz Lecture, 1947).

William W. Morgan   The Partial Vision: Hardy's Idea of Dramatic Poetry (1975)

One of the more puzzling features of Hardy's statements about his
poetic intentions is his frequent use of the designation 'dramatic' to
describe his work – a body of poetry much of which is transparently
personal. In the several introductory statements in his volumes of verse,
he states that he does not often speak as himself in the poems, that they
are 'in a large degree dramatic or personative in conception'.[1] Hardy is
explicit and insistent about this matter, but he is not very concrete or
detailed. It is evident that his principal motivation was to separate
himself from some of his personae, but he appears to be claiming much
more than the simple prerogative of speaking through the masks of
created characters. In the prefaces after *Wessex Poems*, he seems in fact to
associate the dramatic persona with the entire issue of systematic

consistency in mood, tone, and thought, and he is anxious that we should not expect consistency. Most readers doubtless recognise that Hardy uses masks, but it may appear that his prefaces are claiming too much—that he is not so often dramatic as he says he is. Reading the prefaces analytically and in sequence and observing the various forms in which he speaks of the matters of persona and consistency, we learn, however, that Hardy's conception of dramatic poetry is much broader than the usual and that, for him, the dramatic does not stand in simple opposition to the personal. Once understood, Hardy's conception of dramatic poetry becomes paradoxically a key to understanding the authentically personal voice which characterises much of his poetry and provides a significant and clarifying context for reading most of his poetic canon.

Hardy published prefaces or introductions in five of his eight volumes of poetry, and in all five he gave the matter of the dramatic persona a position of some prominence. Introducing *Poems of the Past and the Present*, he explained himself in almost the same words he had used for *Wessex Poems*: 'Of the subject-matter of this volume – even that which is in other than narrative form – much is dramatic or impersonative even where not explicitly so' (*CP*, p. 84). One might wish to puzzle over what is meant by 'subject-matter' and 'other than narrative form,' but the thrust of the message is clear: we are not to expect that Hardy himself will speak in all the poems. Eight years later he returns to the same themes and again some of the same words in the 'Preface' to *Time's Laughingstocks*:

Now that the miscellany is brought together, some lack of concord in pieces written at widely severed dates, and in contrasting moods and circumstances, will be obvious enough. This I cannot help, but the sense of disconnection, particularly in respect of those lyrics penned in the first person, will be immaterial when it is borne in mind that they are to be regarded, in the main, as dramatic monologues by different characters. (*CP*, p. 190)

Here, however, the emphasis is altered, and the message is much clearer. Hardy is saying that poems which are products of his own moods and circumstances and are therefore in some sense personal utterances 'are to be regarded' as the statements of created characters. This is an unorthodox but, as I shall show later, clear and even useful notion of the dramatic persona, and if we remember for now that he has reserved the right to declare a given persona 'dramatic' after the fact, we shall find that Hardy's various statements on the matter are much less teasing and obscure.

In the famous 'Apology' to *Late Lyrics and Earlier* (1922) we encounter a paragraph which does not at first appear to have much to do with the use of the dramatic persona:

To add a few more words to what has already taken up too many, there is a contingency liable to miscellanies of verse that I have never seen mentioned, so far as I can remember; I mean the chance little shocks that may be caused over a book of various character like the present and its predecessors by the juxtaposition of unrelated, even discordant, effusions; poems perhaps years apart in the making, yet facing each other. An odd result of this has been that dramatic anecdotes of a satirical and humorous intention following verse in a graver voice, have been read as misfires because they raise the smile that they were intended to raise, the journalist, deaf to the sudden change of key, being unconscious that he is laughing with the author and not at him. I admit that I did not foresee such contingencies as I ought to have done, and that people might not perceive when the tone altered. But the difficulties of arranging the themes in a graduated kinship of moods would have been so great that irrelation was almost unavoidable with efforts so diverse. I must trust for right note-catching to those finely-touched spirits who can divine without half a whisper, whose intuitiveness is proof against all the accidents of inconsequence. In respect of the less alert, however, should any one's train of thought be thrown out of gear by a consecutive piping of vocal reeds in jarring tonics, without a semiquaver's rest between, and be led thereby to miss the writer's aim and meaning in one out of two contiguous compositions, I shall deeply regret it.   (*CP*, p. 559)

But of course this statement has a great deal to do with the subject as Hardy so broadly defines it. He is here calling our attention to the variety and 'irrelation' which result from his habit of finding numerous isolated moments and incidents worthy of his or our attention. Those 'dramatic anecdotes' to which he so casually refers might be supposed, given his definitions, to include such diverse pieces as 'Weathers' [512*], 'The Fallow Deer at the Lonely House' [551*], and even the clearly autobiographical 'End of the Year 1912' [560]. For it appears that one of the important things Hardy means by dramatic is, rather simply, a *temporary* persona, mood, feeling, fancy, or idea.

With this meaning in mind, it is easy to see that throughout his comments on the subject, Hardy was saying the same thing: that his personae, even when they are versions of himself, are often making statements and expressing states of mind which are circumscribed by time and place and are not, in any permanent or complete sense, the attitudes of the poet himself. 'I also repeat what I have often stated on such occasions, that no harmonious philosophy is attempted in these pages – or in any bygone pages of mine, for that matter' (*CP*, p. 834). This weary last paragraph of the 'Introductory Note' to *Winter Words*, therefore, may be seen as a brief and dispirited restatement of what he apparently thought to be his clear and simple position on the whole matter. Because his personae are often attending to the moment only, they are neither wholly himself nor mutually consistent with one another. We may, especially the professional critics among us, grumble a bit over Hardy's idiosyncratic adaptation of the language of poetic form, but the message behind the idiosyncrasy remains. For Hardy there are no rigid boundaries between the personal and the dramatic; a poem may be both at once. Hence he may be serious and sincere, even private and personal, in a given poem and still conceive of that poem as a dramatic moment fixed in time and place, a temporary version of himself which need not be consistent with the self he presents in another equally honest and personal poem.

We must, I think, take Hardy at his word when he says that his poems are dramatic in this sense as well as in the more conventional sense. One of the strongest impressions we receive as we read through the *Complete Poems* is that of unity within great tonal and formal variety and even philosophic inconsistency. It is precisely because so many of his poems are dramatic moments that the unity and the variety can coexist. As a thinking, responsive human being, Hardy considered himself free to entertain nonce perceptions and fancies for whatever interest or insight they might yield without censoring them first. Similarly, as a poet, he produced numbers of poems built upon these nonce impressions. The result is a body of work unified by its origins in the experience of a powerfully individualised personality but not consistent in either form or content.

Though he does not emphasise it in the prefaces, Hardy wrote, of course, conventionally dramatic poetry also – that is, poetry which is impersonally dramatic because its perspective prohibits direct self-revelation on the part of the poet, and much of it achieves the same kind of isolation in time and place that he claims for his personal poems. More than 10 per cent of Hardy's poems achieve an impersonal dramatic voice by the simple device of an identified narrator other than the poet. Some of these soliloquies and dramatic monologues are among his best known poems ('The Peasant's Confession' [25*], 'The Respectable Burgher on "The Higher Criticism"' [129*], 'The Chapel-Organist' [593*], 'One Ralph Blossom Soliloquizes' [238*]), and in his fondness for the mask of a created character he has occasionally been likened to Robert Browning. Hardy is a competent character-builder (though he cannot match Browning), but his more interesting and impressive achievements in the impersonal-dramatic are built upon a studied lack of emphasis on the character of the narrator rather than upon the creation of a character whose mind becomes the center of the reader's attention. In a number of his poems, for example, he effaces his narrator so completely that there is not so much as a personal pronoun to give the persona an identity. In the best of these, such as 'A Light Snow-Fall after Frost' [702] and 'Life and Death at Sunrise' [698*], the effect of such effacement is to suggest something like a camera recording without commentary. Such poems are intensely visual and rich with closely observed detail; they are usually written in present tense; they customarily are concerned with a situation or an image of stasis or gradual change; often they present a human figure or figures in some sort of relation to nature or natural forces; most important of all, they make only implicit evaluations of the data they present. This sort of impersonally dramatic poem suggests not so much the absence of the poet's editing mind and eye as it does his modest reluctance to place himself between us and the experience—for example, in 'Life and Death at Sunrise':

> The hills uncap their tops
> Of woodland, pasture, copse,
> And look on the layers of mist
> At their foot that still persist:
> They are like awakened sleepers on one elbow lifted,
> Who gaze around to learn if things during night have shifted.
>
> A waggon creaks up from the fog
> With a laboured leisurely jog;
> Then a horseman from off the hill-tip
> Comes clapping down into the dip;
> While woodlarks, finches, sparrows, try to entune at one time,
> And cocks and hens and cows and bulls take up the chime. [698]

Such poetry is not, of course, a mere transcript of sense-data, but it poses rather convincingly as such by its detached impersonality. That is, I think, the point of this particular dramatic technique of Hardy's–to suggest through de–emphasising the persona that the intense experience of sense-data within the frame of a short period of time may be worth the poet's and our attention. He does not profess to know, much less to tell us, the reasons for that worth.

Another dramatic technique of Hardy's – and one which allows him to achieve something like stage drama in short poems – is characterised by an even more thoroughly effaced persona. The technique involves simply presenting the entire poem within quotation marks as if it were being overheard by a silent persona who is part of the poem only by inference. 'In the Restaurant' [347] and 'In the Moonlight' [351] from *Satires of Circumstance* are typical examples. Both are overhead dialogues – the first between a pair of adulterers contemplating flight and the second between a naively sentimental interrogator and a man who reveals in response to questioning that he has discovered his love for the woman by whose grave he is standing only after her death. Through the simplified perspective of the poems Hardy places us in direct contact with a short period in these anonymous people's lives and forces us to confront the situations and issues of their lives as if we ourselves were overhearing their conversation. (The quotation marks aggressively assert the veracity of that conversation.) It is as if we are being led to eavesdrop, and since the themes of such poems are often unpleasant or at least problematic, it is an unsettling experience to be manipulated into confronting them.[2] Inasmuch as the poems are presented to us nakedly, without a preface or a context, they startle with their immediacy; since thematically they are usually built around some sort of moral conflict (Is adultery wrong? Does one who loves too late deserve pity or contempt?), they press us for moral answers which the poet is unwilling or unable to give. That is perhaps the key to Hardy's motivations in using this technique: he knows that he is presenting materials which are meaningless without a moral context, but by placing us in the position of temporary eavesdroppers, he is making that context our responsibility.

Hardy must have anticipated that his readers would have no trouble recognising such impersonally dramatic poems, for he gives them little space in his prefaces. His principal intention throughout his discussions of his personae, as I have suggested, was two-fold: to balk attempts to read his poetry as direct self-revelation and to assert the temporary nature of most of his personae so that he might be relieved of the burden of being consistent. Hence he concentrates on the first-person narrators whom we might be tempted to see as the poet himself. In the preface to *Poems of the Past and the Present*, as we have seen, he tells us that much of the 'subject-matter' of his poems is 'dramatic or impersonative' – by which I take him to mean that the vision of many of his poems (the interplay of the persona's perspective and values with the experience being related or created) is either not his own or is the vision of a particular time only. Without transition he adds:

Moreover, that portion which may be regarded as individual comprises a series of feelings and fancies written down in widely differing moods and circumstances, and at various dates. It will probably be found, therefore, to possess little cohesion of thought or harmony of colouring. I do not greatly regret this. Unadjusted impressions have their value, and the road to a true philosophy of life seems to lie in humbly recording diverse readings of its phenomena as they are forced upon us by chance and change. (*CP*, p. 84).

In addition to emphasising the temporary quality of his 'individual' or personal narrators, this passage offers a partial explanation for their temporary quality, for it presents the poet as a rather passive recipient of life's 'phenomena' – one radically subject to the influence of time and place, 'chance and change.' And, most important, this passage tells us what Hardy would have us attend to in his poetry, the particulars of time and place which define the limits of perception for his narrators. Ultimately, then, Hardy's comments on the dramatic nature of his poetry not only warn us away from a certain approach to it, but they point us in a positive direction as well. As he tells us not to look for consistent and direct self-revelation, he also tells us to look for acute sensitivity to the moment and the scene as they create or prohibit the creation of the context of values for his poems.

Hardy's techniques for exploiting the limiting effects of time and space are remarkably varied in their details, but they may be summarised as the restriction of time and the particularisation of place. Perhaps his simplest technique is to restrict the persona's consciousness to the immediate present or distant past as he does in 'Nobody Comes' [715*] and 'Childhood among the Ferns' [846*]. Without introduction, digression, or conclusion the first poem records a temporal fragment – in straightforward word order: subject, verb, complement. The fragment of time is perceived as a series of processes whose purposes and terminations are unknown to the persona. Leaves 'labour up and down'; the light of the sun fades; the telegraph wire carries messages from others to others; an automobile passes, 'in a world of its own,' while the persona just watches. The closing line continues the pattern of straightforward, linear word order:

> And mute by the gate I stand again alone,
> And nobody pulls up there.   [715*]

The word order, echoing in its form the sense of linear time in the poem, casts 'nobody' in the position of subject and gives it an active status as a perceived entity in the persona's consciousness. The last line, then, suggests that the negative quality 'nobody' actively enters the persona's consciousness in the wake of silence left behind the passing automobile. Just as the leaves labor, the light fades, the wire carries messages, and the automobile passes, so 'nobody' comes. The poem, read thoroughly within its insistently present-tense, linear-time structure, becomes then not a statement or study of loneliness so much as the record of a moment in which the persona – clearly a version of Hardy himself – experienced or apprehended a negative entity. The restriction of time here functions to insist upon the momentary but intensely felt quality of the experience.[3] Similarly in 'Childhood among the Ferns' (and other purely past-tense poems) Hardy insists upon the isolation of the time period by riddling the diction of the poem with adverbial constructions expressing temporal conditions: 'one sprinkling day,' 'as I conned,' 'I sat on,' 'then,' 'as they dried,' 'till death,' 'as I sate' [846*]. These modifiers, spaced almost evenly throughout a poem written entirely in the past tense, serve to particularise and suspend the time of the poem in the past and to obscure the relation between the persona speaking the poem and the version of himself represented in it.

'Childhood among the Ferns' also relies heavily upon the piling up of visual and tactile detail, and that is, of course, a part of Hardy's other major limiting technique, the particularisation of place. Sometimes Hardy works quite broadly to specify the locations of his poems – with his titles ('Near Lanivet, 1872'), subtitles (*Near Tooting Common*, the subtitle to 'Beyond the Last Lamp' [257*]), or subscriptions (BON-CHURCH, 1910, the subscription to 'A Singer Asleep' [265*]). More often, however, he works smaller details of place into the temporal structure of his poems. Usually these details are prominent in the initial (and sometimes the closing) lines, as they are in the following opening lines of 'New Lanivet, 1872':

> There was a stunted handpost just on the crest,
>   Only a few feet high:
> She was tired, and we stopped in the twilight-time for her rest,
>   At the crossways close thereby.   [366*]

Such details may be themselves more isolated and more sharply etched in order to serve as psychological symbols as in 'Neutral Tones':

> We stood by a pond that winter day,
> And the sun was white, as though chidden of God,
> And a few leaves lay on the starving sod;
>   – They had fallen from an ash, and were gray.

In the closing quatrain of the poem the persona specifies the quality of psychological permanence which some of the details have achieved:

> Since then, keen lessons that love deceives,
> And wrings with wrong, have shaped to me
> Your face, and the God-curst sun, and a tree,
>   And a pond edged with grayish leaves.   [9*]

Neither 'Neutral Tones' nor 'Near Lanivet, 1872,' however, is a purely past-tense poem like 'Childhood among the Ferns.' Each of them articulates at least a portion of the present – 'Neutral Tones' in the last four lines and 'Near Lanivet, 1872' in the last two words, 'Alas, alas!' It is fairly common in Hardy's past-tense poems for the closing lines or words to reveal something of the persona's present, but as in these two, the revelation is usually only partial and explains only the persona's present relationship to the specific past experience presented in the poem. Even when they speak partially in the present tense, the narrators of such poems focus upon the past as it impinges upon the present rather than upon the present as it is explained by the past. In such poems, then, even the narrators' present-tense utterances are controlled and limited by their roots in the past. The present-tense conclusions merely reinforce the sense of their limited vision.

In both his impersonal and his personal dramatic poems, then, Hardy is at once avoiding complete and direct self-revelation and accommodating the idiosyncrasies of his highly personalised view of the world. In the impersonal poems other than the conventional dramatic monologues and soliloquies, he effaces his narrator to bring the experience to the fore, and in the personal poems he binds his narrator's vision to the moment so as to restrict its relevance to the particulars in the poem. The two types of his dramatic poetry have a shared element: a kind of incompleteness of vision. The impersonally dramatic are incomplete because they are without a context of values, a framework of moral norms; the personally dramatic, because their vision cannot be generalised beyond the temporal and spatial limits specified in them. In neither, then, is Hardy wholly and directly himself. That is, finally, what Hardy means by dramatic – not wholly and directly himself. His insistence upon the dramatic quality of his poetry is not a deception he wished to practice upon the public; indeed, it is far more accurately seen as a measure of his personal and artistic modesty. It is, further, a serious critical statement about his work – and an insightful one.

SOURCE: essay in *Tennessee Studies in Literature*, XX (1975), 58–65. See also Morgan's 'Form, Tradition and Consolation in Hardy's "Poems of 1912–13"', *PMLA* (May 1974).

NOTES

1. *Complete Poems* (London: 1976), p. 6. Subsequent quotations from prefaces are from this volume, hereinafter cited as *CP*.

2. At least one of Hardy's overheard dialogues is an exception to the general sordidness of theme which I have noted: 'Under the Waterfall' [276*]. It shares with the others, however, the fact that it presents an experience for which it is difficult to construct the appropriate context. One does not know what value to assign to the principal speaker's almost religious attitude toward that day in the past when she and her lover lost their 'chalice' in the stream. Part of Hardy's reluctance to evaluate the experience can probably be explained by the fact that the principal speaker is rather clearly his first wife, Emma.

3. The momentary quality of the experience is reflected also in the fact that Hardy dates the poem fully and specifically: October 9, 1924.

Frank R. Giordano Jnr Hardy's Farewell to Fiction: The Structure of 'Wessex Heights' (1975)

Many years ago Charles Williams stated that in a significant number of his works Thomas Hardy is 'a romantic poet of the first order,' with a 'mind not unlike Shelley's in its hunger for the victory of peace and joy in a belligerent and disconsolate world, a romantic mind.'[1] While Hardy's mind is more typically post-Romantic in its awareness of the impossibility of victory and the illusoriness of peace and joy, in various of his novels and poems Hardy is deeply engaged by Romantic conceptions of nature, memory and imagination, selfhood, and love. The whole question of his relationship to his Romantic predecessors is an open one; and this present essay attempts to begin a discussion of that relationship. I shall relate Hardy's fine poem 'Wessex Heights' to the tradition of the 'greater Romantic lyric'; my interpretation of the poem will develop in conjunction with a description and analysis of its structure.

'Wessex Heights' [261 *] is an interior monologue narrated by a solitary figure, a lonely man haunted by memory. The poem begins with a description of a landscape, 'some heights in Wessex,' which, upon the speaker's meditation of them, reveal themselves to be more than just some heights. The process of meditation leads to considerable revelation about the speaker and his personal situation; in returning at poem's end to description of the heights around Wessex, the speaker indicates that they provide him partial liberation from his oppressive crises.

The speaker in 'Wessex Heights' is experiencing a personal crisis. He has undergone such crises before; and in the past has turned to the heights. The key to this poem, I think, is to define the precise nature of the crisis. And this in turn requires some discussion of the people in the lowlands whom the speaker wishes to avoid. Other questions must also be asked: What do the heights mean for the speaker? Why, specifically, does he go there? And what are the results of his meditation?

Two notable Hardy scholars have addressed themselves to some of these very questions. Professor J. Hillis Miller has written a provocative and closely-reasoned study of 'Wessex Heights' in which he describes the speaker as a memory-haunted victim of his own failure to love; his movement from the lowlands to the heights represents withdrawal in fear and disgust into the emptiness of his own mind.[2] Miller's interpretation presents some controversial opinions as the results of his reading of Hardy's mind. Professor J. O. Bailey, without presenting a full analysis of the poem and relying on his exceptional knowledge of Hardy's life, attempts to discover the actual identities of the various figures and places in the poem.[3] Bailey's findings seem not fully conclusive, as Hardy deliberately conceals and de-emphasises the 'facts' of the speaker's experience in order to accentuate his reaction to them; nevertheless there are many valuable suggestions in his piece.

Less risky than the psychographical and biographical approaches, and perhaps more revealing in the case of 'Wessex Heights,' is an analysis of the poem's structure. Through consideration of the poem's form and its relation to a given tradition and its conventions, this essay will attempt a new reading of 'Wessex Heights.' I emphasise structure because, generally speaking, a poet's use of a standard poetic form is indicative of the subjects, themes, moods that he wishes to treat as other poets have traditionally treated them.

The structure of 'Wessex Heights' is very similar to that which characterises some of the finest Romantic lyrics, such as Coleridge's 'Eolian Harp' and 'Frost at Midnight,' Wordsworth's 'Tintern Abbey,' Shelley's 'Stanzas Written in Dejection,' and Keat's 'Ode to a Nightingale.' In describing the paradigm for what he calls the 'greater Romantic lyric,' M. H. Abrams writes of these poems:

They present a determinate speaker in a particularised and usually a localised, outdoor setting, whom we overhear as he carries on, in a fluent vernacular which rises easily to a more formal speech, a sustained colloquy, sometimes with himself or with the outer scene, but more frequently with a silent human auditor, present or absent. The speaker begins with a description of the landscape; an aspect or change of aspect in the landscape evokes a varied but integral process of memory, thought, anticipation, and feeling which remains closely intervolved with the outer scene. In the course of this meditation the lyric speaker achieves an insight, faces up to a tragic loss, comes to a moral decision, or resolves an emotional problem. Often the poem rounds upon itself to end where it began, at the outer scene, but with an altered mood and deepened understanding which is the result of the intervening meditation.[4]

Abrams makes clear that the 'repeated out-in-out process, in which mind confronts nature and their interplay constitutes the poem,' is the earliest Romantic formal invention to have engendered successors that define a distinct lyric species . . . . The poetic strategy of talking about life, death, joy, love, dejection, or God at the same time as one talks about the landscape remains a vital one in the verse of many post-Romantics, right down to the present.

Let us begin with the question of the poetic function of the heights. Initially, the heights around Wessex are actual parts of the landscape, identified by name, location, and relative size. But by an act of the mythopoeic imagination, these particular local heights become an ideal symbolic retreat, apart from all known places and outside all known times. Like the mountains in the Romantic poetry of Wordsworth and Shelley, the heights symbolise ascent to a realm of imaginative vision, a place where 'one's next neighbour is the sky.' Standing on these heights 'shaped *as if* by a kindly hand' for 'thinking, dreaming,' the speaker presents an imaginative account of his location: 'I *seem* where I was before my birth, and after death may be.' (Italics mine.)

Now Hardy's capacity for exploiting the symbolical potential of landscape is familiar to all of his readers. As early as in *Far From The Madding Crowd*, we have seen Hardy transform a hilltop into the imagination's observatory.

The poetry of motion is a phrase much in use, and to enjoy the epic form of that gratification it is necessary to stand on a hill at a small hour of the night, and, having first expanded with a sense of difference from the mass of civilized mankind, who are dreamwrapt and disregardful of all such proceedings at this time, long and quietly watch your stately progress through the stars. After such a nocturnal reconnoitre it is hard to get back to earth, and to believe that the consciousness of such majestic speeding is derived from a tiny human frame.

I submit that the preceding quotation, from Hardy's famous poetic evocation of Norcombe Hill, a greater romantic lyric in prose and in some ways reminiscent in thought and feeling to 'Wessex Heights,' suggests that Hardy had long shared the Romantic poets' identification of remote elevations as the domain of the imagination. Ultimately we must perceive the symbolic character of both Norcombe Hill in chapter II and the heights around Wessex; the heights must be seen not only as places rooted in geographical reality but as places of the mind, the eternal realm of the imagination. The symbolical force of the heights, neighboring the sky, shaped for thinking and dreaming (recall the importance of the dream as a symbol for the imagination in Keats), seems indisputable.

Miller has recognised the symbolical nature of the landscape.[5] However, he overlooks the Romantic implications of the speaker's presence, in times of crisis, on the heights. Hardy verbally contrasts the 'kindly' shaped heights with the lowlands, where not even the kind friend of the lone man, Charity, accepts the speaker. This contrast between the time-and-space-bound world of the lowlands with the eternal and infinite realm symbolised by the speaker's perspective ('I seem where I was before my birth, and after death may be') is developed in terms of an "internalised quest-romance," a motif that appears in many of the greater Romantic lyrics. Professor Harold Bloom describes this motif:

The Romantic movement [of quest-romance] is from nature to the imagination's freedom (sometimes a reluctant freedom), and the imagination's freedom is frequently purgatorial, redemptive in direction but destructive of the social self. The high cost of Romantic internalisation, that is, of finding paradises within a renovated man, shows itself in the arena of self-consciousness. The quest is to widen consciousness as well as to intensify it, but the quest is shadowed by a spirit that tends to narrow consciousness to an acute preoccupation with self. This shadow of imagination is solipsism, what Shelley calls the Spirit of Solitude or *Alastor*, the avenging daimon who is a baffled residue of the self, determined to be compensated for its loss of natural assurance, for having been awakened from the merely given condition that to Shelley, as to Blake, was but the sleep of death-in-life. Blake calls this spirit of solitude a Spectre, or the genuine Satan, the Thanatos or death instinct in every natural man.[6]

When we recognise the internalised quest motif in 'Wessex Heights,' Miller's judgement of the speaker as a memory-haunted victim of his own failure to love seems unduly negative and moralistic; actually, the poem represents a courageous advance by the speaker, not an evasive, guilty retreat into himself. In the poem's context, the speaker is a man in crisis who goes to the kindly heights because he receives no kindness on the plain. While it is true that he is motivated to withdraw from the haunting memories that plague him on the plain, he goes to the heights because they seem appropriate 'for thinking, dreaming, dying on.' The heights do not represent separation from life; they symbolise a timeless-spaceless perspective, an ideal vantage point above the welter and pain of the lowlands. They are simply another form of life: the life of imagination, that provides partial liberty to a man trying to preserve himself from pain and widen his consciousness.

Now, if we see the heights as an imaginary realm to which the speaker's mind flies—a pre-historical and post-historical domain where the speaker's mind is unimpeded by oppressive past experiences; where the mind is free to think and dream; and where what it sees it creates from itself—then we may interpret this poem and this speaker's motives adequately. Like Keat's narrator in the 'Ode to a Nightingale,' Hardy's speaker takes off in imaginary flight to 'Fade far away, dissolve, and quite forget/ . . . The weariness, the fever, and the fret/Here, where man sit and hear each other groan;/ . . . Where but to think is to be full of sorrow/And leaden-eyed despairs.' The speaker's motives, i.e., thinking and dreaming, identify him with the Romantic poet; even so late a Romantic as Yeats has written, in a passage that seems to illuminate 'Wessex Heights': 'I think that all happiness depends on the energy to assume the mask of some other self; that all joyous or creative life is a re-birth as something not oneself, something which has no memory and is created in a moment and perpetually renewed.'[7]

The speaker's sense of the positive value of the heights for 'dying on' is problematical, until one recollects the death-impulse as it attracts Keats, for example, at the peak of his creative activity as symbolised in his flight with the nightingale: 'Darkling I listen; and for many a time/I have been half in love with easeful Death,/Called him soft names in many a mused rhyme,/To take into the air my quiet breath;/Now more than ever seems it rich to die,/To cease upon the midnight with no pain . . .'

The attraction of death for Hardy's speaker may be interpreted as his 'quest for permanence,' a stay against the painful flux of time and chance, his wish to end his existence on the heights; that is, in the elevated state of imaginative creativity. Such a quest is, as Bloom describes, 'purgatorial, redemptive in direction but destructive of the social self.' In a real sense it involves a redeeming or remaking of the old self of the lowlands. Hardy's chrysalis image in stanza four becomes relevant here. But I shall return to this image at a more appropriate point. Thus, though Hardy's speaker resolves his emotional crisis by going to the heights, he does so at the cost of leaving society and letting go his 'one rare fair woman.'

In discussing the speaker's motives, I have associated him with speakers of other greater Romantic lyrics. That all such speakers are poets is not without bearing, for Hardy's 'Wessex Heights,' as I see it, is one of the many Romantic poems in which the creative process itself is a major concern. The speaker's 'acute preoccupation with self,' which constitutes the six middle stanzas of the poem, results from his purgative efforts to liberate his consciousness in order to create.

The hero of internalised quest is the poet himself, the antagonists of quest are everything in the self that blocks imaginative work, and the fulfilment is never the poem itself, but the poem beyond that is made possible by the apocalypse of imagination. 'A timely utterance gave that thought relief' is the Wordsworthian formula for the momentary redemption of the poet's sanity by the poem already written, and might stand as a motto for the history of the modern lyric from Wordsworth to Hart Crane.[8]

Once all of the shadows and ghosts and phantoms from the poet's past have been left behind, he can 'know some liberty' for his imagination.

Thus far, my interpretation of 'Wessex Heights' has centered upon the opening and closing stanzas, particularly as they reveal the poem's conformity to the structure of the greater Romantic lyric. Like so many of these lyrics, 'Wessex Heights' reveals one of the most illuminating habits of Romantic poetry: 'its tendency to dramatise the searching mind of man, and especially the poet himself as the quintessence of the searching mind, through the symbolic figure of the Wanderer, Outcast, or Solitary.'[9] The middle stanzas present the consequences of an internalised quest for freedom: an expanded, intensified self-consciousness and a heightened sense of isolation. The solitary speaker creates what Hardy would call 'an idealism of fancy,' and he accepts the imaginative solace he creates, in the absence of any substantial solace found in life.[10]

I noted above that the speakers in the 'greater Romantic lyrics' are usually the poets themselves. The intensely personal note of 'Wessex Heights' and the testimony of the second Mrs Hardy require that we assume the speaker of 'Wessex Heights' to be Thomas Hardy himself.[11] Moreover, it is Thomas Hardy in 1896, as the poem's sub-title indicates. William Butler Yeats has somewhere said that a poet writes always of his personal life, though he never speaks directly as to someone at the breakfast table. Like Yeats, Hardy writes out of his evil luck, writes to express what he is not and, for completion of self-fulfilment, desires to be.

This is his period of intense depression when his marriage had become a disaster, his 'impossible love' for Mrs Henniker had come to an end, and his thin skin had been lacerated by the critics of *Jude the Obscure*. Surely these crises are among those that have previously driven Hardy to the heights.

It is clear by the end of the second stanza that the author of *Jude* is an alien in the world 'down there,' an outcast shadowed by the Spirit of Solitude and excessively self-conscious. Certainly his isolation has something to do with the way he thinks. The clanking 'mind-chains,' as Miller suggests (p. 347), may refer to his own ideas, which cause him suffering below; but it is more likely that they refer to the ideas of his Victorian neighbors and critics, who are 'dubious and askance,' like the enslaved, chain-bound occupants of Plato's cave, in refusing to see the light of day because of their customary occupation with shadows. The speaker, who is 'too weak to mend' his own faults, is refused love by 'the lone man's friend,' an allusion perhaps to Emma Hardy, and by the larger community, the uncomprehending readers of *Tess* and *Jude*, because of his idiosyncratic ideas. His painful isolation in the lowlands symbolises the situation of the artist as he is presented in numerous Romantic works and coincides with Hardy's actual feelings after having published *Jude*. The poet is not, I think, guilty of a lack of charity in the lowlands, as Miller states (p. 347); for in the penultimate stanza he enunciates his love for 'one rare fair woman,' which 'in its fullness she herself even did not know.' Rather, the speaker resembles 'The Impercipient,' one who, because he fails to perceive in the same naive Pippa-like manner as the broader community, is scornfully rejected and refused affection:

> Since heart of mine knows not that ease
> Which they know; since it be
> That He who breathes All's Well to these
> Breathes no All's-Well to me,
> My lack might move their sympathies
> And Christian charity! [44*]

The third and fourth stanzas are particularly illuminated by a structural reading; and in turn, such a reading illuminates the biographical content of these stanzas. In the third stanza of this speaker's quest for the expanded consciousness of the poet, he is tracked by phantoms and shadows who are associated with specific places in towns and who speak harshly, sneer, and disparage. We cannot, of course, identify these 'Shadows of beings who fellowed with [the speaker] of earlier days'; though we may surmise that they are similar in kind to the figures and ghosts of stanzas five and six. Now Professor Bailey assumes that these beings are probably actual men and women Hardy knew. An alternate approach to their identification is suggested by Hardy's phrases 'Shadows of beings' and 'myself of earlier days.' That is, some of the beings may be *representations* of, rather than actual, living beings; they may be fictional beings who may or may not have been based on actual people, yet were mental companions of the speaker at a prior stage in life, 'myself of earlier days.' The activities, so baleful and damning when seen as actual sneers and disparagements aimed at the speaker (Miller, p. 347), seem less censorious when considered as the modes of being of, say, some melodramatic or hypocritical creatures of Hardy's fictional world. Let us note that these figures never disparage or sneer *at the speaker*; on the contrary, they 'fellowed' with him. In this stanza, as in later ones, the speaker is laying the ghosts of the past, which ghosts may be his own fictional characters. More specifically, as stanza four relates, he is saying farewell to his life as a novelist; and all the places, events and characters associated with that phase of his life, 'the simple self that was,/And is not now,' are to be avoided as he pursues his new life as a poet. Because of their persistence in his mind, these locations and ghosts, along with the mind-chained critics, are impediments to his efforts to develop, to his attainment of imaginative freedom. Readers of Hardy's 'My Cicely' [31*] have seen an earlier narrator avoiding a particular landscape, the West Highway, 'lest [it] disturb [his] choice vision.'

This interpretation of the stanzas is supported by the theme of development and the chief metaphor of the syntactically and psychologically complex fourth stanza. It is here that the Spirit of Solitude appears, in the form of the simple self, and the speaker's solipsistic preoccupation is most acute:

Down there I seem to be false to myself, my simple self that was,
And is not now, and I see him watching, wondering what crass cause
Can have merged him into such a strange continuator as this,
Who yet has something in common with himself, my chrysalis.

From the speaker's perspective on the heights, the symbolical location
of the poet, he looks down and traces in the present poem his
development through stages. These stages may be compared to Blake's
developmental pattern in which a person proceeds from a state of
innocence (my simple self that was) through experience (of crass causes)
to a higher innocence (the speaker as poet), involving a mature
accommodation of the full experience of the earlier states. The simple
self is not, as Miller states (p. 349), 'an accusing spectator,' disdainful of
the 'strange continuator' the speaker finally becomes; rather, this
simple self is described as 'wondering' at the ultimate change. The
seeming falseness of the latest self need not be construed as damning; the
word 'seems' is important in qualifying the speaker's apparent falseness,
for it is to the simple self, a chrysalis who sees with but partially
developed vision, from the perspective of the lowlands, that he appears
false. The phrase 'crass cause' characterises this simple self, whose
knowledge of both the world and himself is imperfect and limited; while
the speaking self, presumably a fully-developed butterfly with the
expansive perception attained in transcending the limits of time and
space, achieves a fully purgational and redemptive self-
understanding.[12] Once again Yeats can comment on 'Wessex Heights':
'Wisdom is a butterfly/And not a gloomy bird of prey.' After Hardy
reviews and lays to rest his past, the fictional 'ghosts then keep their
distance' and he is liberated for thinking, dreaming, imagining his next
poem.

The biographical meaning of the fourth stanza is now clear. The
simple self is Hardy the novelist, working 'down there' at the inferior
form of art.[13] To that simple self, a chrysalis in the process of
development, the 'strange continuator' Hardy the poet has become,
seems false. The metamorphosis, however, is an accomplished reality
for 1896, a wonderful transformation, the 'crass cause' of which may
have been the unkind reviews of *Jude*.

According to Miller's reading of stanzas 5–6, the speaker is guilty of
betraying the shadowy, ghost-like figures who haunt him with their
'weird detective ways' (p. 347). These figures need not be seen as
victims of the unloving speaker's betrayal. Rather, if we consider them
as actual beings, their existence in the lowlands, the world of shadows, a
finite and imperfect realm reminiscent of Plato's cave, suggests
forcefully that *they* are the victimisers whose mind-chains inhibit the
speaker's imagination and deprive him of love. He has resigned himself

to pensive isolation because, as Matthew Arnold writes in another greater Romantic lyric, 'The realm of thought is drear and cold . . ./ The world is colder yet!' In short, none of the relationships is clearly enough defined to support a judgement of the speaker's inability to love.

Professor Bailey, following Florence Hardy's suggestion that 'the four people mentioned are actual women,' identifies the ghosts and figures in 'Wessex Heights' as Jemima Hardy and Tryphena Sparks.[14] Such a reading, though plausible, has recently been challenged.[15] Aided by Bailey's suggestions, I would interpret the ghosts and figures as characters in Hardy's fictions, created in the earlier and lower stage of his development and prior to 1896. The 'figure against the moon' is Eustacia on Egdon Heath; nobody else sees the figure, for Hardy alone envisioned it. But it is a fictional figure, reminding him of his past and 'inferior' work, in the hierarchical sense, at a time when he wants to write poetry. This figure, then, an impediment to the rhythmical poetry makes his breast 'beat out of tune.' The chiding 'ghost at Yell'ham Bottom' may be either Christine Everard in Hardy's story 'The Waiting Supper' (1887–8) or, less likely, Mother Nature of the poem 'The Mother Mourns' [76].[16] The 'ghost in Froom-side Vale' is Tess. Bailey rightly, I think, sees Little Father Time, from *Jude*, in the ghost 'in the railway train.'

I cannot agree with Miller that the speaker's mood at the end of the poem is one of 'fear and self-disgust' (p. 351); nor that he knows 'all love is folly' (p. 353). Rather, like the intensely sensitive figures found in so many Romantic works, he accepts his painful alienation because as an artist he must and because he recognises the primacy of his imagination's integrity; if he is to move on and create, he cannot dwell in the past. Of course he is lonely and saddened by his suffering in the lowlands, but it is through suffering, as Wordsworth and Keats before him learned, that one defines and realises oneself as a poet.[17] Moreover, through his suffering he has learned to transcend the painful world of finiteness and imperfection. So he chooses to walk on Wessex Heights, 'Where men have never cared to haunt, nor women have walked with me.' His removal to the heights permits him literally to avoid seeing those who peopled his past in the lowlands and, at the same time, locates him symbolically beyond time and space, at the boundaries of his imagination. His mood is altered from his original state of crisis to one of imaginative freedom: in 'Wessex Heights' Hardy accomplished his long-delayed resumption of 'the viewless wings of poesy.'[18]

The foregoing analysis of the structure of 'Wessex Heights' is offered in part to supplement and, at some points, provide alternatives to previous readings. An equally important issue however, has chiefly engaged me here and elsewhere. This is the knotty problem of demonstrating Hardy's poetic artistry in transforming personal experiences of various kinds into formal works of literature. A naturally shy, even reclusive person, and a writer who loved the art of concealing art, Hardy has deliberately erected barriers to the understanding and appreciation of so much of his life and his art. Thus, in a Hardyan irony he never appreciated, so many valuable, seemingly simple poems go unread or mis-read or read simply for the biographical or psychological data they provide. Yet, if we are precisely to define Hardy's stature as a poet, we need to know more about his technical achievement, his use of structured language for the attainment of his fine effects. To this end, the present essay identifies the 'greater Romantic lyric' as the prototype of 'Wessex Heights'; and, implicitly, calls for further examination of Hardy's relationship to other Romantic formal traditions and authors. This identification emphasises the central theme of the poem: the speaker's quest for imaginative freedom. This quest motif, traditional in the greater Romantic lyrics as well as in such works as Shelley's *Alastor* and Keats's *Endymion*, suggests the speaker's pursuit of preoccupations peculiar to the poet. Such preoccupations derive from his unique endowments and permit his entry into realms of experience from which most men are excluded. Simultaneously, they further isolate the poet.[19] 'Wessex Heights,' then, is *not* about a guilt-ridden, unloving traitor, haunted by his past; rather, it is about a lonely writer who would liberate himself from the painful memories of obtuse critics and from the inhibiting preoccupation with his past fictional creations, in order to create in a newer and higher form of art, poetry. Finally, 'Wessex Heights' represents Hardy's formal farewell to fiction and announces his long-delayed but henceforward nearly total commitment to poetry. It seems appropriate that, in announcing his aim, he should employ a structure developed and refined by Wordsworth and Shelley, two of his most valued predecessors. . . .

SOURCE: essay in *The Thomas Hardy Year Book*, No. 5 (1975), pp. 58–65. See also Giordano's 'Hardy's Moments of Revision', in *Budmouth Essays on Thomas Hardy* (Dorchester: 1976), and his 'A Reconsideration of "In a Eweleaze near Weatherbury"' *The Thomas Hardy Society Review* (Dorchester: 1977).

NOTES

1. Charles Williams, *Poetry at Present* (Oxford: 1930), p. 8.

2. J. Hillis Miller, '"Wessex Heights": The Persistence of the Past in Hardy's Poetry', *Critical Quarterly*, 10 (1968), 338–59. This essay will be cited in my text according to page number.

3. J. O. Bailey, *The Poetry of TH: A Handbook and Commentary* (Chapel Hill, N. Car.: 1970), pp. 274–80.

4. M. H. Abrams, 'Structure and Style in the Greater Romantic Lyric', in Harold Bloom (ed.), *Romanticism and Consciousness* (New York: 1970), p. 201.

5. Miller, p. 342.

6. Harold Bloom, 'The Internalisation of Quest-Romance', in Bloom (ed.), op. cit., p. 6.

7. Quoted in Richard Ellmann, *Yeats: The Man and the Mask* (New York: 1948), p. 174.

8. Bloom, p. 8.

9. See David Perkins, *The Quest for Permanence* (Cambridge, Mass.: 1959), p. 27.

10. See F. E. Hardy, *The Life . . .* (London: 1962), p. 310.

11. See Bailey, p. 274f.

12. The butterfly, associated with development, flight, beauty and liberty, is an appropriate Romantic symbol for the poet.

13. See Michael Millgate, *TH* (New York: 1971), p. 352, for a discussion of Hardy's hierarchical ranking of literature.

14. Bailey, pp. 275–7.

15. See Norman Page, '"Wessex Heights" Visited and Revisited', *English Literature in Transition*, 15, 1 (1972), 57–62. Professor Bailey's rejoinder appears after Professor Page's challenge.

16. See R. L. Purdy, *TH: A Bibliographical Study* (London: 1954). Though this figure did not appear in print until 1902, the germ of the poem, and presumably its speaker, occupied Hardy's mind in November 1883.

17. Like Wordsworth, Hardy wishes to avoid the enemy of human tranquillity, the 'passion over-near ourselves, / Reality too close and too intense' (*Prelude*, xi, 57–8). The strategy of both poets is to lessen the strain of present concern by locating it in an immense natural world engulfing these concerns. See Perkins, pp. 40–50.

18. See F. E. Hardy, *The Life . . .*, p. 230. In 1890 Hardy used the phrase from Keats's Nightingale ode as he considered devoting himself thereafter to poetry. When he finally makes his switch, Hardy turns to Wessex Heights as Wordsworth turned to

> . . . yon shining cliffs,
> The untransmuted shapes of many worlds,
> Cerulean ether's pure inhabitants,
> These forests unapproachable by death,
> That shall endure as long as man endures,
> To think, to hope, to worship, and to feel,
> To struggle, to be lost within himself
> In trepidation, from the blank abyss
> To look with bodily eyes and be consoled.

19. I am indebted here, as above, to David Perkins's fine insights; see his p. 28.

SELECT BIBLIOGRAPHY

In what follows Hardy('s) and Thomas Hardy('s) are abbreviated throughout to H('s) and TH('s). Unless otherwise stated, the poetry texts and studies cited below are published by Macmillan.

1. TEXTS

Wessex Poems and Other Verses (1898). *Poems of the Past and the Present* (1901). *Time's Laughingstocks and Other Verses* (1909). *Satires of Circumstance, Lyrics and Reveries* (1914). *Moments of Vision and Miscellaneous Verses* (1917). *Late Lyrics and Earlier, with Many Other Verses* (1922: prefaced by H's 'Apology'). *Human Shows, Far Phantasies, Songs and Trifles* (1925). *Winter Words in Various Moods and Metres* (1928). The 1898 and 1901 collections were first published by Harper.

The first five were printed together as *Collected Poems* (1919) – actually the first volume of *The Poetical Works of TH*, the second being *The Dynasts. Late Lyrics and Earlier* was added in 1923, *Human Shows . . .* in 1928, and *Winter Words . . .* in 1930. *Collected Poems* (1930 edition) was frequently reprinted but not re-set or revised until 1976, when James Gibson edited *TH: The Complete Poems*, adding some thirty previously uncollected pieces, and providing brief notes, full indexes and a selection of variant readings. The poems were also numbered in one continuous series (to which all references in this Casebook are keyed). This is now the standard edition. The same editor's *Variorum* edition was published in 1979.

2. SELECTIONS

The poet himself picked 120 poems for his *Selected Poems* (1916), and in 1927 revised and added to them for his *Chosen Poems* (Published in 1929, now out of print). In 1940 G. M. Young made a new selection entitled *Selected Poems of TH*. Other, shorter, selections were subsequently published. These and Young's volume have been superseded by T. R. M. Creighton's *Poems of TH: A New Selection* (1974; revised edition 1977) – a large and well-annotated selection – and by James Gibson's briefer *Chosen Poems of TH* (1976), also annotated. (In this Casebook, an asterisk after the poem-number in *The Complete Poems* indicates a poem included in the Creighton selection.)

3. HANDBOOKS AND BIBLIOGRAPHY

There are two comprehensive handbooks to H's poetry: J. O. Bailey's *The Poetry of TH: A Handbook and Commentary* (University of North Carolina Press, 1970) and F. B. Pinion's *A Commentary on the Poems of TH* (1976). H. Orel's *H's Personal*

Writings (1966) includes virtually everything H wrote about his poems and on poetry in general. For more detailed bibliographical information, see R. L. Purdy's *TH: A Bibliographical Study* (Oxford University Press, 1954). Gerber and Davis, *Secondary Bibliography* (see Introduction, Note 10) lists with resumés practically everything written about H. up to 1968.

4. Autobiographical and General Biographical Works

The following merit particular mention:

Robert Gittings, *Young TH* (Heinemann Educ., 1975) and *The Older H* (Heinemann Educ., 1978).

Evelyn Hardy (ed.), *TH's Notebooks and Some Letters from Julia Augusta Martin* (Hogarth Press, 1955).

Evelyn Hardy and R. Gittings (eds), *Some Recollections by Emma Hardy with Some Relevant Poems* by TH (Oxford University Press, 1961).

Evelyn Hardy and F. B. Pinion (eds), *One Rare Fair Woman: TH's Letters to Florence Henniker, 1893–1922* (1972).

F. E. Hardy, *The Life of TH, 1840–1928* (1962). Originally published in two volumes: *The Early Life of TH, 1840–1891* (1928) and *The Later Years of TH, 1892–1928* (1930). Though published under the name of H's second wife (at his desire), the bulk of *The Life* is by H himself.

5. Books Dealing Wholly or in Part with H's Poetry

A fuller listing than is possible here (or in section 6 below) will be found in the Introduction and in the Notes to material in Parts Two and Three. Early reviews are presented in R. G. Cox (ed.), *TH: The Critical Heritage* (Routledge, 1970); and A. J. Guerard (ed.), *H: A Collection of Critical Essays* ('Twentieth-Century Views' ser., Prentice-Hall, 1963), has four essays on the poetry.

Few critical works confine their attention to H's poetry; the only one not mentioned elsewhere in this Casebook is J. C. Richardson's *TH: The Poetry of Necessity* (University of Chicago Press, 1977). Of books on H's work in general not mentioned in the Introduction, the following merit attention for their sections on the poetry:

J. Bayley, *An Essay on H* (Oxford University Press, 1978).

D. Hawkins, *TH: Novelist and Poet* (David and Charles, 1976).

F. B. Pinion, *TH: Art and Thought* (1977).

G. Wing, *TH* (Oliver and Boyd, 1963).

6. Essays and Articles

These are numerous and their growth is rapid. (See Introduction and Notes to material in Parts Two and Three; and consult Gerber and Davis, under the appropriate year, for reviews and articles up to 1968). A brief selection only is given here, to supplement the advice given elsewhere:

D. Davie, 'H's Virgilian Purples', *Agenda*, 10, Nos 2–3 (1972).

J. Gibson, 'The Poetic Text', in F. B. Pinion (ed.), *TH and the Modern World* (Thomas Hardy Soc., Dorchester: 1974).

A. J. Guerard, 'TH: The Illusion of Simplicity', *Sewanee* Review (Summer 1964).

J. Levi, 'John Clare and TH', Coffin Memorial Lecture (University of London, 1975).

M. Quinn, 'The Persistence of the Past in the Poetry of TH and Edward Thomas', *Critical Quarterly* (1974).

J. Wain, 'The Poetry of TH', *Critical Quarterly* (1960).

NOTES ON CONTRIBUTORS

HOWARD BAKER: sometime Professor of English, Louisiana State University.

JEAN BROOKS: writer and lecturer, and formerly Head of the Department of English, Rose Bruford College of Speech and Drama, Kent; author of *Thomas Hardy: The Poetic Structure*.

DOUGLAS BROWN: formerly Senior Lecturer in English, University of Reading and, when he died in 1964, Professor-elect in the University of York; author of *Thomas Hardy* (1954) and a study of *The Mayor of Casterbridge* (1962).

SIR EDMUND K. CHAMBERS (1866–1954): civil servant and literary critic. Best known for his studies of the Elizabethan drama, his publications include *The Medieval Stage* (1903), *The Elizabethan Stage* (1923) and *William Shakespeare* (1930).

LORD DAVID CECIL: Goldsmith's Professor of English in the University of Oxford until 1969; he has published numerous works of criticism and biography.

HAROLD CHILD (1869–1945): author and critic, he wrote for the *Times Literary Supplement* and *The Times*, and contributed to the *Cambridge History of English Literature*.

C. B. COX: Professor of English Literature, University of Manchester. His publications include *The Free Spirit*, *Modern Poetry* (with A. E. Dyson), *Joseph Conrad: The Modern Imagination* and the Casebook on T. S. Eliot's *The Waste Land* (with A. P. Hinchliffe). He is currently preparing the Casebook on Conrad's *Heart of Darkness*, *Nostromo* and *Under Western Eyes*.

T. R. M. CREIGHTON: formerly Senior Lecturer in English Literature, University of Edinburgh; his publications include *Poems of Thomas Hardy: A New Selection* (1974, revised edition 1977).

WALTER DE LA MARE (1873–1956): poet and novelist; his essays in literary criticism were collected in *Private View* (1953).

A. E. DYSON: formerly Senior Lecturer in English, University of East Anglia, and General Editor of the Casebook series.

FRANK GIORDANO JNR: Professor of English, University of Houston, Texas. He has written widely on Hardy and has edited a special Hardy issue of the periodical *Victorian Poetry*.

THOM GUNN: English poet; a Cambridge graduate currently living in San Francisco.

SAMUEL HYNES: Professor of English, Princeton University, New Jersey. His publications include *The Pattern of Hardy's Poetry* (1956), and he is currently working on an 'English Texts' edition of Hardy's poetry for the Oxford University Press.

R. W. KING: English literary critic.

PHILIP LARKIN: poet and novelist. He is Librarian of the University of Hull and editor of the *Oxford Book of Twentieth-Century English Verse* (which contains more poems by Hardy than by any other poet).

F. L. LUCAS (1894–1967): formerly Reader in English, University of Cambridge; a prolific author of poetry, plays, short stories and translations from French and Classical literature, as well as literary and dramatic criticism.

CECIL DAY LEWIS (1904–72): poet and literary critic; he was appointed Poet Laureate in 1968. His critical studies include *A Hope for Poetry*, *Poetry for You* and *The Poetic Image*.

ARTHUR S. MACDOWALL (1876–1933): sometime Fellow of All Souls College, Oxford, and subsequently a leader-writer for *The Times* and a regular reviewer for the *Times Literary Supplement*. Living for a time in Dorset, he became a friend and admirer of Hardy, who greatly valued his criticism. In addition to his book on Hardy (1931), he published a literary study on *Realism* and several collections of essays, including *Nature and Man* and *A Detached Observer*.

KENNETH MARSDEN: writer and lecturer; his publications include *The Poems of Thomas Hardy* (1969), and is preparing a study of *The Dynasts*.

WILLIAM W. MORGAN: Professor of English, Illinois State University; he has published several articles on Hardy's poetry, and is currently working on a study of Hardy's poetic rhetoric.

J. MIDDLETON MURRY (1889–1957): literary critic and influential journalist; editor of *The Athenaeum* (1919–21) and *The Adelphi* (1923–48).

I. A. RICHARDS (1893–1979): critic and poet; a founding father of modern criticism in his two classic works, *The Principles of Literary Criticism* (1926) and *Practical Criticism* (1929).

L. E. W. SMITH: Principal of Strode's College, Egham, Surrey; he has published many books for schools, and lectures frequently on Hardy.

LYTTON STRACHEY (1880–1932): literary critic and historical biographer: a leading member of the 'Bloomsbury Group'.

EDWARD THOMAS (1878–1917): after graduating from Oxford he acquired a reputation as a literary critic and book-reviewer. He is now also recognised as a notable poet, on the basis of a fairly small number of poems written during the last three years of his life.

INDEX